Making use of newly available archive material, this book provides the first systematic and accessible overview of church–state relations in the Soviet Union. John Anderson explores the shaping of Soviet religious policy from the death of Stalin until the collapse of communism, and considers the place of religion in the post-Soviet future. The book discusses the motivations of Khrushchev's renewed assault on religion, the Brezhnev leadership's response to the election of a Polish Pope and the perceived revitalisation of Islam, the factors underlying Gorbachev's liberalisation of religious policy, and the problems in this area facing the newly independent states of the former Soviet Union. This study will be of interest to students and scholars of Soviet and post-Soviet studies, religious history, and the politics of church–state relations.

Religion, state and politics in the Soviet Union and successor states

Religion, state and politics in the Soviet Union and successor states

John Anderson

University of St Andrews

CAMBRIDGE
UNIVERSITY PRESS

Published by the Press Syndicate of the University of Cambridge
The Pitt Building, Trumpington Street, Cambridge, CB2 1RP
40 West 20th Street, New York, NY 10011-4211, USA
10 Stamford Road, Oakleigh, Melbourne 3166, Australia

First published 1994

A catalogue record for this book is available from the British Library

Library of Congress cataloguing in publication data
Anderson, John, Dr.
Religion, state, and politics in the Soviet Union and the
successor states, 1953–1993/John Anderson.
    p. cm.
Includes bibliographical references.
ISBN 0 521 46231 2 – ISBN 0 521 46784 5 (pbk.)
1. Religion and state – Soviet Union. 2. Soviet Union – Religion.
3. Religion and state – Former Soviet republics. 4. Former Soviet
republics – Religion. 5. Soviet Union – Politics and
government – 1945–1991. 6. Former Soviet republics – Politics and
government. I. Title.
BL980.S65A53 1994
291′.0947–dc20   93-44304 CIP

ISBN 0 521 46231 2 hardback
ISBN 0 521 46784 5 paperback

Transferred to digital printing 2002

TAG

Published in the year that the Church of England first ordained women, this book is dedicated to those women whose vocation the churches have denied for so long. With Soviet believers they shared in pain and rejection; with them they have the potential to make a major contribution to a rapidly changing world.

Contents

Acknowledgements

It is impossible to thank adequately the many individuals who have contributed directly or otherwise to the production of this book, but amongst those who should be mentioned are: Leonard Shapiro, Dominic Lieven and Peter Reddaway who introduced me to the academic study of what was the Soviet Union, especially the latter who provided advice and materials during the early stages of my research life; Geoffrey Hosking and Christopher Binns who examined a rather incomplete thesis on religious policy under Brezhnev deserve thanks for their comments and advice; friends and colleagues at Keston College (now Keston Research) with whom I had many discussions of the religious question, especially Jane Ellis and Mike Rowe; colleagues at Edinburgh and St Andrews Universities who have graciously accepted my long-term obsession with religious policy in the former Soviet Union.

Financial help has been forthcoming from the Economic and Social Research Council, the Carnegie Trust for the Universities of Scotland, and the Research and Travels Funds of the Universities of Edinburgh and St Andrews. The staff of various libraries and archives have provided valuable help and resources, including the British Library of Economics and Political Science, the library of the School of Slavonic and East European Studies at London University, the Keston College archive (admirably manned by Malcolm Walker), and the libraries of the Universities of Glasgow, Edinburgh and St Andrews. Special thanks must also go to the staff of the State Archives of the Russian Federation (formerly the Central State Archive of the October Revolution), and of the Centre for the Preservation of Contemporary Documentation (formerly the archive of the CPSU Central Committee), both in Moscow.

Thanks also to friends and colleagues in Moscow and elsewhere who discussed these matters and, more importantly, provided a home from home, in particular Natalya Kigai and her many friends (academic, clerical and downright sceptical). Cambridge University Press's referees offered useful comments, and Felix Corley provided a valuable service in commenting critically on the manuscript, though their advice was not always followed. Thanks must also go to my parents who have provided practical and moral support over what must have seemed an endless period of 'student days'. Above all gratitude to Joseph and Caitlin whose antics (and nappies) reminded me that there exists life outside the ivory tower, and Jill who provided constant support and encouragement.

1 Introduction

Easter 1992. A long line of people stretches across Red Square waiting their turn to visit the Lenin Mausoleum. Behind them the red bricks of the Historical Museum to which is attached a huge poster. As had been the case for many years the image is trinitarian, but in place of Marx, Engels and Lenin, are to be found Father, Son and Holy Ghost.

Much has changed in what we used to know as the Soviet Union since this book was conceived. Originally intended as an analysis of the shaping of the state's less than benevolent policy towards religious institutions and ideas, it has been extended to include consideration of the various factors leading to a fundamental change of policy orientation. Conflictual relations between religion and state have been replaced with cooperation and it has been suggested that in some of the former Soviet republics the majority religion is close to becoming the new official ideology. In these circumstances it becomes essential to focus not only on the discrete processes by which state policies have been formed, but to look for long-term trends which may have contributed towards recent developments. At the same time we need to be aware that the apparently radical nature of recent changes may hide some underlying continuities, particularly in the way in which many of the new breed of politicians and officials – sometimes the same under different political names – deal with the religious question.

The aims of this study are threefold. Firstly, to provide a general overview of religious policy in the post-Stalin years. Although recent years have seen a growing number of publications on various aspects of atheism and religious life in the USSR, most have focused on very specific themes – denominational history, the abuse of believers' rights, or new rites.[1] Many of these are illuminating in their own right and this part of my study will very much build upon and supplement the work of other scholars. Yet in developing a new synthesis, and one that

---

[1] See bibliography. A notable exception is Dmitri Pospielovsky's three-volume *A History of Soviet Atheism in Theory and Practice, and the Believer* (Macmillan, 1987–8).

1

emphasises the policy aspect I shall on occasions offer new interpretations or fill out existing knowledge, in particular by making use of material – both published and archival – that has become available since most of the standard works were written. Of particular use here have been the archives of the two councils for religious affairs which have been partially opened for the years 1943–65, local archival material, and the archives of the Communist Party's Central Committee selectively opened in 1992 and covering the period 1953–91.[2] Inevitably no study covering forty years and the treatment of numerous denominations and groups by a wide variety of official bodies can be fully comprehensive. But in painting at times with a relatively broad brush I hope to illuminate some of the major shifts in religious policy and shed light on the often contradictory factors determining both the shaping and implementation of that policy.

A second and central aspect of this book will be a detailed study of policy making in the religious sphere. Of the growing number of publications on the religious question very few discuss this matter in explicit fashion,[3] whilst more general analyses of Soviet policy making have ignored the field of religion. In many respects a study of policy making in the religious sphere is an attractive proposition. This is an area where ideological considerations might be thought to play a larger role than in other, more technical policy fields. And the period on which we focus is one in which two, or possibly three, very distinctive policy styles are apparent. Under Khrushchev there is a renewed and vigorous assault on religious ideas and institutions; under Brezhnev a modification of this policy which replaces assault with attrition; and then, under Gorbachev and after, a fundamental liberalisation of state attitudes towards religion.

In dealing with religious policy making we need to start by raising some very basic questions. What do we mean by 'policy'? Many of the standard texts on policy analysis note the problems associated with the

---

[2] The archives of the Council for Religious Affairs are to be found in the State Archives of the Russian Federation (formerly the Central State Archive of the October Revolution), in *fond* 6991s. We shall refer to the archive under its old name in footnotes, i.e. as TsGAOR, followed by file references. As I was completing this study I was also able to examine a number of local archives' files relating to the work of CRA commissioners in the Moscow, Kostroma, Kaluga and Yaroslav region, copies of which are to be found at Keston Research in Oxford. The Central Committee archives are located in various *fondy* of the Centre for the Protection of Contemporary Documents (TsKhSD), located in the former party headquarters in Moscow's Old Square. Footnotes here will cite either the relevant file numbers or refer to the Protocols of Secretariat, no. and date.

[3] But see the work of Bohdan Bociurkiw who has explored the issue in two articles: 'The Shaping of Soviet Religious Policy', *Problems of Communism*, May–June 1973, pp. 37–51, and 'The Formulation of Religious Policy in the Soviet Union', in J. Wood, ed., *Readings on Church and State* (Waco, 1989), pp. 303–18. The first of these provided the initial stimulus to this study.

assumption that there exist such recognisable entities as 'policies'.[4] Politicians speak about their 'economic policies', but within that broad definition are subsumed 'policies' relating to taxation, public expenditure, credit controls, or imports and exports. Policy can be used to describe a broad political programme or it might be applied to a one-off decision; to a simple proposal, or to what actually happens at the end of the day which might in turn bear little resemblance to the wishes of the 'policy maker'. Policy might refer to major initiatives and changes – such as those initiated in the religious field by Khrushchev or Gorbachev; might refer to a more instrumental fine tuning of existing practice – as under Brezhnev; or even to a period of drift where the state largely abdicates responsibility for decision making in particular fields.

With regard to religious policy making in what was the USSR some of these problems of definition are apparent. The years after 1953 witnessed very little in the way of publicised, programmatic statements on the religious question. If we were to rely solely on legislation and published Central Committee resolutions we would have very little idea of the way in which religion has been handled since Stalin's death. Routine calls to improve atheist work can be found at regular intervals, yet during one period religion was harshly attacked, whilst at another it was treated in more restrained fashion. A survey of the press helps us to fill out the picture. Here we find a broad range of material from the crude, often personal attacks of the late 1950s and early 1960s to the positive profiling of believers from 1987 onwards. To this one can add the numerous samizdat sources which document how the various policy turns were felt on the ground. Such material has been supplemented in recent years by that found in the archives described above. Finally, we should not ignore the vast output of the anti-religious establishment and articles appearing in the more specialist press which often revealed much about official thinking on the religious question.

Using these sources it is possible to suggest that religious policy up until the late 1980s comprised three main elements:

> a socialisation process aimed at the creation of the new Soviet (atheist) man;
>
> the administrative and legislative regulation of religious bodies with the ostensible intention of eventually seeing them disappear;
>
> coping with the responses of believers to official policies, if necessary by repressive means.

[4] See C. Hamm & M. Hill, *The Policy Process in the Modern Capitalist State* (Brighton, 1984), or B. Hogwood & L. Gunn, *Policy Analysis for the Real World* (Oxford, 1984).

Yet it is important to note that religious policy did not operate in a vacuum. Lenin always argued that the struggle against religion should be subordinated to the wider concerns of building socialism, a stance generally adhered to by his successors. For this reason the treatment of religion has often been shaped by requirements in other areas, in our period including the needs of foreign, nationality and dissent policy.

A basic and common sense assumption underlying this study is that policy should be viewed as a process rather than a series of one-off decisions. Religious policy has been in a constant state of flux and amendment throughout the Soviet period, as governments responded to particular circumstances that might arise and the ideological needs of the moment. In part it has been a product of the tension between what Bohdan Bociurkiw calls 'fundamentalists' and 'pragmatists', that is, those committed to a hasty demise of religion by whatever means it takes versus those prepared to take a more long-term view and subordinate religious to other policy concerns.[5] But within each period, and especially under Brezhnev, it is possible to isolate a series of adjustments often affecting very small groups of believers and sometimes made or affected by the decisions of lower level authorities. So, policy as a process, and one which involves not only the decisions of political elites, but the actions of officialdom all the way down the bureaucratic hierarchy.

In discussing the policy process various stages have traditionally been isolated. 'Inputs' relate to those factors and influences which may have shaped the way in which central decision makers act. In the field of religious policy we might include ideological imperatives, the preference of individual leaders, the need to respond to problems raised by past policies, economic concerns, nationality questions, the perceived need to maintain political controls over society, foreign criticisms and pressures coming from within society. As we shall see the relative importance of these has varied considerably over time. It is also useful to examine the extent to which policy was the product of 'debate' within the elite and whether it is possible to detect distinctive policy alternatives being put forward within the institutions and 'interest groups' involved in religious policy making.

Moving to the process of decision making itself, it is important to know which bodies are involved in the process, which institutions are consulted, which political leaders take the central role in influencing decisions. In the most open societies the 'black box' remains the least accessible feature of the policy making process, yet as we shall see it is possible partially to reconstruct the mechanisms through which religious

[5] Bociurkiw, 'The Shaping of Soviet Religious Policy'.

policy was shaped. Moving on to 'outputs' we shall examine the various resolutions, decrees, instructions, laws, newpaper editorials and other documents that announced decisions once made. Although as already indicated many of these were never published at the time, the majority have since become available to researchers.

Finally we need to examine the implementation phase. Which bodies were responsible for putting central directives into practice, to what extent did they or could they exercise 'discretion' in applying those instructions to their own circumstances? Were central disclaimers that abuses were the consequence of local authorities taking the law into their own hand simply a facade to cover repressive policies, or did they in fact have some basis in reality? And how did believers respond to new policy turns and by what mechanisms was this response fed back to those who shaped policy?

Inevitably such a framework imposes a degree of artificial order on a much more chaotic reality, and it is not a scheme which will be adhered to rigidly. Some aspects of the process are more open than others at different stages in the period with which we are concerned. And such a scheme becomes increasingly irrelevant by 1990 as the various state authorities at the centre and in the republics increasingly go their own way or abdicate responsibility for the religious sphere.

A third theme of the book will be that of continuity and change in the religious policy of the Soviet state and its sucessors. To what extent can the recent liberalisation of religious policy be traced back to trends, policies and arguments of the earlier period? What contradictions in official policies contributed to a possible reinforcement of religion in the 1960s and 1970s – for example, did the state's promotion of social change in fact strengthen religion by reducing the preponderance of poorly educated believers within religious communities? In what ways did some of the arguments and debates developing within intellectual and elite circles help to undermine official views of religion and contribute towards changing state attitudes in the late 1980s. And what impact has Soviet practice had on the new models of relations between religion and the state emerging in the post-Soviet world of independent republics?

2   Khrushchev: Towards a new assault

Though now remembered chiefly as a reformer, and perhaps as a precursor of Gorbachev, Nikita Khrushchev was also the man who from the late 1950s onwards presided over a renewed and vicious assault on organised religion.[1] Some indication of what was to come emerged towards the end of 1954 when the first secretary was locked in combat with his chief rival, Georgii Malenkov. A Central Committee resolution of 7 July (not published at the time) criticised the past failings of atheist work in the USSR and called for a revived attempt to overcome religious prejudices. Over the next four months the press carried numerous, often crude attacks on religion. Then, just as suddenly, the campaign was called off by a decree of 11 November which criticised 'errors' in carrying out atheist work, a decree signed personally by Khrushchev rather than the more anonymous Central Committee. This 'hundred days campaign' has never been fully explained. Some have seen Malenkov's hand in this new assault,[2] but others argue more convincingly that it bore all the hallmarks of Khrushchev style *campaignovshchina*. As Joan Delaney Grossman has pointed out, 'the stress on party responsibility for anti-religious work and concern over the bad effects of religious practice on agriculture' took up issues dear to Khrushchev's heart. Equally importantly the brief assault of 1954 bears a striking resemblance to the opening stages of the attack of the late 1950s.[3]

The campaign launched in 1958 went much further in utilising

---

[1] Though occasionally mentioned in passing, few of the standard works on the Khrushchev period devote much attention to this episode.

[2] H. & P. Lazareff, *The Soviet Union between the 19th and 20th Party Congresses, 1952–56* (The Hague, 1959), p. 202

[3] Joan Delaney Grossman, 'Khrushchev's Anti-Religious Policy and the Campaign of 1954', *Soviet Studies*, vol. 24, no. 3, 1973, pp. 374–86; the Central Committee archives do not help here, though they do record Khrushchev as being one of two secretaries (the other being Shepilov) who discussed the July decree at a Secretariat meeting in April 1954. But after that date Khrushchev does not appear to have been present at Secretariat meetings which discussed the religious issue. Centre for the Preservation of Contemporary Documents, TsKhSD, Protocols of the Secretariat, 56, Session of 16 Apr. 1954.

administrative and police pressure to discourage religiosity and undermine the institutional structures of religious organisations. Though not spelt out in any published policy documents, the outlines of this new turn can be clearly documented from the contemporary press, from samizdat sources and from newly available archive material. Less clear, perhaps, is the motivation underlying this campaign promoted by a political leader who initiated a considerable degree of liberalisation in many other areas of Soviet life. The aim of this chapter is in large part to explore the motivations underlying the new assault on religion, looking at both the more pragmatic and concrete reasons noted at the time, and at the central role of Khrushchev's personal commitment to the building of a communist society within the foreseeable future. In addition we seek to reconstruct the way in which religious policy was shaped at the top during this period, focusing on the individuals and institutions involved in that process. Finally, the main, generally unpublished, statements of intent – whether in programmatic, legislative or administrative form – are outlined. In chapter 3 we examine the translation of theory into practice.

Containing religious influence

The inheritance

The official reasoning behind the renewed assault on religion was set out in the first paragraph of the Central Committee resolution of July 1954, 'on large scale shortcomings in scientific atheist propaganda and measures for its improvement':

The Central Committee of the Communist Party of the Soviet Union notes that many party organisations are providing inadequate leadership of scientific atheist propaganda amongst the population, as a result of which this important aspect of ideological work is in a neglected condition. At the same time the churches and various religious sects have revitalised their activities, strengthened their cadres and adapted flexibly to modern conditions, thus reinforcing their influence on some sections of the population.[4]

Various factors were said to have contributed to this situation, but special emphasis was placed upon the impact of the Great Patriotic War.

The Nazis attacked the Soviet Union in June 1941 and, whilst Stalin faltered over how to respond, the surviving hierarchs of the Russian Orthodox Church immediately offered their support to the war effort. Over the next four years religious congregations throughout the USSR

---

[4] 'O krupnykh nedostatkakh v nauchno-ateisticheskoi propagande i merakh ee uluchsheniya', 7 July 1954, in *O religii i tserkvi* (Moscow, 1977), p. 67.

contributed millions of roubles to the Red Army, and religious leaders portrayed the struggle in traditional nationalist terms. On the part of the state overt campaigning against religion was abandoned, and the League of the Militant Godless disbanded. In 1943 Stalin met with the leading hierarchs of the Orthodox Church and effectively promised them a new deal involving the return of some churches and other institutions, a limited right of publication, and the freeing of such religious personnel as had survived the terror of the 1930s and earlier. Simultaneously, religious leaders sought to ensure survival by actively propagating Soviet foreign policy objectives in the international arena during the late 1940s.[5]

Perhaps inevitably the hardships created by war strengthened the position of religious groups. As one writer put it:

war is linked to heavy sacrifices, privations, worries about the fate of relations, dear ones, friends and comrades. Religion is always parasitic on unhappy people and on their losses. It is not then surprising that amongst people who before the war were believers or who until recently had still not broken with religion, under the influence of the sufferings of the war period and the consequent weakening of scientific atheist propaganda, there has been a notable strengthening rather than weakening of religious prejudices.[6]

In this situation religious consolation was offered by many of the illegally functioning religious communities, though their activities were supplemented and increasingly overtaken by the numerous places of worship officially reopened during the course of the war – some as a result of Stalin's *modus vivendi* with the church, some which started to function during Nazi occupation and which remained open when the Red Army returned, and some in the new areas annexed by the USSR as a result of the war.[7]

Quantifying this revitalisation of religious observance is impossible for no adequate studies of religious adherence were carried out, but numerous Soviet sources attest to its reality. Such a revival was hardly surprising, for war often does render religious institutions and values more attractive, and it was perhaps even more likely in a situation where religion had been artifically repressed for many years. This process was to continue in the post-war years as concessions to the officially

[5] See H. Fireside, *Icon and Swastika – The Russian Orthodox Church under Nazi and Soviet Control* (Cambridge, MA, 1971); D. Pospielovksy, *The Russian Orthodox Church under the Soviet Regime, 1917–82*, I (New York, 1984), chs 6–7; W. Fletcher, *Religion and Soviet Foreign Policy, 1945–70* (London, 1973).

[6] S. Khudyakov, 'Vazhnye voprosy nauchno-ateisticheskoi propagandy', *Kommunist* 13, 1954, p. 80. It is worth noting the suggestion here that religion made no inroads amongst those who were convinced atheists before the war.

[7] See A. Zalesski, ed, *Prichiny sushchestvovaniya i puti preodoleniya religioznykh perezhitkov* (Moscow, 1965), p. 168.

recognised religious groups continued, and the number of registered religious communities grew. For example, prior to the war there were perhaps only a few hundred functioning Russian Orthodox churches, but by April 1946 there were 10,544 and by January 1949 some 14,477[8] – though the majority of these were in territories acquired as a result of the war. And although this figure started to drop during the early 1950s, it was only from 1958 onwards that the fall became dramatic.[9]

These reopened religious institutions were strengthened in the years immediately following Stalin's death by an influx of religious activists who had served years in the camps and who in many cases were in no mood for compromise. Amongst the Evangelical communities such people often took the lead in extending religious activities beyond the narrow parameters laid down by the state. Such people were at the heart of the internal church struggle which led to the creation of a militant 'underground' Baptist movement during the early 1960s in response to the Khrushchev campaign.[10] In similar fashion the banned Ukrainian Catholic Church was revitalised by the release of many of its clerics during this period. And even within the Russian Orthodox Church there appear to have been some who sought to use the period after the November 1954 Central Committee decree to broaden the scope of religious activity. Bishop Arsenii of Kostroma, for example, stimulated considerable official activity in 1955–6 when he committed numerous 'violations of the legislation on cults', most notably holding unsanctioned prayer services in the open air and telling one of his priests who said this was not permitted that 'this was an internal church question' and not for the state to determine. The local CRA commissioner also suggested that he was preaching political sermons, by speaking out against Marxist–Leninist materialism.[11]

During the 1950s anti-religious writers adduced factors other than the war to explain the revitalisation of religion. In a paper given at a major Znanie (Knowledge) society conference in May 1957, N. I. Gubanov

[8] TsKhSD, f. 17, op. 132, d.7, contains an album given to Mikhail Suslov by CAROC chairman Karpov in 1948 which reports the existence of 14,329 active Orthodox churches on 1 Jan. 1948. Of these only 3,217 are in the Russian republic.
[9] Reliable figures for the immediate pre-war years are hard to come by, given that even of those registered probably only a minority actually functioned. M. Odintsev reports twenty-five oblasts with no functioning churches and another twenty with only five between them. *Nauka i religiya* 8, 1990, p. 19. Statistics on registered religious communities can be found in the archives of the Council for Religious Affairs located in the Central State Archive of the October Revolution, TsGAOR, f. 6991s. Those quoted here come from op. 2, ed.khr. 180, p. 22.
[10] See W. Sawatsky, *Soviet Evangelicals since World War II* (Ontario, 1981), chapter 2, and a later account appearing in *Moscow News* 13 May 1990.
[11] State Archive of the Kostroma Region (GAKosO), f. 2102, op. 5, d. 24.

isolated a number of reasons underlying the continued survival of religion under socialism. Though arguing that the social roots of religion had been destroyed as a result of the revolution – a claim which, as we shall see, was to become the subject of some debate in later years – Gubanov suggested that continuing socio-economic difficulties continued to play their part in ensuring religion's survival. And even where economic development had achieved much consciousness still lagged behind life. This was particularly the case in agricultural regions where human dependency upon nature rendered people susceptible to religious claims. The effort to overcome religion had not been helped, according to Gubanov, by the human and economic losses of the war, nor by the efforts of the capitalist camp to encourage religion as a means of undermining socialism. Above all it had been weakened by the failures of atheist propaganda since the war years.[12]

This emphasis on the failings of ideological work was perhaps the single most repeated theme in the writings of the 1950s and early 1960s. In particular published sources made much of the cessation of atheist work in many areas, the willingness of party officials to compromise with religion, and their avoidance of participation in anti-religious work. Typical of such material was an article that appeared in *Pravda* during August 1954. Here special correspondent Sergei Kushinsky told of how the priest in the town of Omutninsk, Kirov oblast, received a phone call in the middle of the night asking for an immediate baptism. The priest told the caller to return the next day, but the caller persisted and informed him that he was to baptise the son of the editor of the local party paper. A short while later there was a knock on the door. The baptismal party appeared and turned out to include a number of local party and komsomol secretaries. After the event the priest was instructed to remove the boy's name from the parish register. When the matter came before the party committee all those involved blamed their mothers-in-law! This case happened in 1950 yet Kushinsky notes that, despite some marginal shuffling of personnel, those involved still enjoyed official positions, and there was still no atheist work being carried out in the district.[13]

If the concessions made to religious groups during the war years seem to have confused party activists, so too did the backtracking implicit in the November 1954 Central Committee resolution which criticised excesses in anti-religious work. As Znanie society chairman M. B. Mitin told the May 1957 conference:

[12] N. I. Gubanov, 'O prichinakh sushchestvovaniya religioznykh perezhitkov v SSSR', in P. N. Fedoseev & M. N. Sheinman, eds., *Nauka i religiya* (Moscow, 1957), pp. 50–67.
[13] *Pravda* 4 Aug. 1954.

several organisations of the society and some comrades leading anti-religious propaganda misunderstood ... the decree of 10 November 1954. Individual leaders of society organisations mistakenly evaluated this decree as a call to stop systematic struggle with religious ideology, and as the beginning of the curtailment of anti-religious propaganda.

This mistaken understanding was reflected in the decreasing number of atheist lectures given by society members – from 120,679 in 1954 to 84,039 in 1956.[14]

Reasserting control

One feature of the revival of religion after the war was the reemergence of many traditional customs that had been suppressed during Stalin's assault on the peasantry. In this context it was perhaps not unexpected, especially given Khrushchev's use of agriculture in his struggle with Malenkov, to find that a central theme of the brief 1954 campaign was the alleged loss to the economy caused by religious festivals. The July 1954 Central Committee resolution noted that:

As a result of the activisation of the churches there has been an increase in the number of citizens observing religious holidays and performing religious rituals, and a renewal of pilgrimages to so called 'holy places' ... The celebration of religious holidays is frequently accompanied by mass drunkenness, mass killing of cattle, causing considerable loss to the economy and drawing thousands of people away from work ... Religious prejudices and superstitions undermine the consciousness of a part of the Soviet people and reduces their active participation in the building of communism.[15]

This theme was repeated in the press at regular intervals with some authors seeking to quantify the damage done to the national economy. One Byelorussian report spoke of 'half the potato crop' suffering damage on one collective farm where employees spent too much time celebrating religious festivals.[16] In the Islamic regions problems allegedly arose less as a result of the drunkenness attendant upon feastdays, than from the weakening of workers as a result of fasting, and from the unprofitable sacrifice of huge quantities of cattle.[17]

During the 1954 campaign, as well as later, the press often asserted that not only did religion lead to absenteeism and drunkenness, but that on

---

[14] M. B. Mitin, 'O soderzhanii i zadachi nauchno-ateisticheskoi propagandy v sovre-mennykh usloviyakh', in Fedoseev & Sheinman, *Nauka i religiya*, pp. 7–22.
[15] *O religii i tserkvi*, p. 67.   [16] *Sovetskaya Belorussiya* 31 July 1954.
[17] *Zarya vostoka* 10 October 1954; this view of fasting as weakening workers in the Islamic regions was endorsed by some of those former Soviet citizens interviewed by Rasma Karklins for her *Ethnic Relations in the USSR – The View from Below* (London, 1985), p. 186.

occasion it led to serious criminal activity. In the summer of that year *Trud* recorded the fate of a young woman who, quite unawares, married a Baptist. Gradually he pressurised her into leaving work and turning down an opportunity to go into higher education. When she persisted in her attempts to enter college, the man simply murdered his wife. The paper concluded, rather ominously, that whilst the murderer had been severely punished, the 'dark forces which pushed him into this act remained unexposed'.[18] The truth or otherwise of these stories was less relevant than their purpose. Religious activity was contributing to a whole variety of activities disapproved of by the state and to a considerable degree beyond its control. The time had come to restore order in a sphere which had been given too much freedom since the war. This point can be further illustrated from the repeated injunctions to local party and state organisations to exercise tighter control over the activities of religious organisations.[19]

We can see here a certain logic. Starting from the need for greater social discipline, something violated by the side effects of religious festivals, we move on to the need for a greater degree of political control over religious institutions so that they do not violate the law without punishment and thus raise questions about the state's wider control over society. In addition, if religious organisations were properly controlled fanatical extremists would be less likely to get involved and tragedies involving physical abuse or even murder were less likely to occur. This pursuit of control was, as we shall see, a major feature of the anti-religious campaign of the early 1960s, though one doubts that drunkenness and ritual murder were the major factors contributing to the renewal of anti-religious campaigning.

The national and the international

In contrast with both earlier and later periods factors relating to nationality politics and external influences were not greatly emphasised under Khrushchev, though the relationship between religion and nationalism was raised in various contexts: Roman Catholicism in Lithuania, Greek Catholicism in western Ukraine – both newly acquired areas where resistance to Soviet rule remained strong – Islam in Central Asia, and in the context of renewed 'anti-Zionism'. Typical of such writings was an article that appeared in Lithuania during 1963 in which the author attempted to discredit the role of the Catholic Church in

---

[18] *Trud* 22 Aug. 1954.
[19] *Literatura i zhizn'* 23 Nov. 1960 exposed an illegal printing operation, and reminded readers that the publication of religious literature was only permitted to official church organisations and 'under proper control'.

Lithuania past and present. Before the war 'ideologists of the Catholic Church stirring up nationalist feelings, sought to divert the working people of Lithuania from the class struggle for national and social liberation', whilst today 'Catholic priests drag up the thesis that the concept of "Lithuanian patriot" includes Catholic conscience and sentiment. The clergy still attempt to represent themselves as the sole defenders and guardians of Lithuanian traditions and even of Lithuanian culture.'[20] Similar comments could be found emanating from the Islamic regions of the USSR, with Uzbek first secretary Rashidov warning a 1963 Central Committee plenum that nationalistic prejudices were often kept alive by religious traditions.[21] Yet very little of the available writings suggest that the national-religious link was a major factor motivating the new campaign, although it may well have affected its implementation in certain areas.

The same applies to the international factor, although anti-religious specialists routinely denounced the attempts of imperialist powers to utilise the religious question in their efforts to undermine socialism. P. P. Cherkasin noted that:

By all legal and illegal, overt and secret means, they are fostering the preservation of a false outlook in the peoples' democracies and the USSR. The imperialists are especially active in supporting religion as a well tried bulwark of reaction. Diplomatic actions are undertaken to this end, with demonstrative visits to religious organisations in the USSR by tourists and delegations from abroad, the dropping of leaflets, and the organisation of religious broadcasts.[22]

Press articles detailed the efforts of religious smugglers[23] or Latvian Baptists allegedly used by Western intelligence forces.[24] But such stories served less to motivate a policy than to reinforce a campaign already in motion.

At the most pragmatic level, then, the new attack on religion was described in terms of the need to contain and restrain a religious sector which had revived during Stalin's last years and which showed signs of going beyond official control. But to explain this new turn it is clear that we have to move to a level of analysis that takes account of Khrushchev's own commitment to the anti-religious struggle and its relationship to his attempt to build communism 'in the main' by 1980.

[20] *Sovetskaya Litva* 19 Dec. 1963.   [21] *Pravda* 22 June 1963.
[22] P. P. Cherkashin, 'O sotsial'nykh kornyakh religii', *Voprosy filosofii*, 6, 1958, pp. 29–41.
[23] *Ogonyok* 46, 1963, pp. 30–31.   [24] *Sovetskaya Latviya* 20 Oct. 1954.

Khrushchev and the ideological imperative

A personal campaign?

Issues reach political agendas through a variety of channels. Some stem from factors beyond the control of political elites: popular unrest, public opinion, interest group pressure, natural disasters, or the activities of other states. Others, possibly a minority in most situations, are placed on the agenda by political elites, especially those dominated by an individual whose tendency is to lead from the front. In the case of Khrushchev we can see very clearly this approach, with many commentators noting his brash, single minded and 'adventurist' style. In Breslauer's words 'the First Secretary's public posture as a politician was distinctly confrontational. He attempted to steal the initiative from his colleagues in the leadership by creating a climate of campaignist fervour on behalf of far reaching developmental goals.'[25] Thus it was that he attached his name, and authority, to specific policies, whether it be the Virgin Lands development, de-Stalinisation, the maize campaign, or the backing of quack geneticists such as Lysenko.

Two other features of Khrushchev's political style are relevant here: his authoritarianism and his penchant for thinking on the grand scale. Despite his reformism and general attempt to humanise Soviet society, Khrushchev never quite reconciled the dilemma of the reformer seeking to encourage popular initiative whilst ensuring that it moved in the direction he had chosen. Perhaps inevitably, when things did not slip comfortably into place, it was not difficult for him to slip back into the old bullying ways he had learned under Stalin. More importantly he was inclined to think about political change in broad strokes. Under his guidance Soviet society would not simply advance a few more steps along the road to communism, but would lay down plans that would guarantee its achievement before the end of the century. And if, as all the classic works suggested, the disappearance of religion was a precondition for the creation of a communist society, religious institutions were bound to be affected by the rapid construction of a communist society.

In his memoirs Khrushchev has little to say about religion, recording only the influence that led him to break with the church whilst still at school:

My school teacher was a woman named Lydia Shevchenko. She was a revolutionary. She was also an atheist. She instilled in me my first political consciousness and began to counteract the effects of my strict religious

[25] G. Breslauer, *Khrushchev and Brezhnev as Leaders – Building Authority in Soviet Politics* (London, 1982), pp. 34–5.

upbringing. My mother was very religious, likewise her father ... When I think back to my childhood, I can remember vividly the saints on the icons against the wall of our wooden hut, their faces darkened by fumes from the oil lamps. I remember being taught to kneel and pray in front of the icons with the grownups in the church. When we were taught to read, we read the scriptures. But Lydia Shevchenko set me on a path which took me away from all that.[26]

This decision once taken was one that Khrushchev never appears to have doubted later. As he told a French journalist in 1958 'I think that there is no God. I have long ago freed myself from such an idea. I am an advocate of the scientific world view. Science and belief in supernatural forces are incompatible and mutually exclusive views.'[27]

Despite this rejection of religion, it is difficult from his public utterances to trace any hint of him pushing hardline policies on religion. In an interview given to American journalists in 1957, prior to the anti-religious campaign, Khrushchev made a number of rather conventional points about the use of religion to justify repressive policies under capitalism, but went on to suggest that in the USSR believers enjoy full freedom of conscience. Of course:

if clergymen were to combine their religious activities with political agitation against the Soviet state this would be in violation of the constitution. And the Soviet state will not tolerate such interference.

We still have people who believe in God. Let them believe. To believe or not to believe in God is the personal affair of each individual, a matter for his conscience. All this does not, however, prevent the Soviet people from living in peace and friendship. And it often happens that there are believers and atheists in one family. But those who believe in God are becoming fewer. The vast majority of young people growing up today do not believe in God. Education, scientific knowledge and study of the laws of nature leave no room for belief in God.[28]

Designed for an American audience, this interview also appeared in the Soviet press, and, almost certainly unintentionally, hinted at what was to come. Following a pro forma reassertion of freedom of conscience, it warned clergy of the dangers of going beyond the narrow parameters set out in existing laws – although not of how narrowly they would be interpreted after 1958 – and in its educational emphasis hinted at later interpretations which would make the participation of overt believers in higher education a virtual impossibility.

Nonetheless, we still lack a public commitment to anti-religious campaigning from Khrushchev's own mouth. At both the 21st (1959)

[26] N. S. Khrushchev, *Khrushchev Remembers*, I (London, 1971), p. 18.
[27] *Pravda* 27 Mar. 1958.   [28] *Pravda* 29 Nov. 1957.

and 22nd (1961) party congresses Khrushchev's keynote speeches made only passing reference to the need to overcome 'the survivals of capitalism in peoples' consciousness' or to 'overcome bourgeois ideology'. Yet is is difficult to find any other sponsor for the campaign, with the speeches of other Presidium members revealing no outbursts of anti-religious enthusiasm. Indeed, V. A. Kuroedov, chairman of the Council for the Affairs of the Russian Orthodox Church during the 1960s, has suggested that no single politician was particularly promoting the anti-religious campaign, though he noted that Mikhail Suslov spoke more harshly than most on the issue.[29] Publicly, the most senior figure to address the question in depth was Khrushchev's ideological chief L. F. Il'ichev, but despite Khrushchev's later attempts to blame Il'ichev for the rather crass ideological campaigns of the early 1960s,[30] there is little evidence that he was more than a faithful executor of his master's policies.

Ideological impulse

Ultimately it is within the context of 'building communism' that one has to locate the anti-religious campaign. Though Stalin had effectively relegated communism to the distant future,[31] Khrushchev very soon made clear his intention of hastening the process of transition. Addressing the 20th Party Congress in 1956 he spoke of the USSR as having 'climbed to such summits, that we can see the wide vistas leading to the ultimate goal, a communist society'.[32] Three years later, at the 21st Congress the first secretary spelt out his vision in more detail, 'having built a socialist society, the Soviet people are entering a new period of historical development in which socialism will grow into communism'. He went on to outline some of the features of this new stage, and stressed that to achieve this goal it was essential to carry out a struggle against all 'manifestations of bourgeois views and morals' and to propagate a scientific worldview amongst the whole population.[33] This was developed further at the 22nd Congress in 1961, where it was promised that by 1980 a communist society would have been built 'in the main'. Amongst the various tasks necessary for the construction of a communist society was the creation of a 'new man' fit to inhabit a communist society.[34]

[29] *Lyudina i svit* (Man and the World), 1, 1992, p. 21.
[30] See R. Medvedev, *Khrushchev* (London, 1982), p. 254.
[31] A. Evans, 'Developed Socialism and the New Programme of the CPSU', in S. White & A. Pravda, eds., *Ideology and Soviet Politics* (London, 1988), pp. 85–91.
[32] ibid., p. 91.   [33] *Pravda* 28 Jan. 1959.
[34] See the discussion of Khrushchev and ideology in White and Pravda, *Ideology and Soviet Politics*, pp. 91–94.

Even before the 21st Congress a leading article in *Kommunist* had called for 'the final overcoming of survivals in the consciousness of Soviet people'.[35] After that congress general injunctions to tackle religious survivals were fleshed out by Il'ichev who laid considerable emphasis on the voluntaristic aspects of building communism, i.e. it would not happen simply as a result of socio-economic transformation, but required conscious effort. Indeed, it was essential that the whole people march forward to the ultimate end. Yet he recognised that the objective of making all march to the same tune was difficult to achieve and required considerable organisational work by the party aimed at overcoming 'the survivals of capitalism' in peoples' consciousness. Of these 'survivals' religion was one of the most tenacious and hard to overcome, because it was passed from generation to generation in the relatively impenetrable context of the home.[36] We shall return to Il'ichev's interpretations of the anti-religious campaigns below, but it is worth noting that it was he who enjoyed great prominence in setting out its ideological justification and that his attitude was uncompromising – religion is backward, unscientific, alien to the citizens of a socialist society, and doomed to extinction. In the context of the commitment to build communism within a specific time frame, as well as within a cultural inheritance of violent struggle with non-conformity, it is difficult to see how this attitude could have resulted in anything other than an active assault on religious ideas and, in practice, upon religious communities themselves.

Policy 'debate'

Scholars exploring other policy decisions during the Khrushchev years have noted the existence of debates and arguments within the 'policy communities' and concerned 'public', and have suggested that on occasion these led to the modification of centrally determined policies. In the case of the new campaign against religion, such controversies are harder to find, at least in published and available archive sources. The picture is rather one of a policy strongly backed by the leader, and one which could only be discussed at the margins if at all. This is not to suggest that there was no discussion, but simply that it was one severely constrained by the personal commitment of the leader to the elimination

---

[35] 'Usilit' nauchno-ateisticheskuyu propagandu', *Kommunist* 17, 1958, p. 98.
[36] L. F. Il'ichev, 'XXI s'ezd KPSS i nekotorye voprosy ideologicheskoi raboty', *Kommunist*, 2, 1959, pp. 18–32; cf. his later article, *Kommunist* 14, 1960, pp. 22–40; and leaders in *Nauka i religiya* 10, 1961, pp. 3–10, and 12, 1961, pp. 3–6, and 1, 1962, pp. 3–8.

of religion within the context of 'building communism'. Moreover, it was an area in which no senior politician had a vested interest to represent or defend.

That religion has been the subject of political controversy cannot be doubted. During the 1920s the 'religious question' was one of the issues fought over by the various groups seeking political dominance within the party.[37] Bohdan Bociurkiw has suggested that Soviet religious policy was the product of an ongoing debate between 'fundamentalists' and 'pragmatists' within the political community. The former have stressed the need for a continuous struggle against religion, opposed any form of collaboration with the churches, and supported restrictive legislation and administrative measures used against religious organisations. Their institutional support he saw as concentrated in the party's agitprop apparatus and the Komsomol. The 'pragmatists' are those who have differentiated between religious groups on the basis of their loyalty to the current political line, who have emphasised the need to 'sovietise' religious organisations, and have stressed a gradual overcoming of religious survivals. Their base he saw as lying in certain sections of the party, state and security police. Yet as Bociurkiw points out, neither side denied the basic Leninist premise that the struggle against religion should be subordinate to the building of socialism. Moreover, he suggested that the two trends were in fact complementary insofar as repressive measures conditioned the churches to accept the Soviet system in order to survive, whilst the strengthening of control weakened their capacity to survive.[38]

Though having some validity this interpretation is perhaps too simplistic. In the first place, it is often difficult to identify the position taken by individuals and institutions from their public statements, especially when all proclaim their adherence to the current line of the party. The reading of nuances in the Soviet press is problematic in many respects, particularly if intepretations cannot be backed up with other evidence. It is probably also the case that many within the atheist establishment could not easily be located in the either-or division posited by Bociurkiw. Instead we should speak of a policy spectrum, with individuals and institutions located at various points and perhaps shifting on different issues.

We would also argue that during the Khrushchev period it is not possible to speak of a policy debate as in some sense prior to the adoption

[37] D. Peris, 'The 1929 Congress of the Godless', *Soviet Studies*, vol. 43, no. 4, 1991, pp. 711–32.
[38] B. Bociurkiw, 'The Shaping of Soviet Religious Policy', *Problems of Communism*, May–June 1973, pp. 37–51.

of policy, but rather one as 'licensed',[39] that is, as developing in a very muted fashion once the new turn had already been taken. In this 'debate' there was little room for direct criticism of official policies, although occasionally there are hints of doubt beneath the surface. Moreover, it is a debate in which those backing the hard line favoured by the first secretary make all the running and in which critical voices could only make themselves known behind the scenes or in the context of a public rejection of their views.

Restating orthodoxy

The official view was set out in a *Pravda* editorial during August 1959. Starting with a reminder that 'our party's premise in defining its attitude towards religion is that religion is inimicable to the interests of the working masses, that it is the most conservative form of social consciousness, and that it hinders the active struggle of the people for the transformation of society', it went on to criticise those party members who misinterpreted freedom of conscience as permitting the free dissemination of religious views. This had led many clerics to increase their activities in recent years without any effort on the part of the authorities to stop them. Though the editorial gave the standard warning about the need to avoid insulting believers' feelings, it reminded party workers that the final goal was the 'complete eradication of religious prejudices'.[40]

A key feature of the orthodox position was its emphasis on the fact that religion no longer had any social roots in the USSR. As F. N. Oleshchuk, a veteran of the League of Militant Godless, put it: 'as a result of the Great October Socialist Revolution the capitalist base nourishing religion has been destroyed in our country and a new base has been created in which there is no soil for religion ... religion continues in the form of a survival'. If religion survived it did so not for any objective reason, but because of the continuing unresolved difficulties within the USSR – incompleteness of social transformation, poor propaganda, and the capitalist encirclement which rendered progress slow.[41] The implication of this was that as socialism developed religion would disappear, though not, most authors repeated, 'of itself'. Ideology chief Leonid Il'ichev made this clear in a number of articles published in *Kommunist*, which stressed that party members had to be active opponents of religious

---

[39] A point made in T. Gustafson, *Reform in Soviet Politics – Lessons of Recent Policies on Land and Water* (Cambridge, 1981), p. 158.   [40] *Pravda* 21 Aug. 1959.

[41] F. N. Oleshchuk, 'Religioznye perezhitki i puti ikh preodoleniya', *Voprosy filosofii*, 6, 1954, pp. 76–88.

prejudices. 'Objective factors' were decisive in bringing about the decline of religion, but the 'subjective factor' was crucial in finishing it off.[42]

A further feature of the orthodox position was a willingness to talk about the possibility of finally eliminating religion from human existence and to suggest that this goal might even be in sight. An editorial in *Nauka i religiya* during 1963 spoke of the current programme of communist construction as including: 'the complete and final overcoming of religious survivals and the liberation of people's consciousness from prejudices and superstition. Communism will be an atheist society, where the religious mist is finally dispelled, where people are delivered for ever from fantastic religious representations.'[43] In analysing the religious question the orthodox view tended to stress the totally reactionary nature of any manifestation of religion, and reject any idea of compromise with religion. The commonly held view – including Marx amongst its adherents – that religion had played a progressive role in certain historical periods was treated with suspicion by many writers, if not rejected outright.[44] Such writers were also notable for their favourable treatment of periods such as the 1930s when anti-religious work had been characterised by brutal measures taken against religious bodies. Typical yet again was Oleshchuk who claimed that during this period 'many churches were closed at the request of believers'.[45] Writing towards the end of the Khrushchev campaign Il'ichev expressed a similar nostalgia for the past when noting that in the years 1943–4 a departure from Leninist norms in church–state relations had been permitted, and that this had allowed the churches to reassert themselves.[46]

Such an approach led to a distinctive understanding of the concept of freedom of conscience and interpretation of existing legislation on religion. Again we might quote Il'ichev's 1964 article which described recent years as having seen the return to a proper understanding of the law and the withdrawal of privileges from clerics. In particular he singled out the need to eradicate the organised teaching of religion to children.[47] A yet tougher line was taken by I. Brazhnik, writing in *Partiinaya zhizn'*, who suggested that deviations from Leninist principles had led to the:

granting of illegal privileges and toleration to clergymen; this gave them the opportunity to step up their activites, to violate grossly the legislation on cults, to encourage idlers playing the role of church activists and choristers. In Tajikistan

---

[42] This approach is especially clear in L. F. Il'chev, 'Formirovanie nauchnogo mirovozzreniya ateisticheskogo vospitanie', *Kommunist* 1, 1964, p. 23.

[43] *Nauka i religiya* 6, 1963, p. 2.

[44] See the editorial in *Komsomol'skaya pravda* 1 July 1954.

[45] Oleshchuk, 'Religioznye perezhitki', p. 80.

[46] Il'ichev, 'Formirovanie nauchnogo', p. 29.   [47] ibid., p. 40.

and other Central Asian republics the illegal activities of charlatan mullahs who shamelessly fleece trusting believers is tolerated to this day, and one often encounters mosques disguised as tearooms ...

Though he offered a warning against administrative measures, Brazhnik clearly felt that the law had been interpreted insufficiently strictly.[48] In general, orthodox writers stressed that the law permitted religious organisations one function, 'the performance of religious rites'.[49]

Critical voices

In the context of an increasingly harsh anti-religious campaign those advocating orthodox positions made much of the running, although it is possible to detect within published sources, as well as within the archives, limited evidence of resistance to the new turn. There are, however, problems in interpreting material appearing in the press, something that can be clearly illustrated from a story printed in *Komsomol'skaya pravda* shortly before Khrushchev's fall. Here T. Yakovlev responded in what initially seemed a 'liberal' manner to a letter from a group of students in defence of one of their number marked down for being a believer. Despite repeatedly high performance Oleg was given low grades on the simple grounds that he believed in God, something the students felt – quite rightly in the opinion of the journalist – was unjust. Yet Yakovlev went on to suggest that in fact the students were missing the real point, that they were concentrating on the lesser evil whilst ignoring the main issue. That is, that

one of their friends was living under the heavy yoke of belief in God ... they were dismayed by the injustice but weren't they guilty of a bigger injustice, a bigger cruelty themselves? They came to his defence in a small thing, in the matter of his certificate and grades, but abandoned him in the big thing, in the central question of his life.[50]

Bearing this problem of interpretation in mind it is, nonetheless, possible to isolate hints of dissension from the dominant hard line on religion. From those one might call 'centrists' come suggestions that there remained at least some social factors contributing towards the survival of religion, a rejection of campaigning tactics against religion, an emphasis on more gradualist and educational anti-religious measures, and a tendency to speak in more positive terms of 'atheism' rather than 'anti-religion'. Moderate views were, however, put forward very tentatively, and most of the writers concerned were equally capable of writing in

[48] I. Brazhnik, 'Ateisticheskoe vospitanie – obshchepartiinoe delo', *Partiinaya zhizn '* 24, 1963, pp. 21–26.
[49] According to *Nauka i religiya* editor Kolonitsky, writing in *Izvestiya* 18 Feb. 1961.
[50] *Komsomol'skaya pravda* 6 Sept. 1964.

harsh language when the occasion demanded. Bohdan Bociurkiw has drawn attention to a piece that appeared in *Voprosy filosofii* on the eve of the anti-religious campaign where P. Cherkashin argued that religion still had some social roots in Soviet society.[51] Yet, as we have already seen (p. 13), this same writer could simultaneously make crude claims about the role of capitalist powers in stimulating religious life within the USSR for their own ends.

V. Bukin offered a more psychological approach to atheist work in an article which appeared during 1963 in *Kommunist*, an unlikely source of moderation at this time. He stressed a gradual approach to overcoming religion, one based upon change in 'public psychology', upon 'systematic labour, ideological, moral and aesthetic upbringing' and upon 'drawing believers into active productive and socially useful activity'. Above all he spoke of approaching believers on their own terms and offering them books and articles which they will find interesting, rather than dry, unemotional works which provided no competition to the colourful fare offered by the churches' preachers.[52]

Possible evidence of resistance to or disagreement with official policies can be found in the context not of overt statements, but in those articles attacking incorrect ideas about religion and its future, or lack thereof, in Soviet society. In an article published in *Nauka i religiya* at the beginning of 1963 the writer Konstantin Simonov suggested that religious morality was not without its positive elements. In particular he claimed to have found 'moral truth and moral beauty' in parts of the Bible, and noted that religious commandments included appeals to 'live a moral life and to avoid evil acts'.[53] This was too much for Grigory Simonov, a philosophy lecturer at the Moscow Power Institute, for whom an even-handed approach to religious morality was out of the question and incompatible with genuine atheism. Could the writer not see, he argued, that 'religion only sanctified the existing moral norms, which were to the advantage of the oppressor'. Had he forgotten Lenin's characterisation of any 'flirting with god' as a 'vile abomination'.[54] Some weeks later *Izvestiya* published a review of the letters received in response to Grigory Simonov's article, most of which backed up the philosophy lecturer, though some did apparently suggest that religious morality could be useful in certain circumstances.[55]

Such a debate was rare in that here at least the initial offender had been

---

[51] Cherkashin (1958). Here I follow Bociurkiw's argument in 'Religion and Atheism in Soviet Society', in R. Marshall, ed., *Aspects of Religion in the Soviet Union, 1917–1967* (Chicago, 1971), pp. 47–8.

[52] V. Bukin, 'Preodolenie religioznykh chuvstv', in *Kommunist* 2, 1963, pp. 71–74.

[53] *Nauka i religiya* 2, 1963, pp. 3–6.   [54] *Izvestiya* 25 Oct. 1963.

[55] *Izvestiya* 4 Dec. 1963.

able to express his opinions in print. More usually one has to rely on the critics who attack those with doubtful views on the religious question. Many of those advocating 'compromise' with religion claimed to be atheists and it was this that aroused the ire of many anti-religious workers. Aleksander Osipov, the former lecturer at the Leningrad theological seminary whose conversion to atheism had been something of a *cause célèbre*, quoted a leter from A. Ya. Smirnova:

I myself am a biologist, 64 years old. I am a confirmed atheist, but I was born and raised in a religious climate and studied in the day school of an evangelical church, and religion has always held a certain charm for me…

Above all people must be aware of two things: first that man is a brother and a friend to man (fulfilment of the ten commandments enters into this), and second, that labour is a matter of honour. If all or most people were aware of this, of course we could create communism…

And what if religion and the clergy of all stripes, insofar as they still wield great influence in the world, could do much to raise the moral level of the people. Believers would heed the voice of the priests. They could give leadership to many people and thereby lighten the work of the state … If religion is considered to be the opium of the people, then it should be said that in small doses narcotics are useful, for they soothe people and reduce pain…

Smirnova's argument was at least presented very plausibly, albeit in the process of being set up for refutation by Osipov. For him the idea of religion as some sort of ideal to be emulated by the builders of communism was absurd, and he suggested that it would only be built by hard work, not by following the commandments.[56]

Of course, having pointed to the existence of critical voices it needs to be re-emphasized that they were very much in a minority in public discussion of the religious question and that there is little evidence that they played a role in the shaping of policy. But they did, perhaps, reflect real divisions within elite opinion, and their arguments were gradually to be developed until the late 1980s when they came to dominate the debate and contribute to the demise of anti-religion as state policy.

Bureaucratic politics and decision making

It is one thing to isolate nuances in published writings on the religious question, and quite another to relate them to political or institutional divisions within the policy making establishment. Even attempting to reconstruct the policy making process, at least that relating to key policy turns, is problematic although documents in the Central Committee archives do enable us to shed some light on the ways in which central party bodies operated.

[56] *Izvestiya* 25 Mar. 1964, and responses in *Izvestiya* 30 Apr. 1964.

Clearly the most important bodies here were the leading organs of the Communist Party. No radical new departure in policy was feasible without Presidium support, and there is little to suggest that Khrushchev was not backed by his colleagues in this matter. And as the new campaign unfolded it was from within the Central Committee, in particular the Ideological Commission headed by L. F. Il'ichev, that leadership and direction came. It was from the Central Committee that key guidelines on atheist education were issued and it was to this body that bureaucratic agencies appealed in seeking adjudication or interpretation of the current line.

Much day-to-day work was left to the Secretariat and its various departments, but on occasions matters were referred to the Presidium for decision. These included final approval for all draft resolutions on matters relating to religion and atheism, all legislative changes, and often questions relating to changes in the leadership of religious organisations. For example, in August 1955 the Secretariat decided to pass to the Presidium the request of the Council for the Affairs of Religious Cults to agree to the appeal of the Armenian Apostolic Church to hold a Council attended by foreign guests.[57] Seven years later issues relating to the Armenian Church were again forwarded to the Presidium after a Secretariat meeting attended by M. Suslov and L. Il'ichev heard that the Catholicos had received newspapers from reactionary circles whilst travelling abroad.[58] On 3 January 1962 the Secretariat approved the suggestions of the two chambers of the Supreme Soviet that religious organisations and leaders actively spreading religious rites or encroaching upon the rights of others be held criminally responsible, and forwarded its view to the party Presidium for final approval.[59]

As the anti-religious campaign developed in 1958 and after one sees the Secretariat active in commissioning different departments to draft decisions or in setting up sub-committees to discuss specific issues. In May 1958 the Ideological Commission discussed a memorandum from Agitprop on the need to improve atheist propaganda;[60] five weeks later the commission approved a draft decree approved by Agitprop and forwarded it to the Secretariat.[61] In August 1958 the Commission set up a sub-committee of Central Committee officials and the heads of the two councils on religious affairs to draft a decree on monastic taxes to be issued by the Council of Ministers.[62]

The Secretariat and Central Committee departments also had to

---

[57] TsKhSD, Protocols of the Secretariat, 81, 20 Aug. 1955.
[58] ibid., 29, 26 June 1962.   [59] ibid., 170, 3 Jan. 1961.
[60] TsKhSD, Protocols of the Ideological Commission, 9, 15 May 1958.
[61] ibid., 12, 19 June 1958.   [62] ibid., 14, 26 Aug. 1958.

respond to requests emanating from other bodies or deal with problems that arose in the implementation of religious policy. During late 1959 the Ideological Commission discussed a memorandum from the KGB reporting on disorders and anti-Soviet propaganda at a synagogue in the Moscow region, and commissioned Mikhail Suslov to review the matter.[63] In November 1960 a session of the Secretariat dealt with a note from the Department of Party Organs and Agitprop regarding the construction of a new Catholic church in the Lithuanian town of Klaipeda. Two months later a gathering of the Secretariat attended by Lithuanian first secretary A. Snechkus criticised the Lithuanian Central Committee and Council of Ministers for its 1956 decision to permit construction of this building and recommended that a way be found to halt the work.[64] It was also the agitprop apparatus of the Central Committee that was responsible for the censorship of the press and which ensured that voices critical of official policies did not find their way into print.

The official bodies formally responsible for religious policy at this time were the two councils for religious affairs. During the 1930s responsibility for the administration of religious policy had primarily been the responsibility of the NKVD, but in September 1943, in the context of a war time *modus vivendi* between church and state, Stalin met with the three leading Orthodox hierarchs. One month later TASS announced the establishment of 'a state commission whose function would be that of dealing with the religious problems of the Russian Orthodox Church for which government permission was required'. Its head was to be G. Karpov, an NKVD operative who had previously been involved in the persecution of the churches. One year later the Council for the Affairs of Religious Cults (CARC) was set up to deal with the affairs of other religious groups.[65] Official documents spoke of the councils' role as essentially mediatory and supervisory, and gave no indication that they had any role to play in decision making – though there were references to them drafting laws regulating religious life, and in the Central Committee archives there are frequent references to the Secretariat commissioning the councils to draft decrees or investigate specific problems. In general they was spoken of and viewed as organisations which implemented decisions taken elsewhere, notably in the Central Committee. Certainly from the records of the Secretariat one has the impression of the councils as supplicant – there are numerous

---

[63] ibid., 39, 25 Nov. 1959.
[64] TsKhSD, Protocols of the Secretariat, 167, 17 Nov. 1960 & 171, 10 Jan. 1961.
[65] For more detail see J. Anderson, 'The Council for Religious Affairs and the Shaping of Soviet Religious Policy', *Soviet Studies* vol. 43, no. 4, July 1991, pp. 689–710.

requests for permission to allow religious organisations to organise foreign delegations, hold councils, or to carry out certain measures to limit religious life.

Yet there is also some evidence to suggest that in a very limited way and at certain times both – or at least individuals within them – exhibited an unexpected degree of independence and very cautious, tentative resistance to the new campaign or at least to some of its excesses. There are documents which appear to support the view that Karpov, chairman of the Council for the Affairs of the Russian Orthodox Church (CAROC) was less than enthusiastic about the new attack on religion – though his involvement in repressive activities during the 1930s preclude any view of him as a 'liberal'.[66] Nonetheless, in March 1959, he wrote to RSFSR prime minister I. S. Polyansky complaining about the growing incidence of administrative abuses of believers' rights in various Russian provinces.[67] Two months later a session of the Ideological Commission criticised an instruction letter that Karpov had written for local authorities and reminded him that such documents needed to be cleared with the Central Committee before distribution.[68]

The following year he was removed from his post and replaced as CAROC chairman by V. A. Kuroedov, a man who had worked closely with Presidium member and ideologist Mikhail Suslov first in Lithuania (1940–41) and then in the Central Committee's agitprop apparatus.[69] According to his own account, written three decades later, Kuroedov was summoned to the Central Committee by Secretary Ye. Furtseva and given twenty-four hours to decide whether he wanted the job. His instructions were to 'restore order' in the religious sphere. Despite his later denials,[70] the new chairman turned out to be a man with no qualms about adopting the most restrictive and repressive interpretation of CAROC's role in implementing the new policy turn.

---

[66] In 1957 the Party Control Commission discussed major violations of socialist legality, mass arrests and application of inappropriate methods of investigation utilised by Karpov during 1937–8 whilst working for the Leningrad and Pskov NKVD. For these offences he was to have been excluded from the party but taking account of his good work for CAROC his punishment was limited to a severe reprimand recorded on his party card. *Izvestiya TsK* 11, 1989, pp. 52–3.

[67] Central State Archive of the October Revolution, TsGAOR, f.6991s (all future references to CRA archive from this fond), op.2, ed.khr. 254, p. 29; the Central Committee archives include a critical report he wrote in July 1959 on the over hasty closure of monasteries, although he is attacking the speed of closure not the fact. TsKhSD, f. 5, op. 30, d. 289, pp. 85–8.

[68] TsKhSD, Protocols of the Ideological Commission, 30, 28 May 1959.

[69] Details of Kuroedov's biography can be pieced together from *International Who's Who, 1982–83* (London, 1982), pp. 730–31, and from W. Hahn, *Post-War Politics – The Fall of Zhdanov and the Defeat of Moderation* (Cornell, 1982), pp. 211–12.

[70] *Lyudina i svit* (1992), pp. 20–3.

Within the archives of the Council for the Affairs of Religious Cults (CARC) are to be found possible indications of resistance to certain understandings of the new campaign, and even hints of an attempt to preserve at least a facade of legality in the fight against religion. In June 1964, for example, a session of CARC took the decision to address a complaint to the Central Committee and the Procuracy about an article that had appeared in *Nauka i religiya*. Here Yuri Rozenbaum had suggested that priests performing religious rites over children without the express permission of both parents should be treated as criminally responsible. CARC complained that such a restrictive interpretation was mistaken, because such action was not criminal, and that it was likely to lead to administrative measures against the clergy. They suggest that the Central Committee should ensure that a proper explanation of the law was published in *Nauka i religiya*.[71] The archive from late 1963 also contains a growing number of CARC criticisms aimed at those guilty of abusing believers' rights, with inspectors of the Council pointing to the illegal breaking up of meetings, searches, seizures of literature, and the refusal to register actually existing communities.[72]

It is also worth simply noting at this stage that CARC closed far fewer places of worship than did its counterpart responsible for the Orthodox Church. During the Khrushchev campaign some 40 per cent of Orthodox churches were deprived of registration, but less than 20 per cent of the non-Orthodox. Of course, this may have had nothing to do with bureaucratic resistance, but simply reflect the state's primary aim of destroying the traditional national church, but it is something that should be born in mind in interpreting this period. Yet whilst CARC may have been more hesitant this interpretation should not be pushed too far. The evidence is limited in scope, and that emanating from CARC mostly dates from 1964 by which time more perceptive officials may well have seen the possibility of change at the top – as we shall see, judicial review of some cases of imprisoned religious believers commenced even before Khrushchev's fall.

Further qualification to any suggestion that the councils might have offered any serious resistance to state policy must also come from an understanding of their clear subordinate position. Among other things, they lacked ministerial status, were subordinate to the Central Committee which appointed their leaders and to whom they reported, and appear to have had relatively limited control over their own employees in the provinces. In theory they appointed republican and regional

[71] Decision taken by CARC at its meeting on 5 June 1964. TsGAOR, op. 4, ed.khr. 147, pp. 8–9.
[72] For example, see ibid., p. 120 for critiques of development in Chuvash ASSR.

commissioners, but in practice these positions were on the nomenklatura of local party committees. On occasions the council might reject the choice of local party organisations,[73] but in general they seem to have accepted decisions made elsewhere. As a result most regional commissioners saw their prime loyalty as to party superiors, who generally controlled their future promotion prospects. In these circumstances commissioners were likely to intepret and implement the harsh policy line coming down from the Central Committee with little reference to any, admittedly limited, reservations on the part of the central councils.[74]

One other body whose role in shaping religious policy should be mentioned is the KGB. Though there is little evidence for this period as to its institutional 'views' on the religious question, we can make certain general assumptions. Firstly, as the agency responsible for internal security it was likely to have thoughts about the possible implications for political control of a new attack on religion. And as a major information gatherer the KGB probably revised its views as the new campaign, to many officials' surprise, produced a degree of resistance from some sections of the religious population that had not been anticipated. In particular it may have been concerned that overly repressive policies would push believers into a religious 'underground' which would be far harder to control.

More practically, the KGB was drawn into the decision making process when there was discussion of how best to deal with religious nonconformity. The Central Committee archive contains reports on decisions taken in response to KGB requests, as in January 1963 when it discussed the entry of a group of Pentecostals into the US embassy. On this occasion a group of three, including KGB chairman V. Semichastny, were commissioned to prepare a draft decree in response to this unforeseen action.[75] And just six days later, again in response to a security police memorandum, the Secretariat instructed the KGB to strengthen work aimed at preventing the illegal activities of certain Baptist communities.[76]

The security police also had close links with the two councils for religious affairs, many of whose officials were former operatives of the security forces. The councils in turn also maintained close links with the Lubyanka, for example forwarding to the KGB copies of documents and complaints it received from believers protesting the treatment of

[73] TsGAOR, op.2, ed.khr. 125, p. 39 reports the rejection of Balashov oblispolkom recommendation and asks for another candidate. No reason is given.
[74] Anderson, 'The Council for Religious Affairs'.
[75] TsKhSD, Protocols of the Secretariat, 54, 8 Jan. 1963.
[76] ibid., 55, 14 Jan. 1963.

religion.[77] Finally, the KGB was involved in attempts to infiltrate religious institutions and place its agents in their employ, a process that has been more clearly, if controversially, documented by material from the Central Committee archives that became available in 1992.[78]

From the material presented in the last two sections we can provide some support for Bociurkiw's suggestion of religious policy as the product of a debate between 'fundamentalists' and 'pragmatists', although one would not wish to push this too far. During the Khrushchev years the former were clearly the dominant group, strengthened by the backing of the first secretary. They were to be found largely in the party apparatus, in particular agitprop, and their views were given maximum publicity. Their main channels of expression were the party press and, not surprisingly, publications specialising in ideological and anti-religious material. The 'pragmatists' were more likely to be found in state institutions and at the more scholarly end of the atheist establishment, and such of their arguments as found their way into print appeared in papers such Izvestiya and journals such as Voprosy filosofii. Alternatively they waged their battles behind the scenes in the corridors of the bureaucracy. One should not however, overstate their significance or power. We have insufficient evidence to suggest a full-scale bureaucratic conflict, and none of the more overt statements of a pragmatic view could be described as genuine arguments for a radical liberalisation of policy. For such views one has to turn to a third group, what might be called the 'sceptics', for example writers such as Konstantin Simonov who refused to see religion in purely negative terms. One might also suggest that already there was beginning to emerge a 'public opinion' that no longer saw the point of a state sponsored attack on religion, expressed by people such as the woman who had the temerity to suggest that even opium had its uses. In other words, even during Khrushchev's assault on religion there are hints of a broadening spectrum of views that cannot be subsumed under the 'fundamentalist-pragmatist' divide, a spectrum that was to develop slowly under Brezhnev and more spectacularly under Gorbachev until those who rejected official attacks on religion became the dominant group.

[77] For example, in June 1964 Kuroedov forwarded an anonymous letter suggesting that the state and leading hierarchs had been involved in the murder of Metropolitan Nikolai of Kolomna and Krutitsy. TsGAOR, op. 2, ed.khr. 529, p. 28.

[78] Though most of the material published so far dates from the Brezhnev years, the policy was initiated much earlier. See Izvestiya 22 Jan. 1992 & Ogonyok 4, 1992, pp. 2–3.

Outputs: the 'public' definition of policy

Once politicans have decided, they have to convey the new or adjusted policy course to two different publics. On the one hand there is the general population, especially that section of the population likely to be most affected, and then there is what might be called the implementing public, those groups who have to be instructed and guided in putting theory into practice. What is noteworthy during the Khrushchev campaign against religion is the relative paucity of published 'outputs'. At no stage did a major political figure make a definitive statement on the new campaign, although there were routine comments about the need to strengthen anti-religious work. The only way the general public became aware of the new assault was via the increasing number of articles in the press on the religious question and, more occasionally, through witnessing the sudden demolition or seizure of places of worship. For believers the new turn was more visible in that they found themselves subject to a new wave of pressure, ranging in scope from crude propaganda to physical repression.

During the years 1953–64 only one Central Commitee resolution – that of November 1954 – and only one legal change – the 1962 amendments to the criminal laws relating to religion – were publicised at the time. Many of the other statements of intent only became available later – the July 1954 Central Committee resolution, the 1962 amendments to the Law on Religious Associations, and various secret instructions on the application of the laws issued by the two councils for religious affairs at the behest of the party apparatus. These documents were all aimed at party and state activists involved in implementing policy, and all suggest a harsher attitude towards religion than is implied in published documents.

The 1954 episode

The brief campaign of 1954 was bounded by two Central Committee resolutions, though that of July was not published until the 1960s. Having analysed the revival of religious life in the aftermath of war and the failure of many party organisations to struggle effectively against religion, the former resolution went on to oblige various party and state organisations to carry out certain tasks. In particular it warned against a passive attitude towards religion which underestimated its 'reactionary essence and the harm that it brought' to society. The Ministry of Culture and the Znanie society were enjoined to increase the number of lectures given, and the latter was also instructed to set up a monthly atheist journal entitled *Nauka i religiya*; state publishing houses were told to produce more on the question of religion and atheism; the daily press was ordered to popularise current scientific research which proved the falsity of religious claims; the education ministries were to beef up the atheist content of all courses.[79]

Four months later Soviet newspapers published a further resolution 'on mistakes in carrying out scientific atheist propaganda amongst the population'. This document suggested that there had been violations of the feelings of religious believers in recent anti-religious work, and that many local organisations had unjustifiably interfered in the day to day lives of religious communities. In the press undocumented anecdotes and vulgar abuse of the clergy had been substituted for scientific criticism of religion. The resolution called on party organisations to recognise that most believers were loyal citizens and to carry out anti-religious work in a sensitive fashion. More positively it suggested that atheist work should focus on the popularisation of science rather than overt attacks on religious institutions.[80]

Party documents, 1958–1964

Though there were no printed statements emanating from the party setting out the aims and objectives of the new campaign on religion, various archive sources refer to a Central Committee resolution of 4 October 1958. The draft text available in the Central Committee files, given final approval by the Politburo and passed at a Secretariat meeting on that date, is brief and merely calls upon all organisations to take measures to strengthen atheist propaganda amongst the population,[81] though accompanying instructions reportedly called upon state organisations to take more steps to limit the activities of religious communities.[82]

Six weeks later the Central Committee issued a further resolution (again unpublished) on limiting pilgrimages to holy places. This document noted the growth in the practice of visiting 'holy places' in various parts of the USSR and the way in which these were used to encourage fanaticism by religious activists. In particular the decree attacked the hypocrisy of church leaders who encouraged such pil-

---

[79] 'O krupnykh nedostatkakh v nauchno-ateisticheskoi propagande i merakh ee uluchsheniya', *O religii i tserkvi*, pp. 67–72.
[80] 'Ob oshibkakh v provedenii nauchno-ateisticheskoi propagandy sredi naseleniya'. ibid., pp. 72–7.
[81] TsKhSD, Protocols of the Ideological Commission, 12, 19 June 1958 and Protocols of the Secretariat, 79, 4 Oct. 1958.
[82] V. Alekseev: '*Shturm nebes' otmenyaetsya* (Moscow, 1992), p. 222.

grimages whilst themselves making use of modern medicine and Soviet sanatoria. To meet this challenge all party organisations were enjoined to improve propaganda, the press were to satirise and criticise those who organised such pilgrimages and the myths surrounding 'holy places', and local soviets and legal organisations were to prevent violations of the law. By June 1959 all these bodies were to report to the Central Committee on actions they had taken to fulfil this resolution.[83] Taken in conjunction with the various regulations affecting the rights of the monasteries issued in November and December (see below) it appears that a renewed assault on institutional religion was in the offing.

Turning to the public arena, in particular to the party congresses of 1959 and 1961, we find little evidence of the launching of the new campaign. The 21st Congress held in early 1959 issued a resolution with the very general injunction to:

strengthen the ideological–educational work of the party, raising the communist consciousness of the workers and above all of the growing generation, educating them in the spirit of a communist relationship to work, Soviet patriotism and internationalism, overcoming the prejudices of capitalism in the consciousness of people, and struggle with bourgeois ideology.[84]

Two months later a Central Committee resolution on political work in the Stalino oblast developed this a stage further by adding the call to take yet more measures to improve atheist propaganda.[85]

Though the 21st Congress gave no public indication of the anti-religious campaign, a reading of the party press made it clear that a new offensive was on the way. In August 1959 *Pravda* devoted an editorial to atheist work, reminding readers of the eventual fate of religion – extinction – and calling on party members to hasten this process. Referring indirectly to the earlier campaign, and indirectly confirming Khrushchev's role, it noted that whilst the (July?) 1954 resolution had led to some improvement in atheist work, this remained far from satisfactory. Implicitly the editorial criticised the November resolution which had given some party members the impression that such work should cease. Though 'carrying out the instructions of the party Central Committee' party organisations had revived atheist work in recent times, there remained a need for all ideological institutions to direct their efforts towards 'the final and complete eradication of religious prejudices'.[86]

[83] TsKhSD, Protocols of the Secretariat, 83, 15 Nov. 1958.

[84] *Vneocherednoi XXI s'ezd kommunisticheskoi partii sovetskogo soyuza* (Moscow, 1959), p. 434.

[85] 'O sostoyanii i merakh uluchsheniya massovo-politicheskoi raboty sredi trudyash-chikhsya stalinskoi oblasti', in *KPSS v resolyutsiyakh i resheniyakh s'ezdov, konferentsii i plenumov TsK*, vol. vii, 1955–9 (Moscow, 1971), p. 513.

[86] *Pravda* 21 Aug. 1959.

A number of resolutions issued in 1960 emphasised various aspects of the campaign, one on party propaganda criticising the failure 'to counter effectively religious ideology', in particular amongst the female population.[87] Another entitled 'on measures for liquidating violations by the clergy of Soviet legislation on cults', was approved by the Presidium on 13 January 1960. Amongst the offences it listed were the propagation of anti-Soviet views regarding the communist party's attitude towards religion, fomenting of nationalist feelings, teaching of religion to children, organising pilgrimages, carrying out charitable activities, and encouraging refusal of military service. All this had come about as a result of 'permissiveness' on the part of the leadership of the two state councils. These two bodies were enjoined to remind religious leaders that the state could not be passive in the face of legal violations, whilst the commissioners of the councils were reminded that they were 'to be strictly guided in their work by the interests of the party and the state'. Further injunctions to improve party propaganda followed, with special attention to be devoted to work amongst sectarian groups such as the Pentecostals and Jehovah's Witnesses – both banned groups.[88] As with all Central Committee resolutions local party organisations were expected to follow suit by passing similar decrees and drawing up additional and more specific instructions relevant to the circumstances in their region.[89]

The 22nd CPSU Congress, meeting in late 1961, accepted the proposal to build communism by 1980, and adopted a resolution whose references to religion were slightly more explicit than that of its predecessor. Thus the party was enjoined to use all means at its disposal to propagate a scientific world view and overcome 'religious prejudices'.[90] More importantly, the new party rules adopted by the congresss called on all members to be more resolute in their struggle with bourgeois ideology, a call warmly welcomed by O. P. Kolchina, second secretary of the Moscow obkom, who argued that this was:

right and timely. We cannot draw comfort from the fact that the majority of working people have rejected religion. We cannot help noting that some amongst us, including the young, have been caught up in the snares of the clergy and sectarians, who have stepped up their activities of late ... It should be added, that as a result of complacency, some comrades by their actions create for the clergy conditions conducive to the revival of religious beliefs and the observance of religious holidays. How else can we undertand the attitudes of officials in the

[87] O religii i tserkvi, pp. 77–8.
[88] TsKhSD, Protocols of the Ideological Commission, 36, 1 Oct. 1959 & 41, 6 Jan. 1960 (with attached comment on Presidium approval of 13 Jan. 1960); TsGAOR, op. 2, ed.khr. 420.
[89] GAKosO, f. 2102, d. 41 includes the regional CRA's response to this decree.
[90] O religii i tserkvi, pp. 81–2.

Ministry of Trade who sanctioned the sale of church candles and, before Easter, of sweet Easter loaves, rather diffidently calling them 'spring cakes'.[91]

Editorials in the party controlled press continued to call for an improvement in atheist work throughout the Khrushchev period, but only once did the party apparatus issue a major statement on the anti-religious struggle. Following the June 1963 Central Committee plenum devoted to ideological matters, the Ideological Commission headed by Il'ichev, appears to have been instructed to produce a major set of proposals on atheist work. Written at the end of the year and published early in 1964, 'on measures for strengthening the atheist education of the population' dwelt more positively on atheist education rather than anti-religious work. Particular emphases included the need for better prepared cadres and for more work with young people.[92] After Khrushchev's fall, the excesses of the anti-religious campaign may have been renounced, but this particular product of the Ideological Commission was not rejected and, as we shall see, was in practice to provide the foundation for the development of atheist work during the Brezhnev years.

Legislative and adminstrative acts

As with party documents, published legislative acts are, with the exception of certain changes to the criminal code, notable for their absence. Yet various state bodies issued a series of decrees or instructions further constraining the activites of religious bodies. Many of these became available in the 1970s when a handbook 'for official use only' found its way into samizdat and then abroad.[93] These and other documents are also to be found in the archives of the Council for Religious Affairs and the Central Committee.

The first hints of change came in the shape of three resolutions issued by the Council of Ministers in October and November 1958. The first of these, dated 16 October, called for a reduction in the quantity of land that could be used for farming by monasteries, forbade them to hire labour, and instructed the two state councils on religion to explore ways of reducing the number of monasteries.[94] Another decree published on the same day, and supplemented one month later, had the effect of raising taxes on the incomes of monasteries and ecclesiastical centres.[95] In mid-December the Council for the Affairs of the Russian Orthodox Church,

---

[91] *Pravda* 30 Oct. 1961.   [92] *Partiinaya zhizn'* 2, 1964, pp. 22–6.

[93] V. A. Kuroedov & A. Pankratov, eds., *Zakonodatel'stvo o religioznykh kul'takh* (Moscow, 1971). All quotes here taken from edition published in 1981 in New York by Chalidze Press.   [94] ibid., p. 36.   [95] ibid., p. 95.

following the Central Committee, took a decision to 'liquidate' pilgrimages to 'holy places'.[96]

The more restrictive attitude towards religion was spelt out most
clearly in an Instruction issued in March 1961, ostensibly in the name of
the two councils but in practice drafted by a special commission of the
Central Committee.[97] Entitled 'on the application of the legislation on
cults', this instruction reiterated and expanded on the list of activities
prohibited to religious communities by the 1929 Law on Religious
Associations. (The latter had detailed the rights and obligations of
religious organisations and laid down the procedures by which they had
to register with state authorities before they could begin their activities.
Amongst the activities not permitted to religious associations were
special circles for youth or women, Sundays schools, religious camps,
charitable actions.)[98] It also gave a list of those religious communities
which were not to be registered by the state authorities under any
circumstances – Jehovah's Witnesses, Pentecostals, True Orthodox
Christians, members of the True Orthodox Church, Reform Adventists,
Murashkovtsy[99] – and at the end of the list added 'and others', thus
allowing scope for further prohibition.[100]

Some of these restrictions were to be incorporated into amendments to
the 1929 law by an unpublished ukaz of the RFSFR Supreme Soviet
issued in December 1962. Many of the changes introduced here were in
line with the practices evolving from the late 1950s, for example in
placing more barriers in the way of registration and making it easier to
close religious communities. For example, in the 1929 law only a single
individual had to sign the request for registration; under the newly
amended law the whole group had to sign, thus rendering more
individuals susceptible to pressure during periods of harsh anti-religious
campaigning (Article 6). The amendments also strengthened the role of
the two councils for religious affairs in decisions over registration. This
centralisation would in theory serve to facilitate the implementation of a
uniform policy throughout the USSR (Article 4). Other features of these
changes included the dropping of the right to appeal against church
closures (Articles 37 & 44), and a ban on the celebration of rites in private

[96] TsGAOR, op. 2, ed.khr. 229.
[97] According to Puzin who says that they were in effect documents created by the
Presidium of the Central Committee, but published in the name of the councils.
TsGAOR, op. 4, ed.khr. 168, p. 203.
[98] On the 1929 law see J. Rothenberg, 'The Legal Status of Religion in the Soviet Union',
in Marshall, *Aspects of Religion*, pp. 61–102.
[99] The Murashkovtsy were an underground and militantly anti-communist sect whose
theology combined Chrisian, Jewish and pagan elements.
[100] Kuroedov & Pankratov, *Zakonodatel'stvo*, pp. 150–60.

homes (Articles 43 & 59). Finally, the changes brought about a formal recognition of the place of the two councils in the supervision of religious life, although even this did not become public until the law was further amended in 1975.[101]

This harsh legal and quasi-legal attitude towards religion was confirmed in the various criminal codes adopted by Soviet republics in the period 1958–62. The RSFSR Code adopted on 26 July 1962 introduced three articles dealing specifically with religion: Article 142 on violations of the laws on separation of church from state and school from church, Article 143 on obstructing the performance of religious rites, and Article 227 on infringements of the rights of individuals under the guise of performing religious rituals. Whilst the first two were slightly amended versions of articles appearing in the 1926 code, the third in effect provided a blanket basis for attacking virtually any religious activity outside the framework of worship within an officially recognised religious building. The offences envisaged in the law included:

the organisation or leading of a group, the activites of which, under the appearance of preaching religious dogmas or performing religious rites, are connected with inflicting harm on the health of citizens, or with other encroachments upon the person or rights of citizens, or with inciting citizens to refrain from participating in civic activities or performing their civic duties, or with drawing minors into such a group.

The punishment for such activities was confinement or internal exile for up to five years.[102]

Appointments

In addition to searching for written statements of policy, it is also worth examining personnel changes, to discover whether new turns require different sorts of officials. Symbolic of the harsh turn against religion was the removal of the seemingly less than enthusiastic G. Karpov as head of the Council for the Affairs of the Russian Orthodox Church. As already noted, his replacement Kuroedov, previously a secretary in Sverdlovsk obkom and before that working in various capacities within agitprop, was less sqeamish. Material in the CRA archive suggests that he took a far more rigorous position than Karpov in his dealings with the church. At a meeting with Patriarch Aleksii on 15 June 1960 he suggested that many

---

[101] The law as amended in 1962 can be found in Kuroedov & Pankratov, *Zakonodatel'stvo*, pp. 83–97; the draft *ukaz* was approved at a meeting of the Bureau of the Russian Central Committee on 14 Dec. 1962. TsKhSD, Protocol of RussTsK Bureau, 12 Dec. 1962.   [102] *Ugolovnoe kodeks RSFSR* (Moscow, 1975), pp. 91–2.

of the problems in church–state relations could be resolved if Metropolitan Nikolai, head of the Patriarchate's Department of External Church Affairs department, was removed from office. From various sources it is clear that Nikolai put up at least some resistance to the new campaign (see chapter 3),[103] and it seems that Kuroedov realised that with this troublesome priest out of the way the church would put up little concerted resistance. One month after the meeting the Holy Synod announced that Metropolitan Nikolai had resigned 'on health grounds'. Within a short time he had died in circumstances that led many to believe he had been murdered.[104]

Conclusion

In this chapter we have explored the motivations underlying the new campaign and suggested that its primary cause was Khrushchev's personal commitment to the building of communism, although we have noted other factors that may have contributed to the decision to launch a renewed assault on religion. We have also suggested that the strong central lead on this issue severely restricted the possibility of even veiled debate or questioning of policy, although some of the differences amongst the 'public' that were to emerge in later years can be seen in embryo during this period. The limited nature of debate is hardly surprising, for, unlike some of the policy areas where scholars have detected clearer hints of fierce debate (economic, education and legal reform),[105] religion fell more clearly into the orbit of ideological work of a type that appeared to require little specialist expertise. Hence the need for the leadership to consult or open up debate was less acute. Once the campaign was decided upon, its parameters had to be set and our analysis of the various 'outputs' has suggested a consistent programme utilising educational, administrative and legislative approaches. Its purpose as defined by such documents was to reduce the institutional presence of religion within society, and to limit its influence on the thinking of a Soviet citizenry about to embark upon the great task of building communism. To what extent it succeeded is the subject of chapter 3.

---

[103] TsGAOR, op. 2, ed.khr. 284, pp. 29–30. The CRA archives for the period 1958–60 contain the records of various conversations in which Nikolai attempts to limit the damage to the church. These included an appeal to Khrushchev to use his influence to stop the renewed offensive against religion (ed.khr. 255, p. 40).

[104] On Nikolai's life and death see W. Fletcher, *Nikolai – Portrait of a Dilemma* (London, 1968).

[105] See works by Juviler and Morton (1967), Schwartz and Keech (1968), Stewart (1969), Skilling and Griffith (1971), Brown (1971), Remnek (1977), Gustafson (1981) and others cited in bibliography.

3   Khrushchev: Theory into practice

The campaign outlined in the previous chapter appears to have envisaged a wide ranging attack involving educational, propagandist, administrative and legal means. Party and state bodies were enjoined to carry out various tasks related to reducing the influence of religion, tasks which they performed with varying degrees of enthusiasm, although the strong impulse from the centre ensured that few remained entirely passive. Yet decreeing change was not the same as carrying it out, and a major concern of this chapter is not only with who was instructed to do what but with the question of whether stated goals were achieved. We shall also raise the question of how religious communities responded to the new campaign and, in chapter 4, how did this in turn affect the practice and thinking of state authorities.

Implementation

Research, education, propaganda

Though both the July and November 1954 Central Committee resolutions had stressed the necessity of improving the quality of research on the religious question, it was the latter that appears to have provided a serious stimulus to such work. In July the emphasis had been upon combatting religious ideas by means of mass propaganda aimed at the masses. By contrast the November decree started with a more detailed and quasi-scholarly analysis of the place of religion in bourgeois and socialist societies, and called for a further development of the 'natural, technical and social sciences' in creating a scientific world view.[1] This stress on research work was re-emphasised in 1959 when the Presidium of the Academy of Sciences adopted a resolution 'on the intensification of scientific work in the field of atheism', and subsequently created atheist sectors in various institutions of the Academy.[2]

---

[1] Texts in *O religii i tserkvi* (Moscow, 1977), pp. 67–77.
[2] J. Thrower: *Marxist–Leninist Scientific Atheism and the Study of Religion and Atheism in the USSR* (Berlin, 1983), p. 143; *Voprosy filosofii* 3, 1960, pp. 3–7.

From this period also dates the renewal of interest in the sociology of religion. Though little was published until after Khrushchev's fall, a number of major investigations into religiosity were mounted during his tenure of office. Involved in such work were scholarly bodies attached to the Academy of Sciences, although they were constantly warned that the needs of research should not be divorced from the real world. As P. N. Fedoseev reminded an All-Union atheist conference in June 1959 'the propagandists of scientific atheism must link their research and explanatory work more closely with the tasks of communist construction'.[3] The party's expectations of scholarship remained ambiguous. On the one hand, serious and objective research was required to find out the true state of religious life in the USSR; on the other, it needed results which demonstrated the steady decline of religious adherence under the impact of socialist transformation.

To ensure the achievement of these two potentially contradictory goals it was resolved to bring research work under closer party control, and in November 1963 the Party's Ideological Commission established an Institute of Scientific Atheism to be attached to the Central Committee's Academy of Social Sciences. Its tasks included:

Leadership and coordination of all scientific work in the field of atheism carried out by the institutes of the USSR Academy of Sciences, higher educational institutions and organisations of the Ministry of Culture; to prepare cadres with higher qualifications... to conduct All-Union scientific conferences and create seminars. The academic council of the Institute of Scientific Atheism will include representatives of the Ideological Department of the CPSU Central Committee, of central scientific and ideological institutions, and also of social organisations.

It was also to be responsible for publishing *Voprosy nauchnogo ateizma* (Questions of Scientific Atheism), a twice yearly collection of essays on atheist and anti-religious themes.[4]

The extent to which the various goals of the research programme were achieved is hard to assess. Atheist sectors were set up within many institutions during the 1960s, and *Voprosy nauchnogo ateizma* began to appear in 1966. An analysis of the material published in subsequent years indicates the presence of serious research hidden amongst the essential ideological genuflections and the considerable quantity of hackwork. But the problems of carrying out research were increasingly noted by Soviet commentators, with one critic suggesting that much current work was superficial in its treatment of the complexity of the religious mindset and

[3] *Pravda* 18 June 1959.   [4] *Partiinaya zhizn'*, 2, 1964, pp. 22–6.

far too inclined to generalise on the basis of a study of one or two major religions.[5]

The frontline for the application of research findings was the education system. At the most general level there was a recognised need to improve the intellectual level of the population on the grounds that a better educated citizenry was by definition more likely to be atheistic.[6] But there was also the need for a more specific attempt to inject atheist content into all types of educational activity. Throughout the 1950s there were numerous complaints about shortcomings in this area. During the brief 1954 press assault on religion the Russian education minister I. Kairov reminded a teachers' conference of their responsibilities in this area:

schools must pay very strict attention to rearing our youth in the spirit of militant materialism, in the spirit of atheism...

Religious prejudices are amongst the most tenacious and dangerous vestiges of the past in peoples' minds, and these also affect children and young people. Yet in recent years many schools and teachers have ceased to fight these survivals, and have not paid sufficient attention to the anti-religious education of students.[7]

As the Khrushchev campaign gathered pace questions of atheist education in schools were increasingly discussed. Typical was a rather artificial exchange which appeared in the September 1960 issue of *Nauka i religiya* (Science and Religion). Replacing the opening editorial was a letter to the Russian education minister from seven workers calling for a more militant approach to anti-religious work in the school system. After giving various examples of children whose lives had been poisoned by religion, they argued that the time had come to move from 'a position of neutral, religionless education to an active struggle for the education of convinced atheists, militant materialists and worthy members of a future communist society'. In his response the minister noted that his ministry had in fact taken steps to improve such work, and he reported that in February 1959 a special letter had been sent to all organs of people's education and school directors on this very matter.[8]

At the higher educational level a course on 'the basics of scientific atheism' was introduced for all students in 1959. Initially voluntary, this course required fourth year students to undertake twenty-four hours of atheist instruction. Yet three years later there were complaints that all the course did was provide students with a set of unrelated and often largely outdated facts about the basic history and dogmas of the major religions.

[5] 'Teoriya nauchnogo ateizma – na uroven' sovremennykh trebovanii', *Voprosy filosofii*, 5, 1964, pp. 3–12.
[6] See D. Ugrinovich 'Neobkhodima produmannaya sistema nauchno-ateisticheskogo vospitaniya' in *Kommunist* 9, 1962, pp. 93–100.
[7] *Uchitel'skaya gazeta* 18 Aug. 1954.   [8] *Nauka i religiya* 9, 1960, pp. 3–7.

One critic noted the general failure to integrate atheist studies into the broader world view teaching of higher educational establishments. Though this same writer claimed that students were asking for extra lectures,[9] James Thrower has suggested that the course had to be made compulsory in 1964 because so few students signed up otherwise.[10] Whether these and other measures were successful in winning over children from believing families is impossible to quantify, but it might be suggested that when combined with official sanctions and pressure, they served to make school and college the front line of the anti-religious campaign. Yet it is perhaps worth noting that many of those young intellectuals who began to find religion attractive in the 1960s and 1970s had at least in part been educated under Khrushchev.

If the November 1954 Central Committee decree provided the impetus for research on the religious question, that of July set the tone of the press campaign of that year and, indirectly, for the campaign of 1958–64. The July document instructed party, komsomol, and various social organisations to take further measures to strengthen atheist education: the Znanie Society was to publish a mass circulation scientific popular monthly journal *Nauka i religiya* (Science and Religion); the state publishing house for political literature was to produce classics of Marxism–Leninism on scientific atheism, and also a series of books and pamphlets on the relationship of the party and Soviet state to religion.[11] In 1954 many of these objectives were not achieved because many party workers interpreted the later November decree as cancelling out that of July. For this reason a *Pravda* editorial in August 1959 reiterated the continuing validity of the July 1954 resolution.

Broadly speaking, those bodies enjoined to improve their atheist work were party bodies, the media, and the cultural enlightenment network, though all of these were under the control of the communist party. In general the instructions given to party bodies in official statements were rather vague – they were to 'raise the level' of their work. Yet as with most resolutions emanating from the Central Committee they were doubtless passed down the layers of party structures with specific instructions as to how they should be interpreted at each level.[12]

The most important party bodies responsible for carrying out anti-religious work were the agitprop sections or departments attached to all party organisations. Under Khrushchev many of their functions were

---

[9] *Komsomol'skaya pravda* 31 Aug. 1962.
[10] Thrower, *Marxist–Leninist Scientific Atheism*, pp. 143–4.
[11] *O religii i tserkvi*, pp. 72–7.
[12] On this procedure see A. Pravdin, 'Inside the CPSU Central Committee', *Survey*, vol. 20, no. 4, 1974, pp. 94–104.

taken over by the newly created ideological commissions, though the precise organisational relationship of these two bodies is far from clear. Most of the articles dealing with these bodies simply list the tasks undertaken by them, although a discussion of the experience of Ukraine stressed that the commissions did not provide 'operational leadership' but merely sought to analyse the situation and make recommendations to party committees.[13] During the Khrushchev years there also appeared atheist councils, bodies attached to party organisations but intended to involve the public in anti-religious work. The work of such councils is frequently described in anti-religious publications. For example, the Vyborg council set up in 1961 collaborated with the Leningrad oblast atheist council in carrying out a sociological investigation of religious belief in some twelve large enterprises and fourteen technical schools. Though the survey revealed low levels of religiosity (1.7 per cent), a significant proportion of those polled (32.5 per cent) was said to have an ambiguous attitude to questions of religion and atheism. As a result of this the council recommended that atheist work should concentrate on communists rather than believers, in order that the former be better equipped to combat religious belief or 'indifference'.[14]

The media was the second category of agency called upon by various party documents to improve and increase their atheist and anti-religious output, and as newspapers and other media outlets were closely controlled by the party the response was immediate. During this period radio and television, and the ever popular cinema, began to increase their atheist output, though it is difficult to evaluate the extent and succes of this medium.[15] In the published press the tone of material on religious themes became increasingly hostile, with targets including communists who compromised with religion, fabricated miracles, corruption in the church, child sacrifice, immoral clergy and so forth. In 1956, for example, *Trud* told the story of an agronomist who, passing a house in his village, heard a child's cry. When the screaming persisted the good citizen burst into the house to find a crazed woman who had murdered an eleven-month-old grandson and was on the point of killing a five-year-old. The woman in question was a Pentecostal who after three days of prayer and fasting had attempted to present two of her grandsons as 'gifts to the almighty'.[16]

[13] D. Zemlyanskii & S. Mezentsev, 'Ideologicheskie komissii partiinykh komitetov', *Kommunist* 5, 1962, pp. 78–84.

[14] D. M. Aptekman, 'Problemy effektivnosti v rabote soveta po ateisticheskomu vospi-taniyu pri raikome partii', *Voprosy nauchnogo ateizma*, 19 (Moscow, 1976), pp. 53–63.

[15] This medium is discussed briefly in D. Powell, *Anti-Religious Propaganda in the Soviet Union* (London, 1975), pp. 93–103.   [16] *Trud* 10 June 1956.

As the anti-religious campaign gathered pace corruption within the church became a favourite target. In May 1959 *Pravda* reported the drunken exploits of a Fr Terenty of the Stavropol diocese who had died following an alcoholic binge. Subsequently Archbishop Anthony of Stavropol arranged for Terenty's grave to be opened so that he could get his hands on the silver cross buried with the deceased priest. This same hierarch, according to the party paper, had quite an eye for the ladies, and often used church funds and bribes to build houses for successive girlfriends.[17] Some of these stories contained implicit threats as to the eventual fate of offenders, some of whom did eventually find themselves in court. Factory worker R. Malozemov told *Pravda* about his upbringing in a Baptist family. His parents forbade him to read secular literature, listen to the radio or go to the movies. After rejecting their faith and serving in the army he returned in order to fulfill his obligations as a komsomol member and 'rescue' his nine brothers and sisters. When they were given only the Bible, he gave them fairy tales; when the children were ordered to pray, he encouraged them to laugh. Eventually the children were separated from their parents and, herein lies the threat, the court granted the eldest son custody over the six youngest. The report ends with the young man stressing that the 'roads of happiness are open to us, as they are to everyone in the land of the soviets'.[18]

The press also carried numerous reports on the defection of believers. Best known of these was Aleksander Osipov, one time professor of Hebrew and Old Testament Studies at the Leningrad Theological Academy. In December 1961 he told *Pravda* how after twenty-five years of service in the church he was leaving because study of religion and acquaintance with modern science had convinced him that religion was nothing but illusion.[19] Two weeks later Osipov alleged that bishops assessed dioceses in terms of what income they brought in, and suggested that the majority of those in the monasteries were idlers whose only desire was an easy life.[20]

Evaluating the impact of the press campaign is problematic. Certainly the quantity of published material rose, whether in newspaper, journal or book form. David Powell and Dmitri Pospielovsky separately have documented the trend from official Soviet sources so there is no need here to do more than quote a few examples. In general the number of press and journal articles rose rapidly in 1958 and 1959, then fell off slightly before jumping once more in 1962–3. More concretely, major anti-religious

---

[17] *Pravda* 10 May 1959; numerous other stories dealt with allegations of corruption, bribery, debauchery and clerical collaboration with the Nazis. For example see *Literaturnaya gazeta* 5 Mar. 1960, *Trud* 17 Apr. 1960, *Izvestiya* 3 June 1960.
[18] *Pravda* 28 Nov. 1963.   [19] *Pravda* 6 Dec. 1961.   [20] *Izvestiya* 20 Dec. 1961.

articles in the central press rose from under 30 in 1957 to nearly 200 in 1959, before settling at around 100 per year in the early 1960s.[21] In practice this clearly understates the extent of activity in this field because Soviet bibliographic sources are based upon a limited number of publications, but it does indicate trends. But whilst the numbers rose, many expressed doubts about quality and wondered who actually read these works.[22]

Finally, various public organisations were drawn into the struggle against religion, most notably the Znanie Society. Formed in 1947, in large part as a successor to the disbanded League of Militant Godless, the society had begun to expand its work beyond the narrowly anti-religious. Nonetheless, during the Khrushchev years it was repeatedly enjoined to improve its work in this area, and by its own account greatly increased the number of measures taken. In September 1959 it at last produced the first copy of the monthly atheist magazine *Nauka i religiya*. The unusual decision to commence publication part way through the year perhaps suggested the increasing degree of urgency in anti-religious campaigning. The first editorial reflected this mood in describing the journal as 'a fighting organ of militant atheism' and in its rejection of the view that religion would disappear 'of itself'. Its prime task was described as educational, with articles promised on the history of religion and atheism, on scientific discoveries and their atheist implications, on the practical concerns of propagandists, and reviews of popular literature. Included in the first issue was a discussion of the origins of the universe, a report on contemporary Russian Orthodoxy, an attack on Pope John XXIII, and an extract from Bertrand Russell's *Why I am not a Christian*.[23] In 1961 the Ukrainian branch of the society started to produce a similar journal initially entitled *Voivnichy ateist* (Militant Atheist). Though both promised objective and scientific reporting, their tone over the next four years was to be extremely aggressive towards believers and, after Khrushchev's fall, was to come in for considerable criticism.

Aside from its periodicals, the Znanie society had particular responsibility for organising lectures on atheist themes. In statistical terms its output in this area rose dramatically, from some 120,000 in 1954 through 400,000 in 1959, to 660,000 in 1963.[24] Yet as in other areas there are considerable doubts regarding the quality of such activities, with complaints about poorly prepared lecturers reading outdated

---

[21] Powell, *Anti-Religious Propaganda*, p. 88. The number of books and brochures on atheist themes rose from 119 in 1954 to some 355 in 1962. D. Pospielovsky: *A History of Soviet Atheism in Theory and Practice, and the Believer*, vol. I (London, 1987), p. 104.

[22] *Nauka i religiya* 5, 1963, p. 3.   [23] *Nauka i religiya* 1 Sept. 1959.

[24] *Nauka i religiya* 1, 1960, p. 4; Powell, *Anti-Religious Propaganda* p. 105.

notes of little relevance to an audience often made up of convinced atheists.[25]

In this discussion of educational and propaganda activities we have not gone into great detail or covered the activities of organisations such as houses of culture, libraries and museums, universities of Marxism–Leninism and other pillars of the cultural enlightenment network. Many of these are dealt with by other authors, notably David Powell. Our intent has simply been to relate the intentions of the policy makers to what happened on the ground. For the former there were a number of objectives: to increase the quantity of measures taken, to raise the quality of measures taken, and to reduce the impact and influence of religion on Soviet citizens.

Of these there can be little doubt that the first was achieved. Much noise and effort, or at least impression of activity, is suggested by the published sources. Yet later publications frequently complained about the poor quality of what was produced during these years, in particular – and adding to the criticisms noted in earlier sections – the tendency for anti-religious activity to come in spurts, following central instructions or at the time of religious festivals. Others argued that it was difficult to carry out such work effectively when many party organisations failed to take it seriously.[26] In terms of winning believers to atheism success is yet harder to evaluate. Such statistics as are available do suggest a general decrease in the number of believers, but it remains difficult to ascribe this to propaganda and educational activities alone, for the decline took place during a harsh anti-religious campaign when public confession of faith could lead to discrimination and job loss, and during which the number of open places of worship was radically reduced. Propaganda messages repeated over time probably had some effect in shaping the perception of religion held by ordinary citizens, but it seems unlikely that many believers were genuinely converted to atheism as a result of such measures.

Non-religious rites

Whilst many of the agitprop measures outlined above were simply extensions of methods already in use, the development of new, non-religious celebrations of major rites of passage were to some extent an innovation of the Khrushchev period. Of course, socio-political rites such as May Day and Revolution Day were already focal points of the Soviet calendar, whilst rituals celebrating the key points of human

[25] *Nauka i religiya* 1, 1962, pp. 3–8.   [26] ibid.

existence had some roots in the Bolshevik tradition. During the 1920s various family rites had appeared, with key party workers opting for non-religious gatherings as a 'mass agitational-propagandist measure directed against the influence of religion and the church on the workers'.[27] These measures to celebrate birth, entry into the pioneers, marriage and death continued into the 1930s, but appear not to have been taken terribly seriously by many party workers and lacked much in the way of official support or resources.[28]

Though none of the major policy statements on religion issued during the Khrushchev years paid much attention to new rites, they seem to have been promoted far more vigorously from the late 1950s onwards, with the Baltic states taking a strong lead.[29] In the spring of 1957 the establishment of a secular alternative to Lutheran confirmation was proposed to an Estonian Komsomol Central Committee plenum by a local group, and by June the first experiments were in progress. At the 1958 republican Komsomol conference rites were discussed in very general terms as 'a means of raising the effectiveness of educational work amongst youth'. It was reported that during this year alone some 27 districts had celebrated the secular ritual and that 2,260 young people had taken part.[30] Further evidence of the success of this rite was seen in the rapid decline of Lutheran confirmations from some 10,000 annually in 1957 to around 500 ten years later.[31] A similar decline in religious rite performance was reported from other Baltic republics, although perhaps predictably the fall in participation was least marked in strongly Catholic Lithuania.[32]

---

[27] D. Ugrinovich, *Obryady – za i protiv* (Moscow, 1975), p. 129.

[28] M. N. Zakovich, *Sovetskaya obryadnost' i dukhovnaya kul'tura* (Kiev, 1980), pp. 68–9.

[29] See *Nauka i religiya* 1, 1961, pp. 80–5 for a general discussion of Baltic experience.

[30] N. Baturin, 'Novye sovetskie traditsii – vazhnoe sredstvo kommunisticheskogo vospi-taniya molodezhi', in *Voprosy nauchnogo ateizma*, Vyp. 3 (Moscow, 1967), pp. 245–54; see also F. V. Salo, 'Anti-religious rites in Estonia', *Religion in Communist Lands*, vol. 1, nos. 4–5, 1973, pp. 28–34.   [31] Ugrinovich, *Obryady*, p. 142.

[32] The two state councils for religious affairs kept detailed statistics on both official and unofficial performance of religious rituals. For example the following figures are produced for Lithuania comparing religious and secular ritual participation:

		Baptism (name-giving)	Marriage	Funerals
1958	Church	49,372	18,753	17,399
	Secular	60,975	28,954	28,017
1963	Church	34,756	10,754	15,457
	Secular	57,084	25,345	23,369

The use of new rites appears to have spread quickly from the Baltic states to other Soviet republics. In 1957, for example, the first komsomol wedding took place in the Andizhan oblast, in Uzbekistan.[33] But it was Leningrad that took the lead in the development of new wedding rituals. In October 1958 the komsomol organisation of the 'Svetlana' enterprise made various suggestions with regard to the introduction of new rites and gained support for their initiative of the Leningrad gorkom. After considerable discussion a new wedding rite was created and in 1959 Leningrad became the first Soviet city to open a special wedding palace.[34]

The development of alternatives to baptism in Leningrad dated from 1963 when a letter appeared in *Leningradskaya pravda* noting the continuing use of church rituals by many families. In particular there were still to be found celebrations of this rite by ostensibly communist families, a comment perhaps indicative of the partial success of the anti-religious campaign if even by 1963 communists – or their grandmothers – were prepared to take the risk of having their children baptised.[35] This letter was in turn discussed at a number of komsomol and party meetings and on their recommendation the gorispolkom (town soviet executive committee) took a decision to develop a special rite for new-born children, and to provide a building in which such events could take place. Such rituals were soon being carried out in palaces of culture, and in November 1965 the Leningrad Malyutka (baby palace) was finally opened.[36]

The preceding summary and examples give some indication of the way in which new rituals developed during the Khrushchev years.[37] What is less clear is the extent to which these were spontaneous regional interpretations of the anti-religious struggle or whether they were in fact centrally determined and an intrinsic part of the new campaign. As already noted, new rituals are surprisingly absent from published instructions and decrees before 1963. Much of the published material on new rites goes out of its way to suggest that here was local initiative at work, a theme very much in tune with Khrushchev's emphasis on

This same file includes a wealth of statistical material on ritual participation, for example, detailed social breakdowns of those participating in religious marriages in registered Tashkent mosques. TsGAOR, f. 6991s, Op. 4, ed.khr. 146, pp. 202–10.

[33] N. P. Lobacheva, 'O protsessa formirovaniya novoi semenoi obryadnosti', *Sovetskaya etnografiya*, 1, 1972, pp. 3–13.

[34] V. A. Rudnev, *Sovetskie prazdniki, obryady, ritualy* (Leningrad, 1979), pp. 131–32.

[35] Figures in the CRA archive indicate that as late as 1962 some 30 per cent of new-born in the RSFSR were still being baptised. TsGAOR, op. 2, ed.khr. 529.

[36] Rudnev, *Sovetskie prazdniki*, pp. 119–20.

[37] Far more detail and other examples can be found in C. Lane: *The Rites of Rulers – Ritual in Industrial Society* (Oxford, 1981).

reviving the local soviets and encouraging social organisations to participate in public life.

Nonetheless, new rites were increasingly discussed in the press from the late 1950s onwards – in particular the komsomol press[38] – and were frequently raised at major atheist conferences and seminars.[39] During 1962 the question of religious and secular rituals was disussed within the bureau of the Russian party organisation (and probably in other republican organisations). In March of that year the bureau dealt with a memo from Vladimir Kuroedov on measures taken to reduce participation in religious rites, and commissioned the CAROC chairman and various comrades (including one by the name of Ligachev) to analyse and make proposals.[40] Five months later the same body commissioned the republican propaganda department to make suggestions for improving secular rites.[41] Yet only in 1963 did the Party's Central Committee give a public lead on this matter when the Ideological Commission issued a call for the improvement of atheist work, including 'the more active introduction into the life of the Soviet people of non-religious holidays and rites'. Local soviets were instructed to devote funds to the building of 'palaces of happiness' where the major events of people's lives could be celebrated. In February 1964, after discussions which drew in the two councils of religious affairs,[42] the RSFSR Council of Minsters issued a resolution 'on the introduction of new civil rites into the life of the Soviet people'. A Committee of the Juridical Commission of the Council of Ministers, drawing in bodies such as the komsomol, was to draft new rituals within two months.[43] Finally, in May 1964, the centre's guiding role was given further publicity when the Central Committee convened the first All-Union Conference on the subject.[44]

New, non-religious rituals came to be seen as a potent weapon of socialisation during Khrushchev's anti-religious campaign, although at the time of his fall their development was in its early stages. Though individual republics and cities took initiatives in terms of structures and ceremonies, most of the evidence suggests that they were responding to

[38] For example, *Komsomol'skaya pravda* 2 Feb. 1958, 23 & 24 Mar. 1958, 25 Jan. 1959, 24 Oct. 1959.   [39] *Nauka i religiya* 8, 1960, pp. 82–83.

[40] TsKhSD, Protocols of the RSFSR Bureau TsK, 10 Mar. 1962.

[41] ibid., Prot. 19, 1 Aug. 1962.

[42] TsGAOR, op. 4, ed.khr. 529, pp. 12–19 records that the draft of this decree was sent to CAROC for comment.

[43] Similar resolutions appear to have been adopted in other republics. See *Sovetskoe gosudarstvo i pravo* 5, 1971, pp. 125–8 on Byelorussia.

[44] See P. P. Kampars & N. M. Zakovich, *Sovetskaya grazhdanskaya obryadnost'* (Moscow, 1967), p. 34, & *Nauka i religiya* 1, 1967, pp. 4–9. It was at this conference that many stressed the need to note that new rituals had more than a narrowly anti-religious potential.

a central initiative and one located in the perceived need to combat religion. As to their success there must be some debate. Participation in secular rituals does appear to have increased during these years and most of the published figures indicate a decline in the performance of religious rituals. Yet this latter trend may have been exaggerated. The CRA archive, for example, contains often contradictory statistics on the performance of religious rituals. Thus a single document can give absolute figures suggesting that a minority of Lithuanian children were baptised in 1963, whilst a few pages later reporting that in the same year 60.8 per cent of new-born were subject to religious initiation. The same document also notes relatively high figures for baptism in general during this year, from 30 per cent in the Stavropol oblast, 37 per cent in Moscow city, to 51.5 per cent in the Moscow oblast, and 68.7 per cent in Transcarpathia.[45] Moreover some sources suggest that in the mid-1960s, with the end of overt anti-religious campaigning, participation in religious rituals began to rise again.[46] Success there may have been but, as with the propaganda measures discussed earlier, it cannot be credited to the development of new rites alone nor isolated from the generally repressive nature of the renewed assault on religion.

Control of religious organisations

A key element of the campaign launched against religion in the late 1950s was the attempt to bring surviving religious institutions under yet closer state control and supervision. During these years the state, largely through the agency of the two councils for religious affairs - themselves closely linked to the KGB – sought to circumscribe the activities of religious communities, to ensure the appointment of relatively passive religious leaders and, on occasion, to place informers within the structures of religious organisations. For obvious reasons little of this was reflected in published party documents, except in veiled form in references to the need to ensure that religious communities and activists did not break the law. Yet it is clear from a variety of sources that such interference was purposeful and extensive. Virtually every aspect of religious life was subject to detailed supervision and control by party and state authorities. Central to this control was the instruction issued by the two councils in March 1961 (see p. 35), which effectively restricted the life of the officially recognised religious community to prayer in a registered place of worship. The instruction required the staff of the

[45] TsGAOR, op. 4, ed.khr. 146, p. 206.
[46] V. Alekseev, '*Shturm nebes*' *otmenyaetsya* (Moscow, 1992), p. 244.

councils and of other concerned bodies to do all in their power to ensure that this understanding of freedom of conscience was not breached by religious bodies, albeit with the standard qualifier that administrative measures should not be used against religious communities.[47]

Though control of religious bodies, particularly the Russian Orthodox Church, has been discussed elsewhere, it is worth briefly recapping the ways in which the state sought to implement this policy, especially given that we can now supplement existing sources with material from the archives. To the hierarchs of the Orthodox Church the removal of Metropolitan Nikolai in 1960 indicated that the state meant business, and effectively choked off more overt forms of resistance by the church leadership. Nonetheless, the Council for the Affairs of the Russian Orthodox Church remained determined to ensure that the senior hierarchy's passive attitude was passed on to other bishops, as well as to the whole clerical caste. In November 1960 V. Kuroedov and A. Puzin, chairmen of the two state councils, addressed a memorandum to the Central Committee in which they argued that the Orthodox Church statute adopted in 1945 gave priests too great a role in parish life, in particular in financial and administrative matters. They suggested recommending to the Patriarchate changes in this statute which would bring it into line with Soviet legislation.[48] Seven months later, at very short notice, a Council of Bishops met in Zagorsk and took a decision to amend the church's statute so as to remove the priest from all involvement in the administrative and financial life of the parish. In effect this turned him into a hired servant of the executive committee of the parish, a body easily controlled by the state and often dominated by local unbelievers. None of the bishops arriving in Zagorsk knew why they were there until the meeting opened, and then it was made clear by Patriarch Aleksii that a unanimous approval of the revised statute was expected. An oft-quoted samizdat account of the gathering, almost certainly written by or based on the account of one of the bishops, noted that prior to the Council most of the 'less retiring bishops had been retired' and that present throughout the gathering were three civilians from CAROC whose 'silence was deafening'.[49]

The Council for the Affairs of Religious Cults (CARC) was similarly instrumental in attempts to bring other religious communities under

---

[47] Text in V. Kuroedov & A. Pankratov, eds., *Zakonodatel'stvo o religioznykh kul'takh* (Moscow 1971), pp. 150–60. All quotes used here from edition published in 1981 in New York by Chalidze Press.   [48] TsGAOR, op. 2, ed.khr. 254, pp. 105–6.

[49] *Arkhiv samizdata (AS) 701*. 'Arkhiereisky sobor, 1961' (undated); the Council is discussed in more detail in Jane Ellis, *The Russian Orthodox Church – A Contemporary History* (London, 1986), pp. 53–69; and in D. Pospielovsky: *The Russian Church under the Soviet Regime, 1917–82*, II (New York, 1984), pp. 335–8.

close state control, though in the Baptist case this policy brought to a head discontents that had been simmering during the second half of the 1950s. As the official history of the All Union Council of Evangelical Christian Baptists (AUCECB) published in 1989 put it, 'in December 1959 a plenum of the AUCECB was forced to adopt a Statute on the Union of Evangelical Christian Baptists in the USSR and an Instruction Letter to all Senior Presbyters of the AUCECB'. Baptist chairman Ya.I. Zhidkov told the plenum that the growth of Baptist communities in recent years had caused disquiet amongst 'people adhering to other ideologies'.[50] Amongst other things these documents forbade senior presbyters visiting congregations in their care, from preaching or participating in services without express permission, raised the minimum age for baptism from 18 to 30, and spoke of the prime aim of congregations as satisfying the spiritual needs of their members, not the drawing in of new ones. The history reports that when senior presbyters visited their congregations over the next year they met with considerable dissatisfaction, although only a minority of communities left the union or renounced registration.[51] Those who did leave, however, were to give the state considerable difficulties over the next two decades.

Similar efforts were made to bring other religious communities under close state control and ensure that their activities were restricted. Control took a variety of forms, starting with the collection of detailed information about religious societies, through registration of places of worship and clerics, prophylactic chats with religious leaders, and disciplining – if necessary through the courts – so as to discourage other would be non-conformists. These functions were performed at various levels and by various bodies but, as the following examples suggest, it was generally the councils and their functionaries that played a major role.[52] Though bishops and other church leaders were often called in for conversations with the Moscow office of CAROC and CARC during visits to Moscow, it was generally the responsibility of oblast commissioners to carry out day-to-day work with such people. Early samizdat sources indicate that the state was often successful in using the bishops to maintain 'discipline' within their dioceses.[53] Yet there were exceptions, church leaders who

---

[50] *Istoriya evangel'skikh khristian-baptistov v SSSR* (Moscow, 1989), p. 240.

[51] ibid, pp. 240–4; see the dissenters account in *AS 770* (August 1961 – May 1966).

[52] Most of the standard works contain some examples, though access to the archives has enabled us to fill out the picture somewhat.

[53] Kirov Orthodox activist Boris Talantov accused bishops of paying more attention to the words of the CRA commissioner than Scripture, church canons or the needs of their flock. See translations of some of his writings in M. A. Bourdeaux: *Patriarchs and Prophets – Persecution of the Russian Orthodox Church* (London, 1970), pp. 125–54 & 330–9.

proved more resistant to the new line and who actively sought to promote religiosity in their dioceses. Archbishop Yermogen of Tashkent, well known from unofficial sources, was clearly one such person, and his dealings with the authorities can be fleshed out from documents in the CRA archive. From these it becomes apparent that he spent much of his time in conflict with CAROC's commissioners, as a result of which in July 1958 he was summoned to Moscow for talks with P. G. Cherednyak, deputy chairman of the council. On this occasion the discussions related to Yermogen's dispute with the local soviet over his use of local school children as servers in church.[54] Nine months later Yermogen complained to Cherednyak about the activities of the Kirgiz commissioner who had delayed the registration of priests and frequently tried to reassign them without consulting the hierarch.[55] Finally, in March 1960, Cherednyak warned Yermogen about his repeated breach of the legislation on cults and indicated that the procurator's office was considering taking criminal action.[56] Eventually, and, as the Uzbek CAROC commissioner explained to Kuroedov, 'at the request of the Uzbek government' Yermogen lost his right to serve in the republic.[57] Soon after this his removal from the whole diocese was effected, albeit dressed up as a church decision – two years later he was appointed to Omsk and then in 1963 to Kaluga where he continued to promote religious life in a way that offended the authorities and which eventually led to his permanent removal from office. What is clear from this case is the way in which the authorities slowly upped the pressure – from talks, to summoning to Moscow, to implicit threats of harsher actions – and then utilised the church authorities to give their suppression of the bishop's voice a degree of legitimacy.

The archives of the CRA are full of reports from local commissioners on ways in which they sought to exercise control over religious life in their region. Typical of these was the report given to CARC by its Daghestan commissioner in January 1964. Here we find detailed statistics not only on the number of religious communities – 31 registered (27 Muslim, 3 Jewish and 1 Armenian) and 3 unregistered (2 Shiite and 1 Baptist), but also on the numbers attending services and feastdays. As part of his work the commissioner undertook *komandirovki* (investigative visits) to places where the clergy were most active and gave local workers advice on the Central Committee resolution 'measures to liquidate

---

[54] TsGAOR, op. 2, ed.khr. 227, p. 24.   [55] ibid., p. 29.

[56] TsGAOR, op. 2, ed.khr. 284.

[57] State Archive of the Kaluga Region (GAKalO), contains a series of documents relating to Yermogen compiled when he was Archbishop of Kaluga in the mid-1960s, but relating to his whole career. This letter was dated 2 Sept. 1960.

pilgrimages to so-called holy places' and 'measures for bringing to an end clerical violations of the legislation on cults'. As a result of such work and the petitions of workers in the area a number of holy places had been effectively closed down, as had an unregistered synagogue in Makhach-kala and a registered mosque in Botlinskii raion. The commissioner went on to report how he had perfected control over the Spiritual Board of the Muslims of the North Caucasus located in his region. At his suggestion the chairman of the board had issued a call to all imams to strictly observe Soviet laws on religion. The document ended with a series of recommen-dations, including: a stopping of the call to prayer; the removal of registration from the mosque in Gubdensk where legal violations were common; the development of work with Baptist and Jewish com-munities; the setting up of a secular funeral bureau; and the reactivation of measures to liquidate Sufi brotherhoods. Finally, he suggested that the headquarters of the Muslim Board should be moved from Buinaksk to the republican capital Makhachkala where it would be easier to establish 'close links and control' over the activities of its members.[58]

Special attention was devoted by the councils to the activities of those religious leaders who travelled to or had contacts with countries outside the socialist bloc. The archive contains detailed reports written for the councils by those having made foreign trips,[59] and records the decisions of its own officials regarding permissions for such visits. In 1962, for example, CARC refused permission for Lithuanian bishops V. Slad-kevicius and Yu. Stepanovicius to travel to the Vatican on the grounds that they were not diocesan bishops – the state had recently effectively placed both men under house arrest within Lithuania and deprived them of the right to serve.[60] Those hoping to study abroad were subject to particularly close scrutiny and detailed briefings. An instruction to Muslim students about to leave for Al Azhar in Cairo stressed 'their high calling as citizens of the Soviet country and the responsibilities which go with this calling'. They were to defend the interests of their motherland, avoid giving false impressions about the state of religion in the USSR, and generally preach Soviet socio-economic achievements and the friendship of the peoples. Their behaviour should always be decorous and they needed to avoid night spots. Most importantly, they were requested to report any hostile comments about the USSR to the embassy in Cairo.[61] In such work the KGB also played a key role, with

---

[58] TsGAOR, op. 4, ed.khr. 146, pp. 7–22.
[59] TsGAOR, op. 4, ed.khr. 41, p. 4ff contains the reports of each pilgrim who had recently made the haj, as well as details regarding negotiations between CARC and the Ministry of Foreign Affairs over travel arrangements.
[60] TsGAOR, op. 4, ed.khr. 130, p. 36, on their fate. See M. A. Bourdeaux, *Land of Crosses* (Chulmleigh, 1979), pp. 53–5.   [61] TsGAOR, op. 4, ed.khr. 41, pp. 97–9.

the departments of religious organisations responsible for foreign affairs generally well stocked with KGB agents and informers.[62]

At the local level it was expected, indeed decreed by the 1961 instruction, that local soviets should play a part in bringing religious life under closer control. A prime role here was assigned to the 'commissions of assistance' (*gruppy sodeistviya*) whose origins go back to the 1920s, but which were revived after an April 1960 All-Union meeting of religious affairs commissioners. Attached to local soviet executive committees, they were composed of party and state workers, education staff, pensioners and the 'local aktiv'. Though their formal role was simply one of monitoring the composition and activities of religious communities, it was made clear that they were to do all in their power 'to discover means of weakening and limiting the activities of religious communities and their clergy (within the limits of the law)'.[63]

The new campaign against religion, then, involved attempts to further control and supervise religious life. The evenness of implementation cannot be fully gauged, but a survey of samizdat and archive material for the Khrushchev years suggests that throughout the country the state commissioners, generally in alliance with party and other organisations, did attempt systematically to establish the true extent of religious practice – witness the extreme detail provided by the archive reports on the makeup of individual communities[64] – and to ensure that if allowed to continue it remained within very narrow parameters. These same officials were inclined to report optimistically on their efforts to bring religion under closer control, for with a strong central lead no career minded official wanted to be seen to be left behind. And whilst this latter consideration may have led to some exaggeration, it does seem that this policy of strengthening control met with some success. Many religious leaders were successfully cowed by the campaign, and the more recalcitrant speedily dealt with – usually through church channels. Religious communities at all levels were increasingly taken over at the adminstrative level by people easily susceptible to state pressure. Activities beyond the narrow limits of worship were curtailed and young

[62] See chapter 7.
[63] Quoted in M. A. Bourdeaux: *Religious Ferment in Russia* (London, 1968), pp. 14–15. The Russian text can be found in *AS 774*. The reports of such commissions can be found in various places in the archives of the Kostroma commissioner for religious affairs.
[64] Eg. TsGAOR, op. 4, ed.khr. 27 contains detailed information on religious communities existing in 1951, including the synagogue in the town of Dubna, Poltava oblast. Registered in December 1946 although active before that date, the synagogue consists of two rooms, 42 sq. metres, of a building constructed in 1898. It is some 60 km from the next synagogue. The rabbi Moses Mashov was born in 1884, has no theological education, and only three classes of secular education. The congregation is about fifteen for normal services and thirty on feastdays (p. 61).

Table 1 *Reduction in places of worship*

	1 January 1958	1 January 1964	Total reduction	Percentage reduction
Orthodox	13,430	c. 7,560	c. 5,870	43
Roman Catholic	1,244	1,046	198	16
Lutheran	451	452	+1	+0.1
Reformed	96	86	10	9
Armenian	48	32	16	33
Islam	402	312	90	22
Jewish	135	92	43	32
Buddhist	2	2	0	0
Old Believers (All)	397	336	61	15
AUCECB (Baptists)	2,119	1,663	456	22
Adventists	186	140	46	25
Molokans	17	15	2	12
Others	11	11	0	0
Total	18,521	c. 11,687	c. 6,834	c. 37

people to some extent driven away, at least from the registered communities. Yet at the same time excessive zeal in imposing control brought its own problems, as some religious communities sought to fight back and develop their activities in ways which the state found it increasingly hard to control.

Closure of places of worship

One of the major objectives of the new campaign was to reduce the institutional base of religious organisations by taking away the registration of individual communities. Formally, it was claimed that only those churches would be closed which had become naturally redundant or whose communities had breached the law. But in practice the pace at which religious organisations were reduced in number indicates a considerable degree of intervention by the authorities. From the CRA archives and other sources it is possible to reconstruct with some accuracy the results of this aspect of the campaign, though there do remain gaps. Table 1 gives a breakdown in terms of the impact on individual denominations and enables us to draw a number of conclusions. Firstly they support the view of many scholars that there were actually fewer functioning communities during the mid-1950s than many of the older texts and some Soviet sources suggest. For example, the Russian Orthodox Church claimed to have 20,000 parishes when it applied to join the World Council of Churches in 1961, yet in practice had barely more than half that figure.[65] The table also indicates that somewhat fewer religious communities were closed down than previously thought – just over one third, rather than 50 per cent or more. Moreover, a breakdown by denomination reveals that some groups were hit far more severely than others.[66] The Orthodox Church clearly bore the the brunt of the campaign, losing over 40 per cent of its churches.[67] Other groups hard hit included the Armenian Apostolic Church (33 per cent), the Jews (32 per cent), the Adventists (25 per cent), Muslims and Baptists (22 per cent). A few groups were barely affected in institutional terms, with the Buddhists keeping all of their temples (all two!), and the Lutherans actually making a net gain of one. Overall the non-Orthodox lost less than 20 per cent of their registered religious associations.

If we take a republican breakdown other patterns appear. A majority of registered religious communities (10,178, i.e. c. 54 per cent) within the USSR in 1958 were located within the Ukrainian republic, and of those some 4,370 (43 per cent) were closed down. But within Ukraine the Orthodox were still harder hit, for in a republic in which were situated some two-thirds of its parishes around 48 per cent were deprived of their registration. The Orthodox suffered still more in Byelorussia and Moldavia, losing 56 per cent and 59 per cent respectively. In the Russian republic some 20 per cent were lost. Looking at other republics and the non-Orthodox, the two most seriously affected appear to have been Uzbekistan (20 per cent), Armenia (33 per cent) and Tajikistan (40 per cent). Those in Turkmenistan (0 per cent), Kirgiziya (4 per cent), Kazakhstan (5 per cent), Georgia (0 per cent), Lithuania (7 per cent) and Latvia (7 per cent) were barely touched, whilst in Estonia they made a net gain of eight communities (10 per cent).

In other words, the primary target of the anti-religious campaign – at least with regard to registered religious communities – was denominationally the Orthodox Church, and geographically the Slavic heartland of the USSR. Then came Tajikistan and Uzbekistan where Islam traditionally enjoyed considerable support, and Armenia where religion and national identity were closely linked. There is enough of a pattern to indicate a strong central direction, although it appears that regional

[65] These figures are given a file on the WCC in TsGAOR, op. 2, ed.khr. 421, p. 10. On these inflated claims see the discussion in N. Davis, 'The Number of Orthodox Churches before and after the Khrushchev Anti-Religious Drive', *Slavic Review*, vol. 50, no. 3, 1991, pp. 610–20.

[66] Statistics in the CRA archives are scattered around a considerable number of files including op. 2, ed.khr. 157, 158, 159, 180, 288, 572 & 575, and op. 4., ed.khr. 258, 259, 429, 430, 436, 437, 438, 439, & 440.

[67] A couple of files were unavailable during my visit to the CRA archives, although from various sources I came up with a figure of 7,560 registered Orthodox churches by the time of Khrushchev's fall.

authorities were left considerable discretion as to how many places of worship were closed down. Within the Russian republic Nathaniel Davis has pointed out that the two regions which suffered most heavily – Krasnodar reducing its Orthodox churches from 208 to 77 and Rostov from 213 to 77 – were areas in which the Nazi occupiers had reopened many churches during the war.[68] Otherwise the closure of Orthodox parishes in the central republic reveals little consistency, with figures ranging from over half in the Kirov oblast[69] to none at all in the Vologda region. And from local archival material one has the impression of varying degrees of enthusiasm for the new campaign, with some going through the motions, whereas others, such as the Kostroma region, targeted specific churches for closure.[70] Similar variations can be found in other republics, not always in a predictable direction. For example, in Ukraine three regions lost more than three-quarters of their Orthodox churches, but these included Dnepropetrovsk in the east as well as western regions such as Poltava and Zaporozhe. A further seven Ukrainian regions lost 50 per cent or more of their churches.

Explaining these variations is not simple, even with the amount of documentation available in the archives, but it does seem that a key factor was the enthusiasm of local party authorities for the new campaign and, to a lesser extent perhaps, the extent to which religious leaders sought to resist. The fate of churches in the Kirov region, well known from the samizdat writings of Boris Talantov, brought these two factors together, for it is clear that here the bishop took fright in the face of the new campaign,[71] whilst the local CAROC commissioners and regional authorities pursued the campaign with particular vigour. Indeed, such was the enthusiasm of one Kirov commissioner, D. I. Lyapin, that by early 1964 the central council – perhaps in response to the growing number of complaints addressed to the council from the region – refused to approve a recommendation that he and the local ispolkom had made to take away the registration of one community. In July 1963 CAROC had backed the request based upon the claim that the church had effectively ceased to function, but had since sent an inspector to the region and discovered that hundreds of baptisms were being performed there every year. For this reason they now not only refused to take the community's registration, but criticised Lyapin for his failure to take CAROC guidelines on closures seriously.[72]

---

[68] Davis, 'The Number of Orthodox Churches', p. 618.
[69] These figures bear out the accuracy of the samizdat work of Boris Talantov.
[70] GAKosO, f. 2102, d. 41, p. 5.
[71] See Talantov in Bourdeaux, *Patriarchs and Prophets*, pp. 143–4.
[72] TsGAOR, op. 2, ed.khr. 526, p. 225.

Officially, the removal of registration from religious communities observed all the legal niceties. The protocols of CAROC and CARC meetings during this period provide information on each case, in the form of statements and recommendations from their commissioners. On 5 February 1964, for example, a CAROC session noted a letter from the ispolkom of the Lvov oblast soviet recording a decision of the previous October to take away the registration of the religious association in Borislav, 'as it has ceased its activities', and suggested that the Mother of God church be used as a sports hall. The commissioner reported that there were four other churches in the town, so the council agreed. At this single but typical meeting seventeen other communities were deprived of registration, and a decision to prevent bell ringing in Orenburg was approved.[73] In practice closure was generally imposed upon unwilling congregations through the use of a number of devices. It might be charged that a local 'cult servant' was in breach of the law, as a result of which he would be removed from his parish. Once gone the authorities would lean on the *dvadsatka* (twenty founders) and attempt to pressurise individuals to resign, after which the absence of the legal minimum would serve as an excuse for closure.

During the Khrushchev years there was also an attempt to reduce the number of unregistered religious communities. Information on such communities is by definition hard to come by but the scale of the problem is evident from statistics in the archives relating to 1963. In that year CARC claims to have reduced the number of unregistered Muslim communities from 1,649 to 1,310 – compare this with 312 registered mosques in 1964 – Old Believers from 350 to 252, and Baptists from 1,060 to 1,023. In addition it reported that the number of Muslim 'holy places' still visited had fallen from 275 to 178. On the other hand the documents note that the number of illegal synagogues had risen from 80 to 107, Roman Catholic churches from 38 to 76, and Lutheran churches from 45 to 141.[74] To these figures one must add the hundreds of sectarian groups who were denied completely any legal existence, notably the Pentecostals (800 plus), Jehovah's Witnesses (400 plus), True Orthodox of various types (200 plus) and others.[75] Clearly, in this area the state enjoyed limited success, with even the reported reductions perhaps hiding the continuing extent of the problem. Indeed, official policies during these years may have compounded the problem, for the deprivation of registration did not guarantee the death of a congregation.

[73] TsGAOR, op. 2, ed.khr. 526.   [74] TsGAOR, op. 4., ed.khr. 146, p. 168.
[75] Information on these groups is scattered throughout the statistical files of the CRA. Alekseev, *Shturm nebes*, p. 235 reports the closure of 3,567 mosques (mainly unregistered) in Uzbekistan alone in the years 1961–3.

Alongside local religious communities, the attack bore hard on the monastic and educational institutions of the Russian Orthodox Church. Five out of ten teaching establishments were closed down, as were over three-quarters of the sixty-nine monasteries and convents open in 1958. The legal basis of such closures lay in the various decrees relating to monasteries issued in 1958, but in many cases closure was accompanied by considerable brutality, as pilgrims and monks were forcibly evicted onto the streets and, in many cases, into the courts and labour camps.[76]

Repression

In the effort to reduce the influence of religion in Soviet society the state when necessary was prepared to resort to overt repression of religious activists, going beyond the control and discrimination that believers had come to take for granted. This entailed three basic elements: the disruption of religious gatherings, particularly those of unregistered communities; the harassment of individuals who publicly brought up their children as believers, including the occasional deprivation of parental rights; and the arrest and internment of those alleged to have broken the law.

The brunt of the attack on services was borne by the unregistered communities. Best documented are the assaults on the Baptist groups which went 'underground' as a result of the schism of the early 1960s (see below). In a letter addressed to Khrushchev in 1963 leaders of the Baptist dissidents set out some of the problems facing their communities. They pointed out that prayer meetings were frequently broken up by:

> druzhiniki and militia under the guidance of the KGB. In Kharkov and Zhivoto (Vinnitsa oblast) believers were beaten up, and then those arrested sentenced to 10–15 days. In Kiev the KGB also instigated the beating up of scores of believers ...There have been cases where church buildings have been demolished by bulldozers in raids led by groups of young people and druzhiniki, for example in Vladivostok, Tashkent, Brest and other places ...

The same document provided a general litany of problems facing the churches, including the abuse of believers in the press, discrimination in education and work, the deprivation of parental rights, and one sided trials which had sent many to the camps. Although they criticised the actions of the KGB and militia, much of their ire was directed against

---

[76] See the description of the treatment of monks and pilgrims at the Pochaev monastery in Ellis, *The Russian Orthodox Church*, pp. 139–41, and statistics on theological educational establishments and monasteries, pp. 100 & 124–5. The Seventh Day Adventists also saw their administrative centre closed down in 1960 as a result of a Central Committee resolution. TsKhSD, Resheniye TsK KPSS, 26 Nov. 1960.

regional commissioners of CARC, a body which although charged to uphold the law did as much as any other body to undermine it, through exerting rigorous control over religious communities and seeking to place unworthy people at their head.[77]

Such activities drew in a whole host of law enforcement and social organisations. The various accounts of the persecutions of the Pochaev monastery in the early 1960s note the role of KGB, militia, local party workers, and *druzhiniki* in beating up elderly monks, and in harassing or even raping female pilgrims.[78] Such actions were not only widespread but deemed acceptable by many officials. According to the account of some of the monks of Pochaev, a group who visited the Central Committee in Moscow were told by one official that believers were pyschologically abnormal and that the party supported all methods of struggle with religion.[79] A key role in raids on churches, the seizure of icons or the ridiculing of believers was played by komsomol groups.[80] That relatively crude approaches became common in many parts of the country is also attested by material in the CRA archive. In September 1964, admittedly shortly before Khrushchev's fall, a meeting of the Council for the Affairs of Religious Cults heard a report on the persistent abuse of believers' rights in the Chuvash ASSR, where meetings had been broken up, illegal searches carried out, literature seized, and the rights of believers violated by the refusal to register actually functioning religious communities.[81]

A second focus of the anti-religious campaign that easily turned repressive was the perceived need to reduce religious influence on children, even when that was exercised through the home. Numerous press accounts set out the harm done to children by religious parents, and family members who helped to break this hold were much praised in the press. More concretely, there were a number of cases where children were taken from the parents by the courts. Bourdeaux reported one case taken from the pages of *Sel'skaya zhizn'* which told the tale of a certain Dmitri Sokhranyaev, once an active komsomol member but now a religious fanatic. Initially his local party bureau took no notice, but there came a time when his children removed their pioneer scarves, put on crosses and refused to eat in the school dining room. Consequently they became physically weak, did badly at school, and came close to mental

---

[77] *AS 771*, 'Predsedatelyu soveta ministru SSSR Khrushchevu N. S. i vozglavlyaemomu im pravitel'stvu' (13 Aug. 1963).

[78] Some of the documents on the Pochaev case are translated in Bourdeaux, *Patriarchs and Prophets*, (1970), pp. 96–115.   [79] ibid., p. 114.

[80] Alekseev, *Shturm nebes*, p. 225.

[81] TsGAOR, op. 4, ed.khr. 147, between 116 & 125.

breakdown. Fortunately a court of law intervened 'to save Lyuba, Masha and Dusya' by taking them away from their parents.[82] How many children were affected by such policies is impossible to quantify from existing evidence, though the CRA archives contain information on over twenty families who were deprived of parental rights during this period in cases involving over seventy-five children.[83]

When it comes to the arrest and imprisonment of believers we have partial evidence from official files. From religious sources only the figures produced by the unofficial Baptists appear relatively complete. A reading of the Soviet press from the late 1950s does provide a picture of a series of trials in which clergymen and other religious activists were tried for a variety of offences. A typical story commenced with a 'softening up' of the target – at the Stavropol Orthodox seminary 'in addition to training future churchmen the holy fathers engage in lively commercial activity and make illegal transactions with various swindlers' – continued with a reminder that freedom of conscience did not entail the right to break the law, and went on to demand strict punishment for the offenders.[84] The Orthodox were fairly hard hit by the repressive feature of the campaign, with a number of hierarchs 'retired' and two, Archibishops Iov of Kazan and Andrei of Chernigov, sentenced to three and eight years imprisonment respectively. Both were accused of various forms of corruption, although a samizdat source claims that the latter aroused the anger of the authorities because he refused to sanction the closure of a convent in his diocese. Iov's reinstatement by the church after Khrushchev's fall would appear to indicate the falsity of the charges levelled against him.[85] How the lower clergy was affected is hard to gauge. In 1960 *Nauka i religiya* reported that in Orenburg oblast alone some twenty-six priests were currently before the courts,[86] a figure which if repeated across the country would suggest that hundreds were involved in some form of criminal prosecution. One year later the same journal discussed the case of a Magnitogorsk priest who was sentenced to three years when a baby died shortly after baptism.[87] In such circumstances the majority of priests became more cautious, unwilling to develop religious life in ways that might risk their registration, livelihood or vocation.

The files of the CRA contain information on some 1,234 non-Orthodox believers condemned in the years 1961–4, of whom 806 were sentenced under the religious articles of the Criminal Code (Articles 142, 143, &

---

[82] Bourdeaux, *Patriarchs and Prophets*, pp. 159–60.
[83] TsGAOR, op. 4, ed.khr. 173, p. 183.
[84] *Sovety deputatov trudyashchikhsya* 10, 1960, pp. 19–26.
[85] See *Nauka i religiya* 9, 1960, p. 50, and N. Struve: *Christians in Contemporary Russia* (London, 1967), pp. 311–12.   [86] *Nauka i religiya* 9, 1960, p. 50.
[87] *Nauka i religiya* 12, 1961, p. 65.

227) and the rest mainly under the decree on parasitism. Of the 806 over half were judged in 1962 alone. During the period 1961–4 at least 350 Baptists (a word used in the archive to include Mennonites) were tried, most under Article 227 ('infringement of the rights of citizens under the guise of performing religious rituals'), and received between three and five years. Other groups subject to particularly harsh treatment included the Pentecostals (with over 260 sentences), the Jehovah's Witnesses (215) and the various branches of the True Orthodox Church (with over 200). The same file notes the sentencing of 36 Muslims (all but 2 from Chechen Ingushetia), 27 Adventists, 4 Lutherans, 2 Catholics and 3 Old Believers.[88]

Information on some of these trials can be found in both samizdat documents and the press. Typical of the latter was the report on the trial of Jacob Schneider, an Adventist elder from the town of Orlovka in Kirgiziya, who allegedly travelled around the USSR selling literature on the black market. In his own congregation he had absolute authority, forbidding collective farmers to work on Saturdays, or children to go to school. Consequently the farm had suffered losses when people failed to turn up to gather in the harvest, whilst the effect of his corrupt teaching had been to drive the intelligence and humanity from the very being of the children. For this 'anti-social activity' he was sentenced to six years.[89]

Overall, the number of religious activists sentenced during the Khrushchev years cannot have been less than 1,500 and was probably considerably more given the complaint found on frequent occasions in the CRA archives about the failure of some commissioners to provide statistics on this subject. Add to this the thousands who were subject to administrative punishments – fifteen-day sentences or fines[90] – and the minority subject to direct physical assaults and even murder, and we have the picture of a considerable degree of repressive brutality being directed against religious communities and believers. And whilst the centre may not have been directly responsible for the worst excesses, the tone of the press, the long inheritance of arbitrary action against non-conformists – especially politically easy targets – and the systemic re-

---

[88] TsGAOR, op. 4, ed.khr. 173, pp. 177–8, 180–3. I have excluded from my calculations of religious prisoners those Muslims sentenced for participation in traditional family customs such as the payment of bride price, kidnapping young women for marriage, or polygamy. TsGAOR, op. 4, ed.khr. 168, pp. 50–1 includes information on 709 breaches of this type in Turkmenistan alone between 1961 and 1964.

[89] *Sovetskaya kirgiziya* 27 May 1960.

[90] *Moscow News* 18, 1990, p. 16 reports that between 1962 and 1970 Baptists alone were fined 94,300 roubles by the state for holding illegal prayer meetings, and that such meetings were broken up on 986 occasions.

lationship of the commissioners of the two councils to their local party bosses, did little to discourage such actions.

Feedback

So far we have spoken largely in terms of policies determined by the centre being imposed with varying degrees of success on a largely passive religious community. Yet in practice religious organisations and individuals responded to this pressure in a variety of ways and sought to modify or alter the renewed hostility of the state. Some religious leaders sought to influence the state via official channels and from a position of total loyalty to the regime. This more cautious approach was adopted by the Moscow Patriarchate which early on saw the signs of a new turn and sought initially to put up some resistance. The attempt to hold back the tide was clearly associated with Metropolitan Nikolai of Kolomna and Krutitsy. From the record of talks held at CAROC offices in April 1959 one has a clear impression of the strategy adopted by this perceptive hierarch. Here he argued that foreign churchmen were speaking of a new campaign against religion in the USSR, and hinted that moderation was necessary to forestall criticism.[91] Behind closed doors Nikolai attempted to document the growing abuse of believers and religion in the press, although his detailed memorandum on this subject sent to CAROC in 1959 was rejected as unfounded by Karpov.[92] Patriarch Aleksii's position was less clear and in general he appeared to be willing to take the line of least resistance. When CAROC proposed to close twenty-eight monasteries in early 1959 he accepted quietly, although when further closures were proposed for 1960 he did argue that at least some monasticism should be retained within the USSR.[93] Whilst Nikolai remained in office the Patriarch did occasionally make efforts to limit the damage caused by the new assault on the church, for example directing a personal appeal to Khrushchev to halt the new campaign.[94] Aleksii also proved willing to publicly excommunicate defecting priests in 1959, and to give a speech at a Kremlin peace conference in which he referred rather obliquely to the 'insults and attacks' suffered by the church.[95]

With the appointment of Kuroedov in early 1960 the pressure on the Russian Orthodox Church increased. In June 1960 the new head of CAROC met the Patriarch and criticised the External Church Relations Department of the Patriarchate headed by Nikolai. In particular he

---

[91] TsGAOR, op. 2, ed.khr. 202, pp. 101–2.
[92] TsGAOR, op. 2, ed.khr. 254, contains a report on Nikolai's complaint by the CAROC librarian.   [93] TsGAOR op. 2, ed.khr., 255, p. 36 & ed.khr. 284, p. 15.
[94] ibid., p. 40.   [95] See Pospielovsky, *The Russian Church*, pp. 333–5.

pointed out that in recent times nothing had been done to condemn the 'reactionary policies of the Vatican' or 'to strengthen the struggle for peace'. According to Kuroedov, Nikolai was telling the Patriarch and other bishops that only communists were interested in such work. His allegedly obstructive attitude led the CAROC chairman to 'recommend' the removal of Nikolai, a 'suggestion' that was quickly acted upon by the church.[96] With the most combative hierarch gone, the Patriarch's resistance effectively collapsed, although perhaps one can see a continuation of Nikolai's defensive strategy in the Russian Orthodox Church's willingness to join the World Council of Churches in 1961 – a move that suited both church and state.

In general most of the official religious hierarchies appear to have adopted a 'heads down' policy, seeking to negotiate concessions at the margins but unwilling to risk a direct confrontation with the state. In the case of the Baptists this provoked a crisis within their own ranks, for many congregations proved unwilling to accept the leadership's call to 'end unhealthy missionary tendencies' or to reduce the participation of young people in religious services. In May 1961 dissatisfied elements formed an 'Initiative Group' to agitate for the convening of a new Baptist Congress to repeal the offending documents. Over the next few years some of these congregations broke away from the All Union Council of Evangelical Christian Baptists (AUCECB) and, as a result, lost their registration – though in practice many had never been registered. It was these groups which bore the brunt of the more repressive waves of the anti-religious campaign and whose members frequently found their way into the labour camps. Though there were attempts at reconciling the two groups, by 1965 the *initsiativniki* had evolved into an alternative Council of Evangelical Christian Baptists (CECB), and the schism was effectively rendered permanent.[97]

In many respects the Baptists provided the inspiration for the later development of religious dissent (see chapter 4), though few groups managed the same degree of organisation – including the formation of their own Committee for Baptist Security to parallel the KGB.[98] Within the Orthodox Church public dissent was generally the work of isolated individuals or small groups, although throughout the USSR small groups of believers conducted letter writing campaigns on behalf of their

[96] TsGAOR, op. 2, ed.khr. 284, pp. 29–30.

[97] Fuller accounts of the Baptist split can be found in W. Sawatsky, *Soviet Evangelicals since World War II* (Kitchener, Ontario, 1981), pp. 157–99; G. S. Lyalina, *Baptizm – illyuzii i real'nost'* (Moscow, 1977), pp. 26–55.

[98] See *Moscow News* 18, 1990, p. 16. The CBS 'made sure of the usual routes home of those who watched us, found out their telephone numbers and home addresses, even took their pictures and sent the information to the KGB'.

own churches. A few bishops, priests, monks or laypeople would address complaints about their treatment to the authorities and, towards the end of this period, to international bodies.[99] Many of those involved in both Orthodox and Baptist dissent were veterans of the camps who took the view that passive acceptance had failed to preserve the churches in the 1930s and that therefore this time a more positive response was required.

Whilst some took the road of open protest, many religious communities were effectively pushed beyond the pale by their simple unwillingness to go along with those elements of state policy that they deemed contrary to religious teachings. The initsiativniki continued to work with children and carry out evangelistic work, unregistered Muslim activists ran Koranic schools or organised pilgrimages to 'holy places', Lithuanian Catholic priests continued to catechise despite frequent fines and occasional prison sentences. In the western Ukraine recently released Uniates priests were at the forefront of the campaigns to reactivate the Ukrainian Catholic Church, forcibly merged with the Orthodox in 1946. A 1959 report in the CRA files provides detailed information on the continuing support for this church amongst some section of the population during the late 1950s, and suggests that even some of those priests who had gone over to the Orthodox retained their earlier sympathies.[100]

Alongside the resistance of those immediately affected, there is some evidence to suggest unease within certain sections of the intelligentsia. A number of Russian writers expressed concern, largely after the event, about the wilful destruction of ancient churches. According to Roy Medvedev an appeal from the Moscow intelligentsia on the theme of protecting the national heritage was handed to Khrushchev by Sergei Mikhalkov after the demolition of the Church of the Transfiguration in Moscow. Khrushchev's response was brusque: 'you take pity on a dozen churches, but have you thought about the hundreds of thousands who have nowhere to live'.[101] Though such actions had little impact at the time, they sowed the seed of a more general intellectual concern that was to emerge after Khrushchev's fall and to tie in with a semi-officially sponsored revival of Russian nationalism under Brezhnev.[102]

The new campaign, then, met with a variety of responses from those most affected, as well as from a small section of the 'public' and, behind the scenes, from within the ranks of those implementing the new

---

[99] For more detail see various sections of Bourdeaux, *Patriarchs and Prophets*.
[100] TsGAOR, op. 2, ed.khr. 256.
[101] R. Medvedev: *Khrushchev* (London, 1982), p. 214.
[102] See J. Dunlop: *The Faces of Contemporary Russian Nationalism* (Princeton, 1983), especially pp. 29–36.

campaign. From the CRA archives, particularly from the years 1963–5, we find frequent complaints being addressed to the councils – from believers, but also from its own officials on occasion – about 'excesses' being committed in the anti-religious struggle. At one level such complaints had little impact, for the strong line being pushed by the centre was not contradicted in a fundamental way by any institution or individual within the political or anti-religious establishment. Yet from later sources it is clear that some of those involved in implementing the anti-religious struggle were aware of the possible dysfunctional implications of excessive measures. This perception was in turn to have an effect on the way in which the Brezhnev leadership sought to resolve the religious question.

Conclusion

In these chapters we have sought to provide a comprehensive survey of the anti-religious campaign associated with the name of Nikita Khrushchev. We have seen how the new policy turn, prefigured in the brief press campaign of 1954, developed from 1958 into a wide ranging attack on all fronts – ideological, administrative and repressive. Though all religious groups were affected to a greater or lesser degree, the primary target appears to have been the Orthodox Church in its traditional Slavic heartlands.

From our analysis of the policy process a number of conclusions can be drawn. The strong central push on this issue and the lack of serious policy objections from any individual or group within the elite severely reduced the possibilities of expressing policy alternatives. Whilst writers and others might, directly or otherwise, implicitly criticise certain aspects of the campaign, they had little leverage without allies at the very top. Within the councils for religious affairs there do seem to have been sceptics, people such as Karpov who perhaps felt that excessively aggressive measures might prove counterproductive, but from 1960 until mid-1964 these voices were muted.

We can also draw some interesting conclusions about centre–local relations. Whilst the denials of Moscow officials that abuses were solely the product of over-zealous local authorities cannot be accepted at face value, it does seem true that by the 1950s and 1960s many of the latter were interpreting central directives in harsher fashion than intended by Moscow. CAROC under Kuroyedov certainly wanted to close as many churches as possible, but there is little evidence to suggest that it explicitly ordered the more brutal measures sometimes seen in the country at large. These were the product of the actions of regional and local party organisations in collaboration with local soviets and security agencies which had little to lose and much to gain from being perceived to be vigorous promoters of the central party line on religion. And acting in a wider cultural atmosphere where brutality against non-conformity was the norm, it was not unlikely that attempts to close places of worship would be accompanied by violence should there be even the slightest hint of resistance. This relative independence could, on occasions, serve to protect religious communities for as we noted earlier, in some regions very few places of worship were closed down. But, in general, harsh actions against religious organisations were the norm and the two councils could not entirely wash their hands of responsibility. Until 1964 they did little to curb the actions of local commissioners, and there is not much evidence to suggest that guilty officials were punished – though the Fergana CARC commissioner was expelled from the party for taking bribes (protection money?) from the clergy,[103] and the Bashkir commissioner for 'compromising himself by unworthy conduct'.[104]

Was the campaign successful? Certainly the number of religious institutions was dramatically reduced, and the leaderships of at least some religious organisations further encouraged in their submisssive attitudes towards the state. Simultaneously the 'cost' of belief rose, as discriminatory measures against believers became more common, and as those choosing to bring their children up as believers faced the possibility of punitive action. Moreover, though some of the excesses were curbed, many of the propagandist measures initiated during the early 1960s were continued into the Brezhnev era. Against this, we would have to note the ambiguity of the evidence regarding religious belief, adherence and participation which according to some did decline but which others would argue was simply pushed out of sight of official investigators. In conditions where mass terror was no longer the norm it also became more practicable to resist the new campaign, albeit at a still considerable risk of imprisonment. Indeed, it was ironic that in the post-Stalinist situation created in part by Nikita Khrushchev, the very policy aimed at reducing religious influence had side effects which served to undermine long-term state efforts to destroy religion. Though dissenters remained in a minority, there were sufficient numbers of resisters (overt or covert) within religious communities and in society at large to make the final eradication of religion extremely costly. For this reason the post-Khrushchev leadership was to back away from extremist measures and to seek a more incremental approach to the reduction of religious influence in Soviet society.

[103] TsGAOR, op. 4, ed.khr. 147, p. 115.
[104] TsGAOR, op. 2, ed.khr. 253, p. 155.

4   Brezhnev: Facing up to new challenges

It is frequently argued that the group which seized power in the Kremlin in October 1964 had more idea of what they were against than what they were for. Whilst 1965 witnessed the ending of many of the policies initiated by Nikita Khrushchev, there was little sign of policy innovation. On the surface the Brezhnev regime appeared more conservative than its predecessor, yet in practice there was considerable continuity. Though dissidents were to be treated harshly and Stalin to enjoy a partial rehabilitation, there was no return to the worst excesses of the Stalin years. Nor did the curbing of Khrushchev's unpredictable tendency to place issues on the public agenda preclude the partial evolution of a more 'rational' style of policy making in which specialists were increasingly consulted by the leadership and processes of decision making became somewhat more institutionalised.

This element of continuity minus excess, and cautious incremental policy making very much characterised religious policy during the Brezhnev years. With Khrushchev's fall the closure of churches slowed dramatically, arrests virtually ceased, many believers were released from the camps, and the cruder forms of anti-religious articles disappeared from the press. Yet one should not overstate the break with the past. Many of the atheist programmes initiated by Il'ichev remained in force, some places of worship continued to be closed against the will of believers, and religious activists were subject to repression. This element of continuity was reflected in the ongoing official adherence to the goal of the eventual elimination of religion from Soviet society although, rather like the creation of communism promised by the 1961 Party Programme, this eschatological hope was now pushed into the rather distant future.

In chapters 5 and 6 we analyse religious policy under Brezhnev and his immediate successors – Yuri Andropov and Konstantin Chernenko. The first deals with the reassessment of religious policy that took place during 1965 which led to very little substantive change in the short term, but raised some of the questions that were to recur in the mid-1980s. We also examine the more limited debate on the religious question which followed, and some of the new challenges that arose during this period. In chapter 5 we examine the decision making process, the ways in which the leadership was drawn into discussion of the religious questions, and the policy responses amended or developed to meet changing circumstances.

Reassessment (1965)

In deciding how best to deal with the religious question the new political leadership now had the experience of the Khrushchev years to add to that dating back to 1917. Though there was to be no explicit analysis of the Khrushchev campaign, the fifteen months following his fall were to witness considerable debate on the shortcomings of official dealings with religion in both the press and behind the doors of those institutions responsible for controlling religious life. Implicit in this period of policy 'drift'[1] was the suggestion that the attack on religion was just one more example of the deposed first secretary's penchant for adventurist, campaigning type policies which produced plenty of noise but little guarantee of results.

An analysis of the writings appearing during this period reveal that a number of lessons had been learnt from the Khrushchev campaign about the most appropriate ways to understand and deal with religion. In the first place, it had become apparent by 1964 that despite continued proclamations of the necessity of eliminating religion as a precondition for building communism, this anti-scientific ideology was in no danger of disappearing. The experience of the 1930s and of the Khrushchev campaign had demonstrated that whilst repression might decimate the organisational structures of the churches, it could not in itself destroy religious belief. Indeed, the experience of the early 1960s suggested that it might be counter-productive, for it pushed some religious groups into an 'underground' position and rendered them less susceptible to control.

If an effective means of controlling religion was to be found, scholars writing in the mid-1960s argued that it was essential to understand fully the reasons for its survival under socialism. In 1963 Il'ichev had declared that the social roots of religion had been destroyed and that only educational work was necessary finally to eradicate religion.[2] Such

[1] An expression used by A. Blane in 'Year of Drift', in *Religion in Communist Lands*, vol. 2, no. 3, May–June 1974, pp. 9–15.

[2] L. F. Il'ichev, 'Ocherednye zadachi ideologicheskoi raboty partii', in *Plenum tsentral'-nogo komiteta kommunisticheskoi partii sovetskogo soyuza, 18–21 iyunya 1963g. Steno-graficheskii otchet* (Moscow, 1964), p. 40.

simplistic thinking was rejected by A. F. Okulov, director of the Central Committee's Institute of Scientific Atheism:

Such a superficial approach does nothing but harm to atheist work. The process of overcoming religious ideology in socialist society cannot be considered as requiring merely ideological struggle. It is inseparable from the resolution of the socio-economic and cultural tasks of communist construction. The basis for the full withering away of religion is created in the process of achieving the communist transformation of society.[3]

Other writers distinguished between the 'social roots' of religion which had in fact been broken – because they lay in the very nature of the old exploitative society – and 'social factors', amongst which they included continuing economic difficulties in the USSR.[4] Whilst emphasising the continued role of social factors, atheist writers publishing in the mid-1960s did not underestimate the role of 'subjective factors', in particular stressing the activities of religious bodies which sought to preserve their influence in a variety of ways, including isolation from society, attempting to create an artificial link between religious and national identities, or modernisation of their teachings.[5]

This more nuanced approach amongst the scholars – ironically, in part a result of the research programmes initiated during the Khrushchev years – was to some degree reflected in the pages of the more popular press. Though none spoke of a specific campaign directed against religion, the content of many of the published articles was clearly aimed at earlier excesses. In March 1965 *Nauka i religiya* published an open letter attacking publicist Alla Trubnikova for her simplistic approach to anti-religious writing. The problem with her work, the authors claimed, was that it aimed 'not at religion but at believers' whom she depicted as 'money grabbing, drunken, libertine and parasitic'. In addition her writings lacked 'tact and delicacy', were cavalier with the facts, and gave the false impression that all believers were virulent anti-soviets. Finally, her infiltration of a convent gave substance to the claims of critics that such practices were commonly utilised by the authorities in their efforts to undermine religion.[6] Later issues of the journal carried generally favourable readers' responses to this letter, although one Leningrad

[3] A. F. Okulov, 'Za glubokuyu nauchnuyu razrabotku sovremmenykh problem ateizma', in *Voprosy nauchnogo ateizma*, Vyp. 1. (Moscow, 1966), p. 13.

[4] I. Tsameryan, ed., *Stroitel'stvo kommunizma i preodoleniya religioznykh perezhitkov* (Moscow, 1966), pp. 141–5.

[5] ibid., p. 63; P. N. Mishutis, 'Opyt sozdaniya sistemy ateisticheskogo vospitaniya v Litovskoi SSR', in *Voprosy nauchnogo ateizma*, Vyp.1 (Moscow, 1966), pp. 200–20; P. K. Kurochkin, 'K otsenke protsessa modernizatsii religii v sovremennykh usloviyakh', in *Voprosy nauchnogo ateizma*, Vyp.2 (Moscow, 1966), pp. 5–38.

[6] *Nauka i religiya* 3, 1965, pp. 23–6.

pensioner suggested that as there were so few believers it was less important to be concerned about their feelings.[7]

March 1965 also saw *Komsomol'skaya pravda* raise the issue of discrimination against believers, albeit in somewhat ambiguous fashion. The article in question reported the case of a woman whose husband became a Baptist preacher. Assuming that she too had become a believer the management at her place of work dismissed the woman. Eventually she did join the sect and endured years of misery before finally breaking with religion.[8] Whilst noting the 'liberal' critique of discrimination, we should not ignore the implicit assumption that had she actually joined the sect at the same time as her husband, the dismissal might have been justified.

Amongst the more thoughtful articles appearing during 1965 was one by Lvov atheist G. Kel't which sought to dispel some of the simplistic notions held by many anti-religious workers and to demonstrate the unacceptability of 'storm tactics' in the struggle with religion. For Kel't it was intellectually dishonest simply to dismiss religion as a highly reactionary influence on the development of human society, for many believers had made significant contributions to knowledge. Poor understanding of religion often led atheists into 'boundless fanaticism'. This had happened to the League of Militant Godless which became during the 1930s an 'atheist sect' almost as intolerant as the more extreme religious groups. Kel't reminded her readers that 'closing a church does not turn believers into atheists. On the contrary it strengthens the attraction of religion for people and, in addition, it embitters their hearts.' Equally ineffective was the tactic of producing renegade priests, for believers will assume that just as they formerly deceived their flocks 'for the money', they will now do the same for the atheists. The true triumph of atheism would come, according to Kel't, not when the priests have left their parishes but when the priest is left alone in the church, abandoned by his parishioners.[9]

The past role of the law in dealing with religion was questioned by G. S. Anashkin, Chairman of the Criminal Collegium of the USSR Supreme Court. For Anashkin the way to combat religion was by educational means with the law only utilised in very extreme cases. Above all it was important that 'not one believer should be prosecuted for belonging to a religious sect and spreading its views, if he has not performed anti-social activities for which he can be held responsible

---

[7] *Nauka i religiya* 9, 1965, pp. 14–15 & 10, 1965, pp. 5–8.
[8] *Komsomol'skaya pravda* 25 Mar. 1965. The assumption that a wife should necessarily adopt the beliefs of her husband might be taken as evidence of yet another 'survival of the past'!   [9] *Komsomol'skaya pravda* 15 Aug. 1965.

under the criminal law'. Given that Article 142 of the 1936 Constitution limited freedom of conscience to freedom of worship and anti-religious propaganda, Anashkin was promoting a remarkable open interpretation insofar as he did not restrict the spreading of religious views to the pulpit. Discussing the articles of the Criminal Code relating to religion (Articles 142, 143 and 227 in the RSFSR Code) Anashkin made great play of the distinction between those activities forbidden under all circumstances and those 'permitted but subject to special regulations'. Implicitly criticising the state councils which made much use of the latter, he argued that only the former category of actions should be liable to action in the courts. Thus he could suggest that the membership of an unregistered religious community was not an offence in itself – a view often rejected under Khrushchev – and point out that the only difference between registered and unregistered communities was that the former had guaranteed legal rights.[10]

Alongside the public debates in the pages of the press and specialist journals, considerable discussion was taking place within the corridors of the bureaucracy. The files of the two state councils reveal growing concern over abuses from mid-1964 onwards, and in June 1964 the Council for the Affairs of Religious Cults (CARC) organised a special conference of its commissioners to discuss the violation of believers' rights.[11] Simultaneously the legal establishment was carrying out its own review of court cases relating to the laws on religion. On 12 October 1964 the Supreme Court had organised a special session on this subject, and heard reports on ninety-four cases that had been reviewed in 1963–4. In many of these the condemned had clearly not breached the law and were thus freed. The court also discussed the well-known case of Nikolai Khmara who, according to Baptist samizdat documents, had been tortured and killed whilst in labour camp. Though not fully accepting the believers' version the court heard that Khmara had indeed been brutally assaulted prior to his death.[12]

With Khrushchev's fall this reassessment of past practices gathered pace. Both councils became increasingly reluctant to deprive congregations of registration, and CARC inaugurated a period of discussion within its own ranks. Further stimulus was provided by the willingness of the new political leadership to reconsider its treatment of the religious question. At the end of January 1965 the Presidium of the USSR Supreme Soviet issued a decree 'on several facts of violations of socialist

---

[10] G. S. Anashkin, 'O svobode sovesti i soblyudenii zakonodatel'stva o religioznykh kul'takh', *Sovetskoe gosudarstvo i pravo* 1, 1965, pp. 39–45.

[11] TsGAOR, f. 6991s, op. 4, ed.khr. 147.

[12] TsGAOR, op. 4, ed.khr. 173, p. 269; but these findings were not made public.

legality in relation to believers', a decree which CARC chairman Puzin claimed had stemmed from a report his council had sent to the Central Committee. Of particular concern was the contribution of abuses to the schism that had developed within the Baptist community. At a meeting of the Supreme Soviet Presidium attended by Anastas Mikoyan and KGB chairman Vladimir Semichastny a special commission was set up to consider the complaints of the Baptists and abuses of believers' rights in general.[13]

This concern with 'sectarians' was reinforced at a special meeting held at CARC in March 1965 and attended by representatives of the atheist establishment, the Central Committee, the KGB and other interested parties. The gathering was opened by Puzin who went out of his way to stress the unacceptability of 'administrative measures' and the absurdity of the religious situation in many parts of the country – one church for the thousands of Baptists in Moscow, and not a single mosque in the Chechen Ingush region where Muslims predominated. He also attacked the harsh treatment of many religious believers, criticising in particular the parasite laws which placed them in the same category as prostitutes and speculators. Such actions could only be counterproductive in that they hardened the resolve of those resisting state policy.[14] Jurist Yuri Rozenbaum, earlier criticised by CARC for his harsh interpretations of the laws relating to religion (see pp. 27), attacked the way in which many party workers treated believers as second class, referring to them as 'they' and as 'harmful people'.[15] Virtually every speaker agreed that legality had been breached and believers' rights abused in previous years, although there was a tendency to blame others, with some CARC officials criticising the Council for the Affairs of the Russian Orthodox Church (CAROC) for its tendency to close churches under any possible pretext.[16] All agreed, however, that in future all applications for registration should be treated on their merits and that every effort should be made to persuade religious communities to apply for registration.

In practice CAROC's position began to change, although the protocols of council sessions for 1965 reveal the continued removal of registration from some communities. Nonetheless, the decision to close a church was no longer automatic, and on a number of occasions CAROC reversed closure decisions by local authorities. In February 1965, perhaps in response to the complaints of believers, it approved the replacement of Kirov oblast commissioner I. D. Lyapin who had distinguished himself by his hostility to the churches during the early 1960s.[17]

---

[13] TsGAOR, op. 4, ed.khr. 168, pp. 27–8. [14] ibid., pp. 70–106.
[15] ibid., pp. 149–60. [16] ibid., pp. 172–3.
[17] TsGAOR, op. 2, ed.khr. 565, p. 8 on Lyapin, and throughout on registration decisions.

For its part CARC issued an explanation 'on the registration of religious communities' in mid-October 1965 which explained that recognition should be granted to all communities expressing a willingness to abide by Soviet laws on religion.[18] This more liberal attitude was ostensibly borne out by a further meeting at the Central Committee on 25 October 1965 where the need to end administrative abuses was further reemphasized.[19] Yet by this time one also finds evidence of a growing impatience with the Baptist dissenters, as what the state views as concessions fail to produce a rapid response from the underground communities. Though President Mikoyan had met leaders of the *initsiativniki* in September 1965, the latter remained wary of a registration procedure that would place them under the control of state organs or in association with what they viewed as a compromised Baptist Union.[20] In October 1965 a CARC session which called for a more sensitive approach to sectarian groups also discussed a draft document on 'measures for struggling against the illegal activities of sectarian religious associations'.[21] And as the Brezhnev coalition settled down into a more conservative style in the latter part of that year, there came signs that the tougher approach to religion – albeit without the earlier excesses – was to dominate. Symbolic of this was the appointment of Suslov protégé Vladimir Kuroedov to head the Council for Religious Affairs created out of the two councils in December 1965 – a merger first suggested in 1957 and taken up in early 1964.[22]

Debate foreclosed; debate beneath the surface

As the more conservative tendency came to dominate from late 1965 onwards public discussion of the religious question lessened. Yet the nature and development of the Brezhnev leadership ensured that debate would not entirely cease. In part this stemmed from the lack of a strong 'ideological' impulse comparable to that of the Khrushchev era, an absence which served to reduce the pressure on the anti-religious community to toe a single line. But it also stemmed from the more incremental style of policy making during the 1960s and 1970s which inclined to fine tuning in response to problems as they emerged. Such an

---

[18] TsGAOR, op. 4, ed.khr. 169, pp. 139–40.   [19] ibid.
[20] *Nauka i religiya* 7, 1966, p. 25; *Arkhiv samizdata (AS) 771xxvii* (24 Sept. 1965); W. Sawatsky, *Soviet Evangelicals since World War II* (Ontario, 1981), p. 146.
[21] TsGAOR, op. 4, ed.khr. 169 mentions this document but does not include the text.
[22] TsGAOR, op. 2, ed.khr. 302, p. 30; the earlier merger proposal can be found in TsKhSD, Protocols of the Secretariat, 31, 29 Jan. 1957, and the latter proposal in which it was proposed that Kuroyedov head the new body and prepare draft statutes, in Protocols of the Secretariat, 92, 15 Jan. 1964.

approach to decision making increasingly allowed for a greater degree of consultation and provided more opportunities for various 'lobbies' to canvas their views. Of course this trend should not be exaggerated. As we shall see, there is little evidence to suggest that the general direction of religious policy became a major source of bureaucratic controversy. Nor is it a simple matter to detect the various viewpoints emerging during these years. Nonetheless we can, as in previous chapters, detect nuances and differing emphases that suggest conflicts beneath the surface.

In some respects the ideological factor was important here. Initially the new regime appeared to show little interest in ideological matters, but from 1968 such concerns appeared to make something of a comeback, in part under the influence of events in Czechoslovakia.[23] This renewed emphasis on ideology was apparent in speeches given at republican party congresses in the winter of 1970–1, and in Brezhnev's address to the 24th CPSU Congress in March 1971:

A great project – the building of communism – cannot be advanced without the enormous development of man himself. Communism is inconceivable without a higher level of culture, education, sense of civic duty, and inner maturity of its people, just as it is inconceivable without the appropriate material and technical base.

Comrades, the make-up of the new man, his communist morality and outlook are consolidated in constant and uncompromising struggle with survivals of the past...

The Central Committee feels that it is necessary to intensify our ideological work, above all to make more active and purposeful the propagation of communist ideals...[24]

This call was duly taken up by the Congress resolution which called upon all party members to fight survivals of the past,[25] and by a series of subsequent resolutions, including one – not published at the time – 'on the strengthening of atheist education amongst the workers' (see pp. 109–10).[26]

This same congress also witnessed the emergence of the concept of 'developed socialism' with its stress on the current stage in Soviet development as a lengthy one, and its *de facto* postponement of the achievement of communism to the distant future. What this meant for religion was not explicitly spelt out, but it became increasingly clear that

---

[23] Candidate Politburo member P. N. Demichev explained the events of 1968 in terms of the failure of the Czechoslovak party to combat adequately imperialist propaganda. *Kommunist* 10, 1968, pp. 14–35.

[24] *The 24th Congress of the CPSU – Documents* (Moscow, 1971), pp. 100–101.

[25] ibid., p. 229.

[26] Text in *Ob ideologicheskoi rabote KPSS – sbornik dokumentov* (2nd edn, Moscow, 1983), p. 200.

the eventual disappearance of religion was an equally distant prospect, albeit one that could could still be aspired to.[27] This lack of strong and explicit guidance gave limited space for partial discussion within the anti-religious establishment.

From a reading of the literature of this period one can find a number of issues over which the relevant 'policy community' was divided, although as in previous chapters it might be appropriate to speak of a spectrum of views rather than distinctive policy camps. Here we shall focus attention on three broad areas that were of concern to the 'policy community': the nature and place of religion in socialist society, the function of rites, and the question of the legal and administrative control of religious life.

In terms of the general analysis of religion's nature, place in socialist society and how to reduce its influence differences began to emerge as the Brezhnev era progressed. The traditional view of religion as reactionary and doomed to eventual disappearance was reiterated in the few *Pravda* editorials on the subject published during these years,[28] but it was increasingly realised that finding effective ways of combatting religion remained a complex task. Some hankered after the old ways, with one letter writer arguing that 'we should not stand on ceremony with believers'.[29] Hardline views continued to enjoy some support within the anti-religious establishment. A typical expression of these came from V. Konavelev, a senior researcher at the Institute of Scientific Atheism, who writing as late as 1980 – admittedly a time when the leadership appeared to be shifting in an ever more conservative direction – went out of his way to emphasise the achievements of the Stalin period, lavishing praise on the activities of the League of Militant Godless. This same writer, whose theme was continuity in policy, also gave considerable attention to the 22nd Party Congress and the programme adopted there which he rather unfashionably described as a major development in the struggle to overcome religious prejudices.[30]

If the harsher approach remained in evidence there were also signs that many in Soviet society, and even within the party, were less than enthusiastic about the anti-religious struggle. On frequent occasions throughout the 1970s atheist writers attacked those intellectuals and party members who were content to rely on social change to bring about

---

[27] There was certainly no questioning of the presupposition that the new man had to be liberated from religious prejudices or that religion was 'in its very essence' contrary to a communist world view. *See Nauka i religiya* 11, 1967, pp. 2–3.

[28] cf. *Pravda* 7 Sept. 1968, 18 Aug. 1971, 15 Sept. 1972, 8 Aug. 1981, & 14 Dec. 1983.

[29] *Nauka i religiya* 9, 1984, p. 4.

[30] V. Konavelev, 'Ateizm v sotsialisticheskom obshchestve', in *Voprosy nauchnogo ateizma*, Vyp. 25 (Moscow, 1980), pp. 244–66.

the demise of religion. Worse still were those who had gone beyond quietism on the religious question to participation in religious rites or to a theoretical idealisation of the church's contribution to the development of Russian culture.[31]

One also finds changes in the scholarly perception of the nature and sociological composition of religious communities within the USSR. Stereotyped depictions of congregations made up of elderly, semi-literate women persisted, but a number of studies began to cast doubt on this picture during the 1970s. Typical of these were perceptive studies of Baptist communities by N. Rudakov and G. Lyalina. In the former's 1976 article on the subject it was noted that the *initsiativniki* in particular were often characterised by a strong central core of young, well-qualified urban workers,[32] whilst Lyalina's book-length study of the Baptists noted similar tendencies amongst many congregations – for example, the reform Baptist congregation in Rostov-on-Don where nearly 40 per cent were under thirty.[33] By the early 1980s some writers were even speaking of a 'new type of believer' who was well qualified or educated, a good worker and a loyal Soviet citizen.[34] This growing reassessment of the religious community and its continued vitality also began to have an impact upon policy makers, so that by 1983 Konstantin Chernenko could tell a major Central Committee plenum on ideology that 'a not insignificant proportion of the population remain believers'.[35]

Another subject that appears to have aroused some controversy, especially during the mid-1960s, was the role of new, non-religious rituals in Soviet society. The debate was sparked off by an article in *Nauka i religiya* at the end of 1965 in which D. Balashov suggested that ritual was essential to any society. Yet he warned that secular rites could not be created overnight in order to meet the requirements of a new type of society, for 'strictly speaking rites are not created but emerge over centuries. New rites formed on the basis of old traditions ... albeit with changed content, have been accepted far more quickly than those invented afresh.'[36] This brought a hasty response from traditionalists, with one author claiming that:

in his attempt to liberate the old popular rites from their religious coating Balashov does not make any distinction between rites and forgets that several of them have negative traits unacceptable to us today ... he reduces the whole affair

---

[31] *Nauka i religiya* 4, 1974, pp. 2–3.
[32] N. Rudakov, 'Osobennosti ateisticheskoi raboty sredi posledovatelei nekotorykh techenii baptizma', in *Voprosy nauchnogo ateizma*, Vyp. 19 (Moscow, 1976), pp. 244–56.
[33] G. Lyalina: *Baptizm – illyuzii i real'nost'* (*Moscow*, 1977), *pp.* 41–55.
[34] For example see *Nauka i religiya* 4, 1982, p. 19.   [35] *Pravda* 15 June 1983.
[36] *Nauka i religiya* 12, 1965, p. 28.

to the removal of Christian elements from pagan rites. Yet there remain not a few elements from pre-Christian pagan faiths which do not in any way enrich our lives.[37]

At around the same time a book appeared which took a fairly harsh line on attempts to build new rites on the old: 'New traditions must be new from beginning to end, completely free of any religious survivals ... When we attempt to achieve our ends by utilising religious rites then we not only fail to weaken the influence of religious organisations but in certain cases strengthen them.'[38] Coming from E. I. Lisavtsev, a Central Committee instructor responsible for religious affairs during much of the Brezhnev period, this critique carried some weight though such comments did not preclude the further development of new rites during the 1960s and 1970s.

A further area where differences of emphasis appeared was in the field of the legal administrative regulation of religion. The official position was perhaps best set out in the writings of Vladimir Kuroedov, chairman of the Council for Religious Affairs from 1965 to 1984. In his view the essential principle governing church–state relations was that of non-interference, although this did not exempt religious associations from the duty to observe Soviet laws. Stressing his concern to defend the rights of believers, Kuroedov accepted that in the past there had been abuses, but claimed that when they had occurred more recently his Council had quickly stepped in to redress them.[39]

Though most writers supported a similar position, a close reading of other works provides further evidence that some were arguing for restrictive interpretations of the rights of believers. Notable amongst these was V. V. Klochkov, Director of the All Union Institute for the Study of the Causes of Crime and Measures to Overcome It, who stressed that the prime functions of Soviet legislation on religion were:

> creating the necessary conditions for religious associations and clergy to 'satisfy their religious needs';
> prohibiting activities such as charity which 'go beyond the satisfaction of religious needs';
> protecting other citizens from encroachments on their rights or disturbance of public order under the guise of spreading religious faith or performing rites.[40]

[37] *Nauka i religiya* 5, 1966, p. 58.
[38] E. I. Lisavtsev: *Novye sovetskie traditsii* (Moscow, 1966), p. 156.
[39] *Izvestiya* 31 Jan. 1976; see also his 'Neot'emlemaya konstitutsionnaya norma sotsialist-icheskogo gosudarstva', *Kommunist* 5, 1980, pp. 45–55.
[40] V. V. Klochkov, 'Kontseptsiya svobody sovesti v burzhuaznom i sotsialisticheskom mirovozzreniyakh i zakonodatel'stve', *Sovetskoe gosudarstvo i pravo* 9, 1974, pp. 29–38.

Elsewhere he repeated this stress on believers' rights as restricted to 'satisfaction of their religious needs' and defined the separation of church and state in terms of the 'full exclusion' of the church from activities such as charity and education which could be carried out by the state.[41] Klochkov was to take a similarly hard line on other issues during the early 1980s, attacking Western states for inspiring religiosity in the USSR, and pointing to the reactionary role of religion in Hungary during 1956, Czechoslovakia in 1968, Poland in the early 1980s, and in Ronald Reagan's America.[42]

Ostensibly more direct debate over the legal rights of believers occurred during 1977 when the draft constitution was being discussed in the pages of the Soviet press. Between June and August of that year the central and republican Russian language press printed a number of letters proposing changes in the constitutional articles relating to religion. A Leningrad enterprise director wrote to *Pravda* suggesting that the freedoms proposed should be denied to 'fanatical sects' guilty of causing 'damage to health'.[43] In similar vein *Trud* published a letter noting that 'under the guise of religion there still exist a number of superstitious sects. Their leaders morally and even physically cripple people and force them into the sect.' Such groups should be prohibited by the constitution.[44] Other people expressed concern at the involvement of young people in religious activity, with a Lvov doctor suggesting a banning of the involvement of minors in the performance of religious rites.[45] Finally, a woman from Ashkhabad called for a change in Article 36 relating to equality of all citizens regardless of race, sex and religion, which she felt should oblige all Soviet citizens to struggle against 'religious prejudices'.[46]

Whilst these letters may have expressed genuine conservative standpoints on the religious question, it was noticeable that virtually all the letters published took a relatively hard line. This in turn allowed the leadership to reveal its own moderation on the religious question in a survey of readers letters published in September. Here A. Okulov and P. Kurochkin, respectively director and deputy director of the Central Committee's Institute of Scientific Atheism, spelt out the official response. Whilst agreeing with those who thought religious fanaticism to be unacceptable, they claimed that the law already protected citizens against such groups. They strongly rejected the view that the struggle against religious views should be a constitutional obligation, for what would happen to the minority of citizens who remained under religious

[41] V. V. Klochkov, *Religiya, gosudarstvo, pravo* (Moscow, 1978), p. 245.
[42] *Pravda* 25 May 1984.   [43] *Pravda* 30 June 1977.   [44] *Trud* 19 June 1977.
[45] *Pravda* 30 June 1977.   [46] *Pravda* 10 July 1977.

influence. Equally, they rejected the position of a number of readers that a freedom of conscience clause was unnecessary as the religious problem had been solved. This was simply 'incorrect' although the scientific basis for the resolution of the problem had indeed been laid.[47]

Though there were different views on the legal and administrative regulation of religious life, evidence of substantive debate is limited. Other legal changes affecting religion were not accompanied by even the orchestrated discussion surrounding adoption of the 1977 constitution. Within the establishment there appear to have been periodic discussions of the legislation on religion,[48] and yet the amendments to the 1929 Law on Religious Associations published in 1975 were issued relatively quietly and, on the whole, simply made public changes decreed in 1962 (see pp. 111–12). After that date one can find occasional calls for the 'perfection' of the legislation[49] but no arguments for major rethinking from within the Soviet establishment. From the religious community or, to be more precise, from the dissenting religious communities, came a flood of proposals for enshrining religious freedom in law, proposals that went far beyond anything discussed in the Soviet press. Typical of these was a 1965 memorandum from two *initsiativniki* leaders, G. Kryuchkov and G. Vins, addressed to Brezhnev in his role as chairman of the Supreme Soviet's constitutional commission. Here the authors claimed that various legislative acts as well as administrative practice since 1929 clashed with Lenin's writings on freedom of conscience and the 1918 decree on the separation of church from state. As Article 142 of the constitution also clashed with the UN statement on freedom of information – insofar as it banned 'religious propaganda' – they suggested that the new constitution under discussion should contain a much clearer formulation of freedom of conscience.[50] Though the authorities received this and other suggestions from religious communities throughout the Brezhnev years – and frequently denounced them in the press as slanderous allegations made by religious 'extremists' – there is little to suggest that they influenced the policy makers of this era.

As already suggested in this and other chapters, it is impossible to speak of distinctive parties fighting for their own policy positions.

---

[47] *Pravda* 1 Sept. 1977.

[48] Addressing the academic council of the USSR Academy of Sciences' Institute of State and Law in 1969 Yuri Rozenbaum noted that many of the provisions of existing legislation were obsolete and suggested that a new draft was essential. *Sovetskoe gosudarstvo i pravo* 2, 1969, p. 141..

[49] In 1983 the Interior Ministry's Professor Rudinsky opined that several clarifications were necessary, in particular with regard to the legal status of religious centres and theological institutions. *Sovetskoe gosudarstvo i pravo* 7, 1983, p. 46.

[50] *AS 788* (14 Apr. 1965).

Instead we might speak of what Griffiths has called 'tendencies',[51] policy inclinations which although sometimes linked to specific institutions may well spread across them. Thus we find the official 'centrist' line of Khrushchevism without the excesses promoted by the central party press and by the state's Council for Religious Affairs. At the same time there is evidence to suggest that there were those within the ideological establishment who hankered after more traditional approaches. Notable amongst these was E. I. Lisavtsev, the central committee instructor whose writings take a hard line on many issues – from the creation of new rites to the treatment of 'extremists'. And even the CRA's new-found moderation is hard to take entirely seriously when promoted by men like Kuroyedov, whose enthusiastic participation in the Khrushchev campaign we have already noted.

Divisions also appear to have existed within the legal establishment. In early 1965 we saw Anashkin promoting a minimalist interpretation of the relationship between religion and the law, in which the courts should only intervene when there was clear evidence of criminal activity on the part of religious individuals or communities. Klochkov is a more complex case. There are passages in some of his writings which suggest that he shares Anashkin's critical attitude to the mass of unpublished instructions that regulate religious life, and it is noteworthy that many of his books on the subject virtually ignore the role of the CRA, the major state body which issued such regulations.[52] Yet we have noted his harsh attitude on many aspects of the religious question, and it may be simply that his attitude towards the council and its works is conditioned by a belief that regulation of religious life should be carried out through the courts rather than by state bodies acting in quasi-judicial fashion.

As for more liberal approaches to dealing with religion, these are to be found outside the formal anti-religious establishment, whether in the pages of dissident publications, or in the attitudes struck by the semi-tolerated Russian nationalist writers which we note below.

New challenges: 1 The religious factor

Though the Brezhnev leadership sought to pursue familiar policies aimed at constraining and reducing the role of religious institutions, it was unable to rely solely on the fine tuning of existing practices, and from the very beginning had to face up to a series of new challenges. In post-

---

[51] F. Griffith, 'A Tendency Analysis of Soviet Policy Making', in H. G. Skilling & F. Griffith, eds., *Interest Groups in Soviet Politics* (Princeton, 1971), pp. 335–77.
[52] V. Klochkov, *Zakon i religiya* (Moscow, 1982), p. 151.

terror and post-Khrushchev conditions religion itself became an actor or influence in its own right, in part as a result of the emergence of overt forms of dissent. Secondly, the ever-present linkage between religion and nationalism appears to have been strengthened during these years – in part, as intellectuals in various republics began to explore their roots and to idealise ancient traditions, but also as some saw in religion a means of national defence. Simultaneously, some religious leaders may have increasingly used the defence of national values in an effort to retain the loyalty of their flocks. Finally, the external factor became more significant as a result of unexpected developments in the outside world, notably the appearance of the human rights issue on the international agenda, the perceived revival of Islamic self-confidence and the election of a Polish Pope. Separately or together these three factors posed new policy questions to a political leadership increasingly incapable of coming up with new answers. And the failure to find satisfactory solutions was in some measure to contribute to the more radical rethinking of religious policy under Gorbachev.

Religious dissent

The mid-1960s witnessed the emergence of a wide range of dissenting activity within the Soviet Union. Stimulated by de-Stalinisation, various individuals and groups sought to prevent a return to the harsh repressive policies of the past and to root the idea of individual rights in Soviet society. Following Khrushchev's fall those involved in non-conformist activity were generally left untouched until the summer of 1965 when a number of dissenters and nationalist activists were arrested. Best known of these were the writers Andrei Sinyavsky and Yuli Daniel whose harsh treatment in early 1966 aroused considerable international disapproval and paved the way for later foreign protests concerning Soviet human rights' policies.[53]

Amongst religious believers dissent was very much a response to the Khrushchev campaign, in particular attempts to strengthen state control over Orthodox and Baptist leaderships. At the forefront were the Baptist *initsiativniki* who rejected the official Baptist Council's introduction of two documents aimed at curbing missionary and youth activities. The Initiative Group launched in 1961 to campaign for the repeal of the offending documents gathered the support of a significant minority of congregations and by 1965 had evolved into a rival Council of Churches of Evangelical Christian Baptists (CCECB), effectively rendering the

---

[53] On dissent in this period see C. Gerstenmaier, *The Voices of the Silent* (New York, 1972).

schism permanent. Though the fall of Khrushchev brought the release of most Baptist prisoners and meetings with A. I. Mikoyan, who promised that their complaints would be looked into, by early 1966 a new campaign had been launched which would return many activists to the camps.[54]

Within the Orthodox Church, 1965 was the year in which dissent went public, with Archbishop Yermogen of Kaluga's call for a repeal of the 1961 decisions of the Council of Bishops. In the same year appeared the well-known open letters of Frs Gleb Yakunin and Nikolai Eshliman criticising state interference in church life. These and other documents produced around this time were particularly critical of the passivity of the church hierarchy in the face of the Khrushchev persecutions.[55] Orthodox dissent, – or that portion which became known at this stage, for the CRA archive contains evidence of numerous complaints from ordinary believers – was largely the work of a few individuals, with the names of Gleb Yakunin, Anatoli Levitin-Krasnov and Boris Talantov constantly re-appearing. More significantly, perhaps, the Orthodox dissidents were not subject to harsh repression during the late 1960s, unlike the Baptists whose new-found organisational skills brought a sharp response from the state. Only in 1969 were Talantov and Levitin-Krasnov arrested, and even then the latter was sentenced for his general human rights activities rather than for religious activities as such.[56]

From the late 1960s human rights activity in the USSR mushroomed, with the appearance of numerous groups committed to a variety of causes. At the beginning of the 1970s the authorities launched a new campaign to limit the activities of dissenters, but this was moderated in the middle of the decade as the Soviet state sought to pursue a foreign policy of detente with the West. Religious dissent continued to develop throughout this period, with more and more groups drawn in. Though more flexible registration policies adopted by the CRA drew some of the 'underground' Baptists back into a legal position during these years, a hard core of irreconcilables remained and reiterated their determination to continue their activities until such time as the church was genuinely free of state interference and there were no Baptist prisoners. In the forefront of the no-compromise movement was the Council for Prisoners' Relatives whose regular bulletins documented the fate of Baptist

---

[54] On the Baptist schism see Michael Bourdeaux, *Religious Ferment in Russia* (London, 1968).

[55] Some of the key documents can be found in Michael Bourdeaux, *Patriarchs and Prophets* (London, 1970).

[56] ibid., various pages; on Levitin Krasnov sentencing see *Chronicle of Current Events* (*CCE*) 10 (31 Oct. 1969), in *Khronika tekushchikh sobytii* Vyp. 11–15 (Amsterdam, 1979), p. 243. Further references are to the English edition published by Amnesty International unless otherwise stated..

prisoners, and the harassment of their families.[57] The scope of Baptist non-conformity diversified considerably during the Brezhnev years, ranging from the organisation of summer camps for young people, the creation of Sunday schools, the setting up of their own counter security service, and the establishment of a printing press. The latter, entitled *Khristianin*, aimed to provide a wide range of religious literature for Baptist communities. Though presses were discovered and those involved imprisoned in 1974, 1980, 1984 and 1985, new presses and printers sprang up elsewhere.[58]

The 1970s also witnessed the development or continuation of dissent amongst other groups, including Pentecostals, Adventists, Catholics and even Buddhists. The Pentecostals, until 1969 and generally later, refused registration by the state unless they joined the official Baptist Union and subject to harsh repressive measures, increasingly saw the solution to their problem in terms of emigration. By 1977 over 20,000 had applied to leave, with 970 having taken the more radical step of renouncing Soviet citizenship.[59] Amongst the Adventists problems centred around a split similar to that which had affected the Baptists, albeit one of longer duration. In 1976 the True and Free Adventists formed a group to struggle for defence of their rights and to combat 'the despotic religion of atheist-materialistic evolution'.[60]

Orthodox dissent gathered pace anew in the mid-1970s. In 1975 Fr Yakunin and lay activist Lev Regelson addressed an appeal to participants in the World Council of Churches meeting in Nairobi documenting the discriminatory nature of Soviet legislation on religious matters. Rather pointedly they asked why the WCC was capable of expressing concern about every form of injustice in the world except persecution of believers.[61] In December of that year Fr Yakunin was instrumental in forming the Christian Committee for the Defence of Believers' Rights which though Orthodox in composition set itself the task of studying the situation of all religious groups and defending those subject to harassment or persecution for their faith.[62] Over the next three years the

---

[57] John Anderson, 'Renewed Harassment of the Council of Prisoners' Relatives', *Religion in Communist Lands*, vol. 14, no. 1, 1986, pp. 99–100; copies of the bulletins can be found in Keston College archive.

[58] These presses were found in Latvia, Dnepropetrovsk, Krasnodar, Alma Ata and Moldavia. See CPR Bulletins 18 (1974), pp. 2–3, 79 (1980), pp. 48, 84 (1980), p. 11, and *Keston News Service* (*KNS*) 238 (14 Nov. 1985).

[59] On the Pentecostals see W. C. Fletcher, *Soviet Charismatics – The Pentecostals in the USSR* (New York, 1985).

[60] On the Adventists dissent movement see M. Sapiets, *True Witness* (Keston, 1990).

[61] *AS 2380* (16 Oct. 1975).

[62] *Documents of the Christian Committee to Defend Believers' Rights* (DCCDBR, produced by Washington Research Centre), vol. 1, p. 1.

committee published dozens of documents which suggested that ordinary Orthodox believers were less passive than traditionally thought in defence of their churches. Numerous items detailed the attempt to open churches, get rid of immoral clerics, or protest the blatant interference of state agencies in the internal life of parishes throughout the Soviet Union. Similar appeals from most other religious groups were also publicised by the committee. Simultaneously members of the committee sought to raise more general issues, for example, submitting a detailed proposal for an amended article on freedom of conscience during the constitutional debate of mid-1977.[63]

Though religious dissent was not entirely new, it acquired a new intensity during the 1960s and 1970s as a growing number of religious believers and communities proved unwilling to accept their status as second-class citizens. Not all groups were affected equally – amongst the Muslims, and the smaller Lutheran and Reformed communities there were few examples of overt dissent. Some groups were more introverted, preferring to limit their activities to self-defence, whereas others were more prepared to link up with different religious groups, and secular or nationalist dissidents in a wide-ranging critique of official policies in the field of human rights. Dissent as a whole never affected more than a small minority of Soviet citizens, yet by the mid-1960s the authorities were faced with the prospect of civil disobedience on the part of thousands of its citizens. Such actions had to be checked if other citizens were not to follow suit, but in post-terror conditions repression and the more overt forms of control had to be handled carefully so as not to drive more people into the arms of the dissenters.

Renewal

A second factor which may have strengthened religion's impact upon policy makers during the Brezhnev years was the development of what might be called religious renewal. Some have spoken of religious 'revival' or 'renaissance', whilst others are more sceptical, pointing out that there was no mass return to the church and that even those who found religion attractive did so for a variety of reasons, that were not always narrowly 'religious'.[64] Nonetheless, it is possible to isolate a number of developments that helped, directly or indirectly, to strengthen or preserve religious influence in Soviet society.

Firstly, there undoubtedly evolved a fashion for religion amongst

[63] *DCCDBR*, vol. 1, pp. 23–26.
[64] See the discussion in Jane Ellis, 'The Religious Renaissance – Myth or Reality', in E. Shirley & M. Rowe, eds, *Candle in the Wind – Religion in the Soviet Union* (Washington, 1989), pp. 251–77.

certain sections of the population. During the 1970s the Soviet press was full of complaints that 'amongst several parts of our youth over recent years there has appeared a certain fashion for religious objects – icons, crosses, etc'.[65] In April 1976 *Komsomol'skaya pravda* published a letter from a tenth grade member of a school komsomol committee who had caused something of a scandal by coming to a dance with a cross around her neck. She asked 'why all the fuss' when numerous komsomol members do likewise without believing in God.[66] One month later the paper reported that this item had elicited 1,140 responses, some defending the girl on the grounds that the cross was an ancient Russian symbol which could not in itself give reason to doubt the wearer's ideological convictions, against which others argued that as a komsomol member she had set a bad example to others.[67]

Religion also rooted individuals in their cultural past, offering rich rituals that contrasted with the drabness of everyday life, and for many provided a source of alternative values. In particular, some were won over by the moral dimension of religious life in reaction to: 'negative phenomenon in social life, violation of the principles of socialist legality or communist morality ... As a result of contact with these young people experience a spiritual trauma that may give birth to scepticism or nihilism, or they may turn their gaze to the church.'[68] Young people in such situations were said to be easily won over by clever pastors or foreign religious centres sending literature or broadcasting into the Soviet Union.[69] Such young people were also at the centre of the creation of the numerous religious discussion groups which sprang up in many cities during the 1970s.[70]

The renewal of religion was also evident in the changing demographic structure of many religious communities to which we have already alluded. Whilst the elderly and the female still predominated, this trend was far less pronounced than hitherto. In the first place, the reproduction of religiosity within the family does not appear to have been dented by official socialisation programmes. During August 1979 this phenomenon was discussed by the Central Committee's Secretariat which concluded that the weakening of propaganda activities in this sphere had contributed to the growing number of young people to be found participating in religious rites or attending illegal religious schools or camps.[71] Young

[65] *Nauka i religiya* 11, 1977, pp. 2–6 pursues this theme.
[66] *Komsomol'skaya pravda* 14 Apr. 1976.   [67] *Komsomol'skaya pravda* 12 May 1976.
[68] *Zarya vostoka* 18 Aug. 1982.
[69] Cf. *Gudok* 27 Feb. 1974, *Komsomol'skaya pravda* 4 Apr. 1981.
[70] Best known of which was the Christian Seminar associated with Aleksandr Ogorodnikov and Vladimir Poresh.
[71] TsKhSD, Protocols of the Secretariat, 172, 21 Aug. 1979.

people from non-religious backgrounds were also proving susceptible to religious influence. Many 'sectarian' congregations attracted young working-class males in considerable numbers, whilst in the cities some Orthodox and Catholic parishes witnessed an influx of young and not so young intellectuals during this period. One author on a visit to an Orthodox Easter service in Moldavia noted: 'Of course, most were old people; then slightly fewer middle aged. There were even less young people, but the word less does not signify quantity and is only used for comparison. Very many young people stood there with kulich awaiting the arrival of the priest.' Amongst them the author noted two acquaintances, a teacher and an engineer.[72] Many authors noted that 'the proportion of educated believers had grown'[73] whilst a statistical report prepared by the CRA in 1984 revealed that over the previous five years the number of adult baptisms in the Russian Orthodox Church throughout the USSR had grown by 36.8 per cent – the number of infant baptisms rose by only 1.6 per cent.[74]

Changing public attitudes towards religion, evidenced in both literary works which portrayed believers in a favourable light, and surveys which suggested that many citizens if not believers were indifferent to the struggle between religion and atheism[75] raised further problems for the state. By the late 1970s it faced a revitalised or partially revitalised religious community at a time when its ability to mobilise counter-attacks was being weakened by the evolution of an increasingly uninterested public. In such circumstances should it maintain its traditional hostility towards religion, or should it seek some modus vivendi with all believers bar the 'extremists' who sought the establishment of 'bourgeois freedom of conscience'?

Bargaining

In the case of the Russian Orthodox Church it has been argued that by the mid-1970s a limited degree of influence over policy had been acquired via a tacit bargain in which the church offered unquestioning loyalty in exchange for continued existence and occasional concessions.[76] Dissidents might argue that too much was conceded to Caesar in

---

[72] *Molodezh Moldavii* 29 Apr. 1982. [73] *Nauka i religiya* 4, 1982, p. 19.
[74] *Istoricheskii arkhiv*, 1, 1993, p. 143.
[75] For example, one poll of 300 young people revealed that less than half ever thought about the question, whilst 24 described atheist propaganda as useless. *Molodoi kommunist* 1, 1977, pp. 70–3.
[76] This view expressed in private by Orthodox hierarchs often appeared in Western journalistic writing. For example, the *Guardian's* Martin Walker spoke of the return of Moscow's Danilovsky monastery to the church in the mid-1980s as a 'reward' for the 'understanding' reached between church and state. *The Guardian* 1 June 1985.

exchange for very little of substance, but some atheist writers appeared to support the view that religious institutions, and the Orthodox Church in particular, used their tolerated position to advance the cause of religion.

Some pointed to the reinforcement of political loyalty by an emerging 'modernisation' of religious teaching which from the mid-1950s onwards increasingly pointed to the similarities between the social forms created in 1917 and those of the early church.[77] More importantly, perhaps, the church was seen as utilising its support for foreign policy as a means of strengthening religious influence at home. Thus the church was always willing to support 'progressive' or condemn 'reactionary' regimes and movements as defined by the Soviet state. Equally, it was prepared to deny allegations of infringements of religious liberty whilst participating in international religious gatherings. But this very public supportive stance was often seen as disguising skilful attempts to renew religious life at home. The well-known report on the church written for the Central Committee by CRA deputy chairman V. Furov in the mid-1970s noted the activities of Archbishop Nikolai of Vladimir and Suzdal who 'skilfully represented the church' at international gatherings and said what was required at meetings with foreign delegations, yet encouraged his diocesan priests to preach more sermons! When it was proposed that the Uspensky cathedral in Vladimir be closed for restoration work a flood of petitions came from believers who appeared to think the church was to close. On investigation these were found to have been instigated by Archbishop Nikolai.[78]

Ironically the opportunity for such efforts by the church were created by the state's own decision to utilise religion for its own purposes. In February 1978 Kuroedov, for example, wrote to the Central Committee suggesting that the party permit the Orthodox Church to celebrate the sixtieth anniversary of the Moscow Patriarchate on the grounds that this would provide a useful opportunity for: 'the propaganda of the peace loving foreign policy of the CPSU and the Soviet government, for the Soviet form of life, the democratic essence of the socialist structure, freedom of conscience in the USSR, and also for discussion of the aggressive policies of the imperialist states.'[79] If the state could use the church, it was also possible for the church to benefit to some degree from this unequal bargain.

---

[77] See *Zhurnal Moskovskoi Patriarkhii*, 7, 1967, pp. 33–8; this tendency to equate communism and Christianity was also perceived in the speeches and writings of Patriarch Aleksii I analysed in P. K. Kurochkin, *Evolyutsiya sovremennogo russkogo pravoslaviya* (Moscow, 1971), p. 174.

[78] *Vestnik RKhD 130* (1979), p. 285; on fears that the restoration might be a cover for closure, see I. Ratmirov, 'Restavratsiya ili diskriminatsiya', in Keston College archives.

[79] TsKhSD, f. 5, op. 75, d. 270, p. 11.

Above all, however, the Russian Orthodox Church sought to preserve its influence by stressing its historical role as the national church at a time when the authorities were flirting rather uneasily with Russian nationalism in a bid to reinforce an ever-more unconvincing official ideology.[80] Throughout the Brezhnev years church publications backed up the arguments of many writers who saw Orthodoxy as an essential part of the national heritage, and made use of key anniversaries in an effort to bolster its own position. Typical of these was the 600th anniversary celebration of the victory of Kulikovo field which fell in 1980 and was the subject of numerous celebrations by the church.[81] The state's response to this development was ambiguous, in large part dependent upon the ups and downs of the 'Russian party', but the atheist establishment expressed increasing disquiet. As one work put it:

In connection with the growth of interest in ancient monuments in recent times, theological apologetics for the centrality of religion to cultural and artistic development have been strengthened. In contemporary theological literature the evaluation of ancient monuments has advanced a series of conceptions. One is to utilise them for a rehabilitation of Christianity, purifying and freeing them from the dirt of the past 'sins' before mankind and giving them historical respectability; then propagandising the aesthetic ideals of Christianity which allegedly have an absolute value; thirdly they are singled out for direct use in the ideological struggle against an alternative, atheist evaluation of religious monuments.[82]

As we shall see, the church's use of its nationalism was to come under sharp attack during the early 1980s as Yuri Andropov rose to prominence within the political elite.

What is less clear are the concrete ways in which this loyalty and promotion of values which, to a greater or lesser degree, coincided with those of the state actually helped the church. It is sometimes claimed that it was during these years that the Russian Orthodox Church became to some extent a privileged church, even a *de facto* quasi-state church. Yet the evidence for such a claim is thin. True it was not on the whole subject to the crude and virulent press assaults that had characterised the Khrushchev years and which continued to be launched against many other religious groups. But on the ground its adherents gained little. Indeed, in the matter of places of worship they saw their numbers continue to decrease during these years, albeit at a much lower rate than previously and with the occasional new registration during the 1970s. If

[80] On Russian nationalism see S. Carter, *Russian Nationalism* (London, 1990).
[81] On the Russian Orthodox Church's celebrations see *Zhurnal Moskovskii Patriarkhii* 12, 1980, pp. 2–27.
[82] Yu.B. Pishchuk & V. G. Furov, 'Ob otnoshenii k kul'turnomu naslediyu proshlogo', in *Voprosy nauchnogo ateizma*, Vyp. 22 (Moscow, 1978), pp. 217–32.

there was any real bargaining by the Russian Orthodox Church, and indeed by other religious groups, it was largely at the margins. A religious delegation about to attend an international meeting might suggest to the CRA that the release of a religious prisoner or the opening of a church might make good propaganda for the Soviet Union, as well as benefitting the church. This may have happened prior to the 1983 WCC Congress when a priest was permitted to visit imprisoned Orthodox dissident Fr Gleb Yakunin, a fact made much of by Orthodox participants in the congress.[83]

Of the three ways in which religion as such began to impress itself upon the official consciousness, it might be suggested that the latter was the least significant, although dissent and renewal both served to back up the timid claims of the official religious leaderships for their views to be taken into account. Taken together, however, they ensured that religion presented new challenges to a regime that seemed, at least with hindsight, unaware of the changing social reality over which it presided.

New challenges: 2 Religion and nation

In the early 1970s Brezhnev was to announce that the nationality question had been solved,[84] yet during the same period Soviet ethnographers were showing a greater sensitivity to the survival and complexities of national self-awareness. Many pointed to the mutual dependence and reinforcing nature of religious and ethnic identities. Simultaneously, various sources suggest that the political leadership was also becoming more concerned with the link between religion and nationalism, and its possible political salience. We have already touched on this question briefly in connection with Russian Orthodoxy, and our focus here will be on Catholicism in Lithuania and Islam in Central Asia – in a later context we shall deal with the Uniates of Western Ukraine.

Religion and nationalism in Lithuania

Official and samizdat sources disagreed fundamentally over the contribution of religion to national identity in Lithuania, with the latter stressing Catholicism as playing a crucial role in the formation, consolidation and defence of national self-consciousness and the former depicting this linkage as simply a stage in the development of the state.[85]

[83] *KNS 180*, 11 Aug. 1983, p. 11.
[84] L. I. Brezhnev, *Leninskim kursom*, IV (Moscow, 1974), p. 56.
[85] Ya.V. Minkyavicius, *Katolitsizm i natsiya* (Moscow, 1971).

Above all, atheist writers saw the attempt of religion to associate itself with the nation as an attempt to hold back the tide of modernisation and secularisation and to preserve its threatened influence.[86]

Evaluating the sense in which Lithuanians identified themselves in religious terms during the Brezhnev years is extremely difficult, with such figures on adherence and rite participation as are available needing to be treated with some caution. One Western study based on Soviet documentation suggested that as many as 50 per cent of native Lithuanians might be believers.[87] And in 1982 a Lithuanian writer noted that around 40 per cent of children were still being baptised in the republic.[88] A large number of Lithuanians retained some connection to the traditional church during the Brezhnev years and many saw religious involvement as a way of expressing and maintaining their commitment to the nation. This was evidenced by both the widespread nature of religious dissent in this small republic and, towards the end of the 1970s and under the influence of the protest movement, by growing participation in major religious festivals.[89] Such activities in turn served to strengthen the image of the church as defender of national traditions and customs.

The religious dissent movement began to develop in the late 1960s, although Lithuanian priests had conducted letter-writing campaigns during the 1950s. In 1968–9 a number of documents outlining the persecution and petty harassment of believers were sent to the authorities. A 1970 report directed to the Central Committee by the Council for Religious Affairs noted the appearance of these documents and general activisation of Catholic clergy. In response a meeting had been held within the republican party's agitprop department attended by state and party officials, including the deputy chairman of the republican KGB, which concluded that the complaints of the priests were groundless and that their influence needed to be combatted.[90] During the same period priests appear to have become more active in carrying out their traditional (but currently illegal) pastoral activities – catechising children or visiting

---

[86] ibid., pp. 253–61.
[87] K. Girnius, 'Some Soviet Statistics on the number of Catholics in Lithuania', in *Radio Liberty Research* 312/79, 18 Oct. 1979.
[88] L. K. Shepetis, 'Ateisticheskomu vospitaniyu – deistvennost'' i nastupatel'nost'', in *Voprosy nauchnogo ateizma*, Vyp.32 (Moscow, 1985), p. 35.
[89] The number of those taking communion during the Marian feasts held in May at Zemaiciu Kalvarija is reported to have risen from 6,944 in 1966 to 22,100 in 1980. *Chronicle of the Lithuanian Catholic Church (CLCC)* 46, 25 Dec. 1980, (edition cited here produced by Lithuanian Catholic Religious Aid in New York).
[90] TsKhSD, f. 5, op. 62, ed.khr. 38, between pp. 70 and 82. The same source noted that the CRA had undertaken a study of over 220 sermons delivered by Catholic priests during recent years.

the sick. In their protest activities the Lithuanians appear to have been influenced by the example of secular and religious dissidents in other parts of the USSR. In addition they were given a psychological stimulus by the results of Vatican II which, although imperfectly known, placed greater emphasis than hitherto on the role of clergy and laity in the everyday life of the church and consequently reduced their dependence upon potentially controllable bishops.[91] During this early period the republican authorities veered between concessions and repression. In 1969 the CRA permitted the consecration of two new bishops, but in 1970–1 a number of priests and lay people were imprisoned for teaching religion to children.[92]

The potential strength of Lithuanian Catholic dissent as compared to that of other groups was demonstrated in late 1971 when a memorandum calling for religious freedom was signed by over 17,000 before the KGB managed to disrupt the venture. The following years saw riots in Lithuania and the self-immolation of Romas Kalanta, both of which brought home to the authorities the extent of discontent in the republic. Growing central concern was exhibited when Mikhail Suslov, party boss during the 1940–1 occupation, paid a visit in 1973.[93] Yet for all the state's pressure dissent flourished throughout the 1970s, with the appearance of the samizdat *Chronicle of the Lithuanian Catholic Church* documenting the repressions directed against the church and its defenders. By the end of the decade tens of thousands of ordinary citizens and as many as two thirds of priests had signed petitions and appeals calling for greater religious freedom. The state responded with campaigns to close down the Chronicle, with attempts to use the bishops to discipline erring clerics and with virulent press assaults on 'extremists'.

In early 1978 Moscow began to show greater interest with a Central Committee delegation paying a visit and calling for more work to be done to hinder clerical influence on young people and to reduce the growing number of those involved in illegal religious communities.[94] Following this visit the Lithuanian Central Committee issued a decree 'on further improving atheist work and control over the observance of legislation on religious cults' (28 June 1978). This made much of the need to combat the church's efforts to depict itself as the defender of morality and of national identity, as well as attacking the attempts of 'hostile foreign

[91] Republican CC secretary Barskauskas attacked clergy who 'had begun to interfere in social life' and 'spread ideologically unsound sermons and memoirs' as a result of Vatican II. *Voprosy nauchnogo ateizma*, Vyp.10 (Moscow, 1970), pp. 151–66.

[92] *CLCC 1* (19 Mar. 1972).

[93] His speech as reported in *Kommunist Litva* 12, 1973, pp. 4–15 made some rather general reference to the need to combat bourgeois nationalism, but doubtless he was more explicit in private.   [94] *CLCC 39* (22 July 1979).

centres, the reactionary part of the clergy ... to speculate on the religious feelings of believers, to revitalise nationalist and religious survivals, and to push them into the path of political opposition'. It went on to instruct various bodies to improve anti-religious propaganda, strengthen educational work with the clergy, more rigorously enforce the law and prevent illegal actions such as the catechism of children.[95] This was at a time when increasing pressure was being placed on other religious communities, but in the Lithuanian case the axe took a little longer to fall for a new factor had entered the game – the election in October 1978 of a Polish Pope.

Religion and national identity in Central Asia

The extent to which Central Asians identified themselves in terms of Islam became a subject of increasing scholarly debate during the 1980s. The traditional view had tended to depict religion as the key factor in regional self-identificiation, with 'Homo-Islamicus' depicted as both unassimilable and a potential threat to Soviet rule.[96] Other writers have suggested that the dramatic socio-economic changes brought about by Soviet rule, combined with the repression of most manifestations of religious life, had significantly altered the Islamic identity of Central Asia's populace. Moreover, even if it were possible to speak of a strong Islamic identity there was no evidence to suggest that this was being transformed into political nationalism.[97] Though this reassessment was valuable in stressing the complexities of identity in modernising societies and in cautioning against assuming a natural jump from the sense of identity to nationalistic activity, it clearly underestimated the strength of Islam in some parts of the region. At the heart of the problem lay what might be described as the 'rationalist fallacy', the belief expressed by Alastair McAuley that 'the more deeply modern-secular structures penetrate, the more developed a society becomes, the more widespread the appeal of reformism, the more restricted the field for fundamentalism'. Though he accepted that the socio-cultural dislocation attendant on rapid modernisation might equally provoke conservative or radical responses, he argued that Central Asia had developed well beyond the point where a traditionalist response was conceivable.[98] Events since

[95] TsKhSD, f. 5, op. 75, ed.khr. 270.
[96] See H. Carrere d'Encausse, *Decline of Empire – The Soviet Republics in Revolt* (New York, 1979); Alexander Bennigsen & Marie Broxup, *The Islamic Threat to the Soviet State* (London, 1983).
[97] A. McAuley, 'Nations and Nationalism in Central Asia', in C. Keeble, ed., *The Soviet State – The Domestic Roots of Soviet Foreign Policy* (London, 1985), pp. 42–56.
[98] ibid., p. 52.

then have suggested that McAuley may have overstated his case, but it is worth looking at his suggestion that Islam was relatively unimportant in Central Asian identities at this time, utilising sources then available.

In this connection a point commonly made by students of Islam needs to be reiterated, i.e. that the status of 'Muslim' indicated a holistic identity, one which brought together religion, politics, society and culture. Religion was not and is not a separate and distinctive sphere, although individual 'Muslims' might vary in the degree of their involvement in religious activity. At the most basic level this was borne witness to in Central Asia by the almost universal observance of circumcision and Muslim burial, and the traditional unwillingness of the population to emigrate or intermarry with non-Muslims.[99] Of course such practices are not in themselves evidence of explicit religious belief, nor should it be forgotten that many of the customs observed in the region are highly syncretic in nature and based on large-scale ignorance of Islamic doctrine. Yet the self-identification as 'Muslim' remained. Thus an atheist lecturer active in Kirgiziya during the mid-1960s recalled that after one talk he was asked if he was a Muslim. His response that as he did not believe in God this was impossible brought the immediate rejoinder 'how can you say that, you are a Kirgiz' – and this in a republic where Islam's roots were much weaker than in many parts of Central Asia. The same author noted a poll taken at the Kirgiz state university which revealed that of 102 students some 52 thought of themselves as 'Muslim', either because they were thus described by their parents, or simply because they were Kirgiz. For this writer this tendency was reinforced by the tendency of many Soviet authors to speak of 'the Muslim part of the population'.[100] Others suggested that this identity confusion was reinforced by clerics who maintained 'that to reject the traditions of Islam was to reject the traditions of the nation'.[101]

During the 1970s there was a resurgence of interest amongst Central Asians, or at least amongst their intelligentsias, in the history and culture of their region. As with the Russians this 'nationalist' tendency included a more positive evaluation of the religious elements of that heritage. The region's press increasingly carried reports on the loving restoration of old mosques and other ancient monuments from the mid-1970s onwards.[102] On occasions celebratory events brought forth contradictory analyses. Thus the 1,000th anniversary of Abu Ali ibn Sina – better know in the

---

[99] See M. Rywkin, *Moscow's Muslim Challenge* (London, 1982), chapters 5–7.
[100] *Nauka i religiya* 3, 1967, pp. 50–2.
[101] E. Bairamov, 'Islam i natsional'nye traditsii', in *Agitator* 24, 1966, pp. 42–5; N. Ashirov, *Islam i natsiya* (Moscow, 1975).
[102] cf. *Pravda vostoka* 21 Mar. 1978 & *Kommunist Tadzhikistana* 21 Aug. 1980.

West as Avicenna – which fell in 1980, was duly recorded by the atheist press which stressed his contribution to neo-materialist scholarship, and the religious press which praised his Islamic learning.[103]

The confusion of the national and the religious could also be seen in some literary works, notably those of the Kirgiz writer Chingiz Aitmatov. In *The Day Lasts more than a Thousand Years* the hero Yedigei tells his boss that he needs time off to say prayers over his dead friend:

Say prayers? You, Buryannyi Yedigei?
Yes, me. I know all the prayers.
And this after, what, sixty years of Soviet rule?
What's Soviet rule got to do with it? People have been praying over the dead for centuries. It is a man that has died, not a beast.[104]

When they reach the burial site a grave is dug in the traditional fashion with a side recess and when Yedigei calls on the funeral party to face Mecca for the prayers, not even the most cynical of those present sniggers or refuses.[105]

What we are suggesting here, then, is not that Islam provided the sole identity of the average Central Asian – who might also identify with family, clan, tribe, ethnic group – but that it retained its hold well into the Brezhnev years and that it may even have been strengthened towards the end of this period. This cannot be quantified in any way but, as we shall see, from the late 1970s onwards the political leadership seems to have become more concerned with the possible politicisation of Islam, as demographic trends, economic difficulties and events in the wider Islamic world appeared to raise questions about the future stability of the region. From about 1978 both central and regional press begin to devote more attention to the 'Muslim question', with special attention devoted to the actions of illegal or unofficial Islamic activists allowed more freedom by political elites increasingly independent of Moscow in the day-to-day management of their fiefs.[106] Occasionally they mounted campaigns against specific phenomena – as happened during the mid-1970s in Turkmenistan where a propaganda offensive was waged against the payment of 'bride price'[107] – but in general such activities were characterised by their noise rather than their effectiveness. Nonetheless, under stronger central direction, various regional organisations took more

[103] *Nauka i religiya* 9, 1980, pp. 24–31 & *Muslims of the Soviet East* 2, 1980, pp. 3–5.
[104] Ch.Aitmatov, *The Day Lasts more than a Thousand Years* (London, 1980), p. 21.
[105] ibid., pp. 239–43.
[106] See S. P. Poliakov, *Everyday Islam – Religion and Tradition in Rural Central Asia* (New York, 1992).
[107] See John Anderson, 'Out of the Kitchen, Out of the Temple – Women, Religion and Atheism in the USSR', in S. P. Ramet, ed, *Religious Policy in Soviet Union* (Cambridge, 1993), pp. 206–28.

actions to combat religiosity during the late Brezhnev period and after. For example, in early 1978 the Kurgan-Tyube obkom of the Tajik party adopted a resolution on containing the growing influence of unregistered clergy, noting in particular the expansion of their activities in the field of religious education of children.[108] In January 1980 CRA chairman Kuroedov reported to the Central Committee on his organisation's efforts 'to neutralise the attempts of international reaction to utilise Islam in the struggle against socialism, which was especially clear in connection with events in Iran and Afghanistan'.[109] Throughout these and other documents and press articles runs the constant anxiety that religious revitalisation, especially amongst Catholics and Muslims from the late 1970s, might link up with nascent nationalist strivings. In the 'Islamic regions' such fears may have been exaggerated at the time, but in politics perceptions of problems often play an important role.

In this section I have suggested that in certain parts of the USSR during the Brezhnev years there is some evidence of a renewed linkage of religious and national identities which impacted upon the consciousness of the political elite. There was no sign of a mass political nationalism based upon religion about to overthrow the Soviet state, but there were subtle changes taking place in part as a result of official policies. Despite denunciations of and campaigns against 'bourgeois nationalism', it does seem to be the case that within certain limits republican leaderships enjoyed greater leeway as to how they managed their fiefs in our period. In conditions where mass terror was absent and some scholarship was possible, one fruit of this was a cautious re-exploration of the past by national elites. And this, perhaps inevitably, led to a reassessment of the religious roots of national cultures. In some areas it went yet further, as in Lithuania where religious dissent aided by a more independent minded religious leadership began to attract those who saw in faith a means of defending national interests. Though the state could harass religious activists it did not appear, at least until the end of the 1970s, to have the will or power to crush them completely. And this in turn stemmed from a desire not to be seen to be acting against Lithuanians as such, in a situation where many closely linked religion and nation. This sensitivity was only exacerbated by developments in the wider world from the late 1970s onwards, although the growing pre-eminence of Andropov in the early 1980s led to a clamp down on nationalism, religion and dissent.

[108]   TsKhSD, f. 5, op. 75, ed.khr. 270, pp. 15–16.
[109]   TsKhSD, op. 77, ed.khr. 126, p. 172.

New challenges: 3 External influences

From the very advent of Soviet power foreign states and public organisations had been active in condemning abuses of religious rights in the USSR. Yet only in the 1960s and 1970s did this become an issue which Western governments sought to place on the diplomatic agenda in any coherent fashion. In part this stemmed from greater awareness of human rights abuses resulting from the entry of more journalists into the country and the evolution of the dissenting movement from the 1960s; in part it proved a useful stick with which to beat the Soviet Union as part of ongoing East–West conflict. As issues and personalities became better known, pressure groups in the Western states started to lobby governments to link better relations with the USSR to specific improvements in this area and to establish some form of linkage – for example, of emigration to trade. This whole process became further institutionalised as the Helsinki process developed in the mid-1970s and effectively legitimised the discussion, however ritualised, of human rights in the international arena.

Though the effect of such pressure on Soviet policy makers is hard to assess and remains a subject of considerable debate,[110] one can isolate a number of areas where it might have had some impact. Firstly, detente and closer contacts between East and West do appear to have affected the activism of religious believers. By the 1970s most religious groups were addressing appeals to Western governments and international organisations, and attempting to relate government practice to the various international agreements signed by the Soviet Union. Foreign radio stations brought them news of such documents, as well as the actions taken on their behalf by Western well wishers. They also provided news of other groups defending religious or human rights within their own country and thus encouraged the coming together of such groups.[111] Hopes were further strengthened by the growing influx of sympathisers visiting the USSR during the 1970s, who brought statements of support, literature and material help, but who unintentionally gave at least some

---

[110] On whether or not Jewish emigration was affected by foreign pressures see the views presented in *Soviet Jewish Affairs*, vol. 16, no. 2 (1986), pp. 70–1; V. Zaslavsky & R. Brym, *Soviet Jewish Emigration and Soviet Nationality Policy* (London, 1983); L. Salitan, *Politics and Nationality in Contemporary Soviet–Jewish Emigration, 1968–89* (London, 1992).

[111] It might also be noted that the GULAG system also encouraged this closer awareness and sympathy between traditionally hostile groups, witnessed by Alexander Ginzburg's experience of meeting Adventist leader Vladimir Shelkov in the camp system and consequent decision to devote special attention to the plight of the smaller Protestant groups when he was setting up the Moscow Helsinki groups. See M. Sapiets, *True Witness*, pp. 72–3.

religious activists an inflated expectation *vis-à-vis* the ability of Western governments to help them. Nonetheless, it probably was the case that for a few years in the mid-1970s the detente process and potential Western denunciations of Soviet human rights practices did serve to increase the 'costs' for the state of excessive levels of repression. Conversely it is hard to believe that the decline of detente and the increase in attacks on human rights and religious activists that occurred in the late 1970s were entirely unconnected.

Foreign pressure, then, was capable of providing 'supports' for religious and human rights activities within the USSR but could provide no guarantee of success; it could influence policy at the margins, but over the long run a Soviet leader committed to preserving the pride of a superpower could not be seen to be pressurised unduly by foreign powers. Indicative of the extent and limitations of foreign influence was the liberalisation of official emigration policies which appeared responsive to Western pressures during the 1970s, but which changed dramatically in the early 1980s with the collapse of detente.

If Western rhetoric and pressure on the human rights and religious issue was something that the Soviet state gradually came to terms with, the same could not be said about the surprise election of a Polish Pope in October 1978. Though Stalin was reported to have sneeringly asked 'how many divisions has the Pope', Moscow had always treated the Catholic Church with considerable suspicion. Despite more nuanced writings on that church after Vatican II, there remained the feeling that Soviet Catholics maintained an allegiance to a body with universalist claims and a central organisation beyond the frontiers of the USSR. Initially there was little press comment on the cardinals' choice, but in January 1979, Foreign Minister Gromyko met John Paul II in Rome, ideas were exchanged and some opportunity provided for the leadership to size up the new pontiff.[112] As we shall see, 1979 witnessed a flurry of activity within the Central Committee apparatus in response to the selection of a Polish Pope. Of particular concern was the likely impact of this event on Rome's policy towards the Soviet bloc. During 1980 the number of press articles on the new Pope's impact on Vatican policy began to increase, with many noting that whilst pledged to continue the line of Vatican II he was in fact developing a more conservative stance on issues such as personal morality and political theology.[113] In time this

---

[112] *Sovetskaya Rossiya* 25 Jan. 1979; Janis Sapiets suggested that the Pope proposed a recognition of Soviet–Polish borders in exchange for the filling of vacant bishoprics in Latvia and Lithuania, and possibly the nomination of a Lithuanian cardinal. *CARIS Report* 2, 1979, (26 Jan. 1979).

[113] Cf. *Pravda Ukrainy* 20 May 1980; *Sovetskaya Litva* 24 Sept. 1980.

critical aspect was to become stronger, in particular after the Pope called for a renewal of Christianity throughout Europe, 'from the Atlantic to the Urals', an effort which one Lithuanian author suggested was to be spearheaded by Polish priests. In addition it was charged that the Vatican was preparing for this new crusade by strengthening contacts with the Russian Orthodox Church and by encouraging the activities of 'extremist priests' in Lithuania and Ukraine.[114]

Soviet writings of the early 1980s made much of the fact that the new Pope's election had stimulated opposition forces within the USSR and Eastern Europe, an assertion borne out by samizdat sources which expressed elation at the Pope's election and which led groups such as the Pentecostals, traditionally hostile to Catholicism, to begin addressing appeals to the Roman pontiff.[115] Amongst those groups revitalised by the event were the Ukrainian Catholics or Uniates. Forcibly merged with the Russian Orthodox Church in 1946 (and 1949 in Transcarpathia), the Uniates had continued an underground existence since that time, periodically launching campaigns for legalisation.[116] Uniate activism on this issue appears to have been renewed from the late 1970s onwards, helped by the Pope's overt support for the eventual freedom of this church. Indeed, at a time when virtually all other manifestations of dissent had been crushed there emerged in September 1982 an Initiative Group to campaign for legalisation.[117] Though committed to the campaign for recognition, the statements of many of the leaders of this group made it clear that they saw the only long-term prospect for both church and nation in the creation of a truly sovereign Ukraine.[118]

This combination of dissent and nationalism, stimulated by events beyond Soviet borders, was something that had been foreseen by Moscow as a possible consequence of the papal election. At a meeting of Soviet bloc ideological secretaries held in East Berlin during July 1979, the election of John Paul II appears to have been discussed with Ukraine identified as a probable focus for renewed Catholic activities.[119] Soviet concern was accentuated by two Ukrainian Catholic synods held in Rome during 1980 where the renunciations of the decisions of the 1946 Lvov council which merged the Uniates into the Orthodox Church were

---

[114] V. Nyunka, 'Vostochnaya politika vatikana', *Kommunist* (of Lithuania) 2, 1982, pp. 62–6.
[115] One such document dated 25 May 1979 can be found in the Keston College archive.
[116] For a general overview see B. Bociurkiw, 'The Suppression of the Ukrainian Greek Catholic Church in Post-War Soviet Union and Poland', in D. J. Dunn, ed., *Religion and Nationalism in Eastern Europe and the Soviet Union* (Boulder, CO, 1987), pp. 97–119.			[117] *AS 4897* (1982).
[118] *AS 5410*, Summer 1984, pp. 40–52.
[119] I. V. Polok, 'O praktike raboty po protivodeistviyu katolicheskoi i uniatskoi propagande', in *Voprosy nauchnogo ateizma*, Vyp. 28 (Moscow, 1981), p. 203.

supported by the Pope.[120] Two years later a major conference on nationality questions held in Riga heard official anxieties expressed by Leonid Kravchuk, then head of the Ukrainian propaganda department, who spoke of:

a plan to resurrect the Uniate church and utilise it for religio-nationalist opposition; to increase the activism of the Catholic communities; to influence the Orthodox with the aim of encouraging their evolution towards Catholicism; to unite all anti-Soviet elements under the banner of religion and encourage religious dissent... [121]

As we shall see, this concern was to be translated into a ferocious campaign of denigration and harassment of the Ukrainian Catholic Church during the first half of the 1980s.

During the Brezhnev years external factors impinged on Soviet religious policy in a way they had not hitherto. Although the actions of outside powers did not in themselves determine policy or shift it in a major way, they did serve to stimulate the hopes and activities of religious believers themselves. For example, the relative success of Jewish activists in utilising Western support for their emigration campaigns undoubtedly influenced the 20,000 or more Pentecostals who sought to leave during the 1970s, although without family or homeland abroad their hopes were always likely to be disappointed.[122] On one occasion religion's impact on the elite was changed by a single event, the election of a Slav Pope who was far less cautious than his predecessor in his dealings with the Soviet bloc and whose election further stimulated the forces of dissent and nationalism within many parts of the region. For these reasons it is legitimate to describe external factors as one of the new challenges facing the Brezhnev leadership that required more than the usual delegated fine tuning so characteristic of much policy making during this era.

Conclusion

In this chapter we have isolated some of the factors that impinged upon the Brezhnev leadership's thinking about the religious question. Whilst halting the worst excesses of the Khrushchev campaign, it faced the need to come to terms with some of the questions thrown up by the experiences of the early 1960s. Could religion be eliminated by decree or was such an

[120] ibid., pp. 84–104.
[121] L. M. Kravchuk, 'Ateisticheskoe vospitanie trudyashchikhsya i zadachi kontra-propagandy', in *Neprimirimost' k burzhuaznoi ideologii perezhitkam natsionalizma* (Moscow, 1982), pp. 35–50.
[122] In the case of the Pentecostals the state could not save face by pointing to humanitarian reasons for permitting native Russians or Ukrainians to leave their homeland. If them, who next?

approach counter-productive in post-terror conditions insofar as it merely stimulated opposition and revitalised religious communities? To what extent did religion retain deep roots in Soviet society and, if so, how could these be tackled by a propaganda apparatus that had perhaps lost touch with the changing nature of religious communities? In addition it faced new challenges. Why were young people and intellectuals beginning to find religion attractive, and how was this strengthened by the perceived connection between faith and national identity? And what to do when the continued ability of religion to survive varying policies of propaganda, control and repression, was further reinforced by developments in the outside world? How the party sought to resolve these questions is the subject of chapter 5.

5 Brezhnev and after: Combatting religion

The political leadership and decision making

In examining the central policy making process we face many of the same problems as were noted in chapter 2 relating to source material. Some gaps can be filled in from documents contained within the Central Committee archives, but there remain many omissions, not least the absence of Politburo minutes which might enable us to determine the precise role of the leadership in this area. Nonetheless, a number of conclusions can be drawn from available sources.

In general it appears that the day-to-day fine tuning of policy in at least some areas – atheist propaganda, new rituals and elements of the control process – were left to subordinate bodies, including the ideological establishment, the Council for Religious Affairs and its commissioners, the KGB, or local organisations. Each of these bodies produced a steady stream of reports and documents for the Central Committee, but the majority of these appear to have been simply noted and filed. Typical of such documents was the lengthy report on non-Orthodox denominations produced by deputy CRA chairman A. I. Barmenkov in late 1969, which provided detailed statistical information, reported on the political loyalty of individual churches, and highlighted problem areas.[1] These may have served to influence the fine tuning of policy, but in general this was done at the level of the Central Committee department. Within the Ideology Department a key figure appears to have been instructor E. I. Lisavtsev, whose signature appears on many documents coming to or issued by this department – albeit below those of the Secretary or section head present at the time. Nonetheless, Lisavtsev appears to have played a key role, representing the Central Committee on the editorial boards of the chief atheist publications *Voprosy nauchnogo ateizma* and *Nauka i religiya*, attending

[1] TsKhSD, f. 5, op. 62, ed.khr. 38.

conferences, and acting as troubleshooter – as late as 1986 being sent to areas where atheist propaganda had fallen down.[2]

Certain issues, however, required the approval of the Secretariat or Politburo. In June 1969, for example, the Secretariat discussed the possibility of the prime minister sending official greetings to a meeting of religious organisations about to take place in Zagorsk, and sent the draft text of the message to the Politburo for approval.[3] More importantly the Politburo was involved in the field of appointments, in late 1965 selecting Vladimir Kuroedov – a man who had previously worked with senior Politburo members Mikhail Suslov and Andrei Kirilenko – as head of the new Council for Religious Affairs. The Politburo also appears to have exercised *nomenklatura* responsibilities with regard to the selection of a new Patriarch in 1971. Patriarch Aleksii had died in the previous year and eventually, in May 1971, the party Secretariat had given permission for the convening of a Sobor to elect his successor.[4] According to Kuroedov's later and rather questionable account the CRA and the KGB put forward rival candidates – Metropolitans Pimen of Krutitsy and Kolomna, and Nikodim of Leningrad and Novgorod respectively – thus requiring the Politburo to make a choice. Kuroedov sought to promote his candidate by lobbying Suslov and prime minister Kosygin, in particular by pointing to the pro-Catholic sympathies of Nikodim. In the event Pimen was the only candidate and was 'elected' unanimously.[5]

Around the same time, and perhaps not unrelated to the publicity surrounding the selection of a new Patriarch, the Central Committee discussed the adoption of a new decree on atheist education – the first since 1958. At the 24th CPSU Congress in March 1971 Brezhnev had called for a rejuvenation of ideological work, and in the following months a series of resolutions in this area were prepared. The initial draft of one 'on strengthening the atheist education of the workers' was discussed by the Secretariat on 13 July 1971. P. Kapitonov was commissioned to produce a final draft for approval by the Politburo which was accepted three days later although not published at the time.[6]

In many of these areas the Politburo and Secretariat was largely operating in conformity with long established practice. For example, the Central Committee retained a key role in censoring religious publications

[2] *Pravda Vostoka* 8 May 1986 reports his presence at a major atheist conference in the Namangan region (Uzbekistan) whose party organisation had come under frequent attack over the previous twelve months from both central and regional bodies for the poor quality of its atheist work.
[3] TsKhSD, Protocols of the Secretariat, 73, 18 June 1969.
[4] TsKhSD, Protocols of the Secretariat, 4, 18 June 1971.
[5] *Lyudina i svit* 1, 1992, p. 22.
[6] TsKhSD, Protocols of the Secretariat, 9, 13 July 1971.

and press comment on religious questions. Veteran Soviet journalist Alexander Bovin recalled his experiences as a correspondent in Poland when he wanted to write on religion: 'I wrote a series of three articles, and one was about religion. I had to go there several times to agree it with their Central Committee, and then I had to do the same with our Central Committee, then again with their Central Committee, then again with our Central Committee ...'[7]

On occasions, however the party apparatus had to adopt new approaches to deal with new challenges. Of growing concern to the leadership was the emergence of overt religious dissent, often uncowed by threats of repression. During the mid-1960s the leadership appears to have devoted some time to discussing the problems raised by the reform Baptist movement, with various committees on the question drawing in members of the political elite such as Anastas Mikoyan, chairman of the presidium of the Supreme Soviet, and Vladimir Semichastny, chairman of the KGB.[8] Religious activism must have come up at other times during Politburo discussions of dissent, as KGB chairman Yury Andropov (appointed in 1967) sought guidance or freedom to deal with non-conformists in his own more flexible way. By most accounts Brezhnev had little interest in the religious question,[9] and within the Politburo it appears to have been Mikhail Suslov who, fearing the loss of long term control over Soviet society, kept the anti-religious flame alive whilst seeking to avoid the 'storm tactics' of the Khrushchev years.[10]

Leadership concern with the religious question appears to have increased during the late 1970s, with the election of Pope John Paul II in October 1978 acting as a major stimulus. The immediate response of the Secretariat was to commission Oleg Bogomolov to produce a report analysing the implications of this new turn. Dated 4 November 1978, this document apparently focused on the likelihood that this conservative pontiff would increase criticism of Soviet human rights' practice, and suggested that one option would be to warn the Vatican that such an approach might lead to new restrictions on the churches in Eastern Europe. Alternatively silence might be bought in exchange for concessions to the church.[11] A flurry of activity followed with CRA chairman Kuroedov flying to Warsaw to discuss developments with his Polish counterpart in February 1989,[12] whilst in April the CRA issued a series

---

[7] Quoted in B. McNair, *Glasnost', Perestroika and the Media* (London, 1991), p. 121.
[8] See chapter 4, p. 83.   [9] *Lyudina i svit* 1, 1992, p. 21.
[10] According to former party worker V. Alekseev in '*Shturm nebes' otmenyaetsya* (Moscow, 1992), pp. 244, 248.
[11] According to a report in the Catholic paper *Our Sunday Visitor*, 9 May 1993.
[12] TsKhSD, f. 5, op. 76, d. 186.

of decrees on combatting Catholic extremism.[13] In October 1979 a Secretariat session (whose participants included Mikhail Suslov, Konstantin Chernenko, Mikhail Zimyanin and Mikhail Gorbachev) discussed the necessity of taking measures to combat Vatican policy towards the socialist bloc and set up a commission to draft a decree on the matter 'taking into account opinions expressed at the session of the Secretariat'. The commission's membership was to include CRA chairman Kuroedov and KGB deputy-chairman Viktor Chebrikov.[14] During November an unpublished decree 'on measures to counteract the policy of the Vatican in relation to the socialist countries' was issued by the Central Committee.[15] Secretariat interest in this question remained high well into the 1980s. Less than a year after the issuance of this decree the party apparatus returned to the matter, approving a propaganda document on the Catholic question to be propagated by all foreign agencies of the USSR.[16] Around the same time the Central Committee discussed an agreement with its Czechoslovak counterpart to hold a special meeting to discuss means of combatting the revival of Catholic and Muslim activities.[17] In response to this concern other bodies were also taking action. A report produced by the CRA on its fulfilment of a 1979 CC decree on ideological work noted that it had undertaken a series of education measures in Catholic regions in response to the anti-Vatican decree and the 'anti-socialist, anti-communist activities of John Paul II'.[18]

A further religious issue taken up by the Politburo related to the perceived resurgence of Islam in the outside world and the fear that this might spread to the demographically dynamic population of Central Asia. Such matters were almost certainly discussed during Politburo debates over the decision to invade Afghanistan. Concern was also evident in Brezhnev's speech to the 26th Party Congress in early 1981 where he stressed, with Islam in mind, that communists respected the views of religious believers.[19] Increasingly, leading political figures linked religion to the campaigns of imperialist powers to undermine the Soviet Union. Addressing a Moscow party plenum in mid-1981 Viktor Grishin noted that:

---

[13] I am grateful to Felix Corley for reporting the contents of these documents which he saw in the Lithuanian archives.

[14] TsKhSD, Protocols of the Secretariat, 181, 23 Oct. 1979.

[15] TsKhSD, Protocols of the Secretariat, 184, 13 Nov. 1979.

[16] TsKsSD Protocols of the Secretariat, 219, 15 July 1980.

[17] TsKhSD, Zapiski otdelov TsK, ministerstv, vedomstv i dr.organizatsii s soglasiyem sekretarei TsK KPSS (30 July 1980).

[18] TsKhSD, f. 5, op. 77, ed.khr. 126, pp. 172–3.

[19] *Ob ideologicheskoi rabote KPSS* (Moscow, 1983), p. 60.

In recent years reactionary churchmen, especially Catholics, Muslims and sectarians have become more active. Inspired by Western propaganda they speculate on the religious feelings of believers, organise illegal meetings for those of similar mind – into which they attempt to draw children and young people – demand unlimited rights to propagate religion and resort to slanderous fabrications and provocations.[20]

More specific targetting of Muslim groups was left to others, but a reading of the published materials from the late Brezhnev period adequately confirm central leadership worries over both Catholicism and Islam.

The hardening attitude to religion appears to have been connected to the rise of Yury Andropov within the elite. From late 1979 the KGB waged a harsh campaign against religious and other forms of dissent, and during the same period calls for ideological 'hardening' (*zakalka*) became more insistent. In August 1981 *Pravda* published its first editorial on atheism since 1972,[21] and one month later the Central Committee issued a decree on strengthening atheist education. The focus of official concerns was indicated by an accompanying instruction issued to the CRA to take special action to improve political-educational work within Catholic and Muslim theological institutions.[22]

On the ideological front the major event during the early 1980s was the June 1983 Central Committee plenum, the first to be entirely devoted to ideology for twenty years. Delivering the keynote speech Konstantin Chernenko stressed the need to take further measures to create the 'new man' and raised a number of issues having a bearing on the religious question. In particular he attacked foreign 'centres of ideological influence' which sought to utilise religious sentiments and impart to them an 'anti-Soviet and nationalist bias'. This same speech also contained a thinly disguised attack on Russian nationalist tendencies as revealed in literary and artistic works, reflecting Andropov's personal distaste for this phenomenon as well as having implications for the position of the Russian Orthodox Church.[23]

From the above discussion it is evident that although religion was not a major issue of political concern or intra-elite political debate, it remained on the agenda of the Brezhnev leadership and its immediate successors. What is less clear is the extent to which bodies such as the KGB and CRA were drawn into the decision making process at the centre. We know that the status and role of the security police increased

[20] V. Grishin, *Voprosy partiinogo-organizatsionnoi i ideologicheskoi raboty* (Moscow, 1984), pp. 5–10.   [21] *Pravda* 8 Aug. 1981.   [22] *Izvestiya* 22 Jan. 1992.
[23] *Pravda* 15 June 1983; on Andropov and Russian nationalism see J. Dunlop, *The New Russian Nationalism* (New York, 1985).

under the headship of Yury Andropov, with representation in the leading political organs growing and its activities being given ever more favourable coverage in the press.[24] And during this period the KGB as a whole and Andropov in particular (from 1973) would have been drawn into Politburo discussions of how to deal with religious dissent. Above all the KGB played a key role as provider of information to the elite, supplementing (and perhaps supplanting) the reports of the CRA with its own reports based upon the work of operatives and informers within both state agencies – including the CRA, one of whose deputy chairmen was usually a secret police officer[25] – and religious bodies themselves.[26]

KGB reports contained in the Central Committee archives are generally not available to researchers, although one does find there references to KGB reports on specific situations. In February 1970, for example, the Secretariat responded to a memorandum from the security police on the religious situation in Daghestan by ordering the local obkom to take up the issues raised.[27] Four years later Yury Andropov, by then a Politburo member, directed a report to the Central Committee on the politics of the Vatican and its attempts to draw closer to the Russian Orthodox Church, something he viewed as undesirable[28] – a stance that clashes with Kuroedov's depiction of the KGB backing the pro-Catholic Metropolitan Nikodim for Patriarch in 1971.

The KGB was also drawn into the campaign against the Vatican launched in the wake of the election of Pope John Paul II. Whether it was involved in the plot to assassinate the Polish pontiff remains a subject of some controversy, but there can be little doubt that it did participate in actions aimed at undermining papal influence, both within the socialist bloc and the wider world. Former London KGB operative Oleg Gordievsky quotes a number of documents which he received in 1984 instructing intelligence agents to adopt measures to counteract the influence of the Vatican. Of particular concern was the attempt to revitalise the Uniates of Eastern Europe and Ukraine, and the evolution of closer links between the Vatican and the Orthodox churches. To combat this, KGB officers were to attempt to discredit papal policies in this region, encourage those forces in the Catholic church sceptical about the more conservative ideas of John Paul II, 'to take steps to expose John Paul II as the protegé of the most reactionary circles in the West', and to

[24] See Amy Knight, *The KGB – Police and Politics in the Soviet Union* (London, 1988), pp. 83–5.
[25] According to K. Kharchev, CRA chairman 1984–9, in *Ogonyok* 44, 1989, pp. 9–12.
[26] *Izvestiya* 22 Jan. 1992.
[27] TsKhSD, Protocols of the Secretariat, 91, 24 Feb. 1970.
[28] TsKhSD, f. 5, op. 67, d. 963.

expose any links between the Vatican and capitalist intelligence services.[29]

Though the involvement of the Council for Religious Affairs in religious policy making was clearly subordinate during the Brezhnev years, it was not without some part to play. Firstly, it played a key role as informant, providing the Central Committee with regular reports on the state of religious life in the Soviet Union. Best known of these is the detailed 1974 report of deputy chairman V. Furov on the Russian Orthodox Church, a document which characterised the hierarchs in terms of their loyalty to the state and promotion of religiosity, and provided valuable information on the ways in which the CRA sought to control religious life. But this was but one amongst many provided by the Council to the Central Committee, reports which included information on individual denominations, statistics on religious organisations, lists of measures taken by the council, or accounts of religious delegations travelling abroad. In preparing such reports the CRA had an opportunity to influence policy in that the way it shaped such documents could affect leadership perceptions of the religious question. The 1969 report on non-Orthodox denominations prepared by Barmenkov notes, amongst other things, the strength of Catholic communities in Byelorussia and the numerous complaints from believers in this republic, going on to suggest that some of these were not without justification.[30] By making this point the Council began to lay the groundwork, deliberately or otherwise, for the registration of Catholic communities in Byelorussia during the second half of the 1970s. In the case of the Furov report we can see the CRA attempting to demonstrate both its success in controlling religious bodies and the continued problem areas which necessitate the continued existence of the Council.

The Council also played some role in the various sub-commissions organised to deal with specific problems by the Central Committee. The records of the Secretariat reveal that Kuroedov was often present when religious matters were discussed, and we have already noted his appointment to a commission to draft an anti-Catholic decree towards the end of 1979. In theory the CRA was also a means through which the demands of the religious leaderships could be channelled to the political elite, though there is little evidence as to how seriously the Council took this role. But in practice it was less as decision maker than as implementing agency that the Council played a role in policy making, for its actions and interpretations of the central line – insofar as they were

[29] C. Andrew & O. Gordievsky, *More Instructions from the Centre – The Secret Files on KGB Global Operations* (London, 1992), pp. 46–52.

[30] TsKhSD, f. 5, op. 62, ed.khr. 38, pp. 65–95.

followed at the local level, something which became increasingly less certain during these years – helped to determine the reactions of religious communities which in turn shaped the later adjustment or even alteration of policy.

Outputs: the 'public' definition of policy

Party documents

The earliest indication of some of the concerns of the leadership came in 1967 when *Pravda* published an article coauthored by M. Morozov and E. Lisavtsev, of the Central Committee's Propaganda Department. After a standard warning against the use of 'administrative measures' the authors went on to suggest that religion was a highly complex phenomenon with deep social and psychological roots, in turn reinforced by the intrigues of clerics and imperialist propaganda. The 'decisive role' in combatting religion belonged to the practical activities of the Soviet state in pursuit of socio-economic transformation, but this did not preclude a whole range of educational measures designed to free people from 'religious prejudices'. Such actions had to be carried out under firm party *kontrol* and by well prepared cadres.[31] Though hardly revolutionary in content this article set the tone for many of the official statements of the Brezhnev years, and most of its themes reappeared in the five *Pravda* editorials on religion and atheism between 1964 and 1985.

In 1971 the paper stressed the need to place atheist work on a 'scientific footing' by making use of the results of sociological investigation and well trained cadres.[32] One year later *Pravda* was to be found attacking those communists who publicly supported atheism yet behind closed doors participated in religious rites.[33] These last two editorials followed the appearance of a Central Committee resolution on atheism. Issued in July 1971, but not published until later, this decree noted that in many parts of the country 'party organisations and ideological institutions have weakened their attention to the atheist education of the population and have frequently permitted a compromising attitude to the spread of religious views'. In particular it noted the participation of communists in religious rites, and the idealisation of religious customs to be found in certain artistic and literary works. All of this was said to have been carefully utilised by clerics and sectarian preachers to strengthen their influence upon the population. To combat this the decree enjoined all party and social organisations to raise the level of their atheist work.

[31] *Pravda* 12 Jan. 1967. [32] *Pravda* 18 Aug. 1971. [33] *Pravda* 15 Sept. 1972.

Simultaneously local soviets and administrative organs were to ensure the strictest observation of the legislation on cults and to 'take the necessary measures' to bring an end to the activities of those believers who violated Soviet laws.[34]

In considering this decree the question arises as to why it should appear at this time and why it should remain unpublished for some years? By 1970–1 Brezhnev was increasingly dominating the leadership group and perhaps, following his predecessors, felt the need to develop some form of distinctive ideological stance. It was during this period that the phrase 'developed socialism' began to be used more frequently and, following the 24th CPSU Congress, at least five resolutions dealing with ideology were issued by the Central Committee. All noted that the party's concentration on economic tasks during the late 1960s had led to a neglect of ideological questions.[35] Combined with the shift towards detente with the West and the awareness that this might increase the risk of ideological contamination,[36] a renewed stress on combatting an alien ideology such as religion was perhaps to be expected. The failure to publicise this decree presumably stemmed from the nature of its intended audience, party and state workers. It was such people who were attacked for their compromises with religion, and warned that the curtailing of the excesses of the Khrushchev years did not absolve them from responsibility for participation in anti-religious work.

During the mid-1970s the party made very little public comment on the religious question. Decrees on lecture propaganda and ideological work issued in 1978 and 1979 respectively paid scant attention to religious matters, and only in the early 1980s did the party press once more take up the question with any seriousness. As already noted the Central Committee produced a decree on atheist propaganda in 1981, but the text of this document and other resolutions on the religious question – such as that of 5 April 1983 on 'the ideological isolation of the reactionary part of the Muslim clergy'[37] – have yet to become available. And published resolutions such as that produced by the 1983 plenum on ideological matters contained little more than generalised injunctions to improve work in this area.

[34] I was first alerted to this decree by an editorial in *Sovetskaya Kirgiziya* 1 Sept. 1973.

[35] *Ob ideologicheskoi rabote*, pp. 199–215.

[36] In February 1974 *Nauka i religiya* was to warn that detente would enable more foreigners to become acquainted with Soviet reality, but that there would also be more opportunities for 'diversions based upon religion'.

[37] Alekseev, *Shturm nebes*, p. 263.

State documents

Here, as before, we have to deal with three broad categories of output: changes in civil law, in criminal law, and further unpublished instructions issued by the Council for Religious Affairs. The latter type of material was included in the law book on religion 'for official use only' which we quoted earlier which reproduced the changes to the 1929 Law on Religious Associations made in 1962, amendments made to republican laws in 1968–9, and a series of unpublished instructions issued by the CRA and its predecessors.[38] Amongst these was one issued in October 1968 which enjoined all those concerned with religious matters to keep better records on the number, type, activities etc. of religious associations in their area.[39] Changes to republican legislation issued around the same time all appear to be based upon the assumption that control over the observance of the legislation on cults had become lax in recent times. The details have been discussed in considerable detail by Sawatsky,[40] and for our purposes it is sufficient to note the repeated injunctions on the need to establish firmer control over religious bodies. Most of these instructions and administrative changes remained in force until the late 1980s, although in 1978 Kuroedov wrote to the Central Committee suggesting that the 1961 instruction (discussed in chapter 2) was only partially relevant and not fully compatible with the 1977 constitution. His request to update the instruction was approved by the party, although once again the text of any document subsequently approved is missing.[41]

The major publicised change in civil law came in the mid-1970s when the Law on Religious Associations was subject to some amendment. The decision to amend this law had been taken by the Central Committee in 1972, with the following year proposed for its publication,[42] but in practice the updated law did not appear until 1975. Moreover, in terms of content the new document did little more than make public changes introduced in 1962. Of these perhaps two have significance for our purposes. Firstly, the public recognition of the role of the Council for Religious Affairs in the administration of religious policy, and then the shift of responsibility for registering religious communities to that Council. Under the 1929 law religious communities could not legally function until they had been registered by local soviets. Article 4 of the

---

[38] V. A. Kuroedov & A. Pankratov, ed., *Zakonodatel'stvo o religioznykh kul'takh – sbornik materialov i dokumentov* (Moscow, 1971).   [39] ibid., pp. 133–50.

[40] W. Sawatsky, 'Secret Soviet Lawbook on Religion', *Religion in Communist Lands*, vol. 4, no. 4, 1976, pp. 24–34.   [41] TsKhSD f. 5, op. 75, ed.khr. 270, p. 1.

[42] TsKhSD, Protocols of the Secretariat, 25 Apr. 1972.

1975 version formally transferred the final decision on the granting or withholding of recognition to the CRA in Moscow.[43]

Initially it was samizdat writers who noticed this trend towards centralisation in registration procedures, a development they viewed in a negative light. One Orthodox document noted that now believers had lost the faint hope that they might achieve results – for example, the opening of a church – by means of exerting pressure on local authorities.[44] Official sources countered with the argument that centralisation might provide believers with protection against occasional abuses by such bodies.[45] This official view that this presaged improvements should not be ignored for from the mid-1970s the overall reduction in the number of places of worship came to an end, and from then until the advent of Gorbachev the total may even have increased slightly. From that point onwards the CRA did indeed begin to take a more flexible attitude to registration and on occasions to criticise those local officials who overstepped the mark though no serious legal action was taken against those abusing believers' rights.

Alongside the legal change came the 1977 constitutional revisions mentioned earlier. Here the regime's intent to depict itself as moderate on the religious question was perhaps borne out by two features of the revised Article 52. In the first place freedom of conscience was now 'guaranteed' rather than simply 'recognised', and secondly, the freedom to carry out 'anti-religious propaganda' was replaced by the less offensive 'atheist propaganda'.[46]

In the sphere of criminal law the only changes affecting religion came in the context of the anti-Baptist campaign in 1966 and related to the more restrictive interpretation of existing clauses in the criminal code. In March of that year the Presidium of the RSFSR Supreme Soviet issued a number of resolutions clarifying what were to be considered offences under Article 142 of the code ('violation of the laws on separation of church from state and church from school'). Amongst these were to be included the refusal of religious leaders to register their communities, violation of the rules laid down for the performance of rites, and the organisation of special groups for young people, children or women which had no relation to religious worship – the penalty being an administrative fine of 50 roubles. A further edict (*ukaz*) elucidated those actions liable to criminal punishment, including: dissemination of

[43] *Vedomosti verkhovnogo soveta RSFSR* 3 July 1975, pp. 487–91.
[44] G. Yakunin & L. Regelson, 'General'nomu sekrataryu Vsemirnogo soveta tserkvei Filippu Potteru', 6 Mar. 1976 (in Keston College archive).
[45] Cf. CRA chairman Kuroedov in *Nauka i religiya* 1, 1978, pp. 22–5 and deputy chairman Furov in *Nauka i religiya* 10, 1979, pp. 15–18.
[46] *Konstitutsiya (osnovnoi zakon) SSSR* (Moscow, 1983), p. 18.

written appeals and letters calling for the non-observance of Soviet legislation, the organisation of public meetings or processions which violated public order, systematic and organised teaching of religion to children, and discrimination against believers. The final edict provided for up to three years imprisonment for second offences under Article 142.[47]

From these various party and state documents one has the impression of a leadership committed to the struggle against religion, but in a less offensive and militant style than that associated with Nikita Khrushchev. In particular, it was concerned that party activists should not forget that the religious and communist worldview were fundamentally incompatible, and that they had a duty to combat religious ideas. Alongside this went a determination to bring religious institutions under much firmer control, whilst seeking to limit repressive measures to the more overt opponents of official policy.

Implementation

Education and propaganda

Most of the educational and propaganda programmes developed during the Brezhnev years had their roots in Khrushchev's anti-religious campaign. It was in the early 1960s that atheist education became a constituent part of political education in higher educational establishments; it was in the 1960s that the party called for more serious research into the religious question; it was in November 1963 that the Central Committee's Ideological Commission called for the creation of an Institute of Scientific Atheism, a body which started life the following year; and in 1966 the long promised *Voprosy nauchnogo ateizma* (Questions of Scientific Atheism) began to appear. Despite this continuity there is some evidence to suggest that the drive and enthusiasm declined once the centrally directed campaign came to an end. An increasing number of specialists were working in this field, yet the 1971 Central Committee resolution could complain of a general weakening of effort in educational institutions and instruct the relevant ministries to remedy this.[48]

In the research field there were frequent calls to place atheism on a 'more scientific basis' and in August 1971 *Pravda* suggested that one way to do this was through the further development of the sociology of religion.[49] But although genuine scholars were attracted to this field during the Brezhnev years, their research was considerably restrained

[47] *Sovetskaya Yustitsiya* 9, 1966, p. 28.   [48] *Ob ideologicheskoi rabote*, p. 200.
[49] *Pravda* 18 Aug. 1971.

or distorted by ideological considerations. Survey work was especially problematic, as respondents were all too aware of the possible 'costs' of openly proclaiming religious adherence.[50] Moreover, some sociologists wrote quite explicitly of the development of sociology as contributing 'to the perfection of the system for managing the process of overcoming religion and the affirmation of a scientific world view amongst the workers of our country'.[51] In these circumstances it was hard to gauge the reliability of such data as was published, and it seems that on occasions 'undesirable' results were simply not reported. Nonetheless these same findings contributed to the academic reassessment of the vitality of religious life in the USSR which in turn impacted upon the thinking of the reforming leadership which came to power in the mid-1980s.

Anti-religious propaganda during the Brezhnev years was equally very much a continuation and development of the programme set out in Il'ichev's 1963 'measures for strengthening the atheist education of the population'. Party documents and newspaper editorials during this period made frequent pleas for an improvement of existing activities, although warnings against complacency suggested that at least some party workers took the end of the Khrushchev campaign as a signal to cease all actions in this area.[52] In March 1969, for example, the Secretariat discussed a memorandum produced by the Party Control Commission on the failure of many party organisations and members to take seriously the party statute with its injunctions to struggle with religious ideology.[53] Reading the literature of this period one finds three broad emphases: the need to improve the training of atheist cadres, the improvement of mass measures such as lectures, and the development of individual work with believers.

On the first the frequent complaint was that all too often those involved in atheist work were poorly trained for this task. To meet this criticism a vast array of institutions developed further training programmes during these years. The extent of such activity is revealed in a study of the Byelorussian republic where between 1964 and 1972 the following measures were carried out:

> from 1964 the republican agitprop initiated a two-year course for preparing atheists, held within the BCP higher school – this trained about 300 atheists a year;

[50] See C. Lane, *Christian Religion in the Soviet Union – A Sociological Study* (Cambridge, 1978).
[51] I. N. Yablokov, *Metodologicheskie problemy sotsiologii religii* (Moscow, 1972), p. 2.
[52] See the already cited *Pravda* editorials.
[53] TsKhSD, Protocols of the Secretariat, 68, 5 Mar. 1969.

during 1966 a series of day courses for leaders of atheist councils were held in each oblast involving some 2,000 people;

in September 1971 the republican party's Central Committee issued a resolution on atheist education establishing a branch of the Institute of Scientific Atheism whose main responsibility would be the training of atheists;

throughout this period 448 special seminars were organised, drawing in some 9,000 individuals.[54]

Other sources report similar ventures in other republics.[55] Yet for all the efforts, in reality or on paper, there remained doubts as to the utility of such training exercises. In late 1983 a *Pravda* editorial entitled 'Atheist Propagandists' lamented the fact that so many of those involved in such work were 'incompetent to do so' and that all too often their training only fitted them to combat a simplified form of religion that was not characteristic of modern believers.[56]

Similar problems arose in the attempt to improve the conduct of mass measures, whether in the form of press articles, media programmes or public lectures. In the press there was still a tendency for long periods of relative quiescence, interspersed with sharp rises following major ideological pronouncements – as happened after the 1971 decree and the 1979 Central Committee resolution on improving ideological work (See Figure 1). In the lecture hall, after a fall in the mid-1960s, the number of lectures given rose again from the early 1970s, reaching a total of some 3,000 a day (1 million every year by the end of the decade.[57] Yet, over and over again, complaints were heard that the rise in quantity was not paralleled by one in quality. Critics spoke of lectures that did not take account of local circumstances – on e.g. Orthodoxy in Bukhara – or provided unconvincing critiques of religion. It was pointed out that believers rarely attended lectures, with one survey showing that of those at lectures only 4.1 per cent were religious, and 6.7 per cent 'waverers' between faith and unbelief.[58] The cause of atheism was rarely helped by the tendency to time lectures to coincide with religious meetings or to advertise titles offensive to the sensibility of believers.[59] From 1978,

[54] R. P. Platonov, *Vospitanie ateisticheskoi ubezhdennosti* (Minsk, 1973), pp. 170–2.
[55] *Nauka i religiya* 11, 1981, pp. 13–14, reports a correspondence course initiated by the University of Kiev's Philosophy Faculty in 1977. This differed from traditional courses in permitting students a considerable degree of specialisation, for example allowing those from Western Ukraine to focus on the banned Ukrainian Catholic Church.
[56] *Pravda* 14 Dec. 1983.　　　　　　[57] *Nauka i religiya* 6, 1978, pp. 2–3.
[58] *Partiinaya organizatsiya i ateisticheskoe vospitanie* (Moscow, 1975), pp. 147–8.
[59] cf. *Nauka i religiya* 8, 1968, pp. 2–5; V. A. Saprykin, *Sotsialisticheskii kollektiv i ateisticheskoe vospitanie* (Alma Ata, 1983), p. 85.

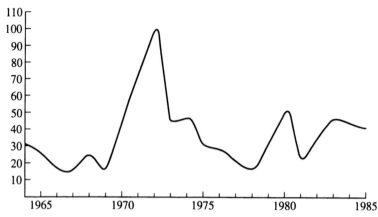

Figure 1   Major press articles
Source: *Letopis Gazetnykh Statei*

following a Central Committee resolution on lecture propaganda, some effort was made to improve this work. Lecture cycles were developed to enable subjects to be explored more fully,[60] and attempts were made to exercise some control over lecture propaganda by introducing panels of reviewers.[61]

The other main emphasis of atheist activity that looked likely to be developed during the Brezhnev years was individual work with believers, an approach which allowed the atheist to take account of the age, sex, occupation, and religious affiliation of 'her' believer. But there were very real problems attendant upon this method,[62] which required atheists with time, patience and a good knowledge of the subject's belief system, as well as a means of establishing contact with someone who was likely to be suspicious of any official figure sent to 'enlighten them'.[63] There was also the danger of counter-influence as a poorly prepared atheist came into contact with believers who were articulate, good workers and popular with their colleagues.[64] Nonetheless, during the 1970s such approaches reportedly continued to enjoy some success with one source claiming that of 180 people who had broken with religion in one part of the Ukraine, 144 had done so as a result of individual work.[65]

---

[60] *Nauka i religiya* 2, 1981, pp. 16–18.
[61] *Nauka i religiya* 10, 1981, pp. 8–9 & 7, 1982, pp. 4–8.
[62] For a general overview see the collection *Individual'naya rabota s veruyushchimi* (Moscow, 1967 & 1974).
[63] *Kazakhstanskaya pravda* 10 Feb. 1983 profiles an activist involved in such work and notes how he developed contacts by finding something the believer and he had in common – a hobby, a book etc.   [64] *Nauka i religiya* 9, 1966, pp. 14–18.
[65] *Partiinaya organizatsiya*, p. 53.

We have given anti-religious activity a fairly cursory treatment here, in part because it is well covered elsewhere, but mainly because many of the measures utilised during this period largely continued those of previous years. From the printed sources, the overall impression is that whilst on paper the sheer number of actions taken increased, there was an ever present concern over their quality. Nearly all the sources speak of the tendency to formalism in such work, of inappropriate methods, and of declining enthusiasm amongst party workers. It also seems likely that the actual carrying out of anti-religious activities was persistently undermined by the sheer number of organisations involved. Even within the party itself one could find three bodies charged with coordinating atheist work – branches of the Institute of Scientific Atheism, local atheist councils and the various agitprop organisations. To these one should add the wider range of social organisations, most notably the Znanie Society. On occasion this duplication led to open hostilities between the various bodies. In 1981, for example, the director of the Moscow House of Scientific Atheism could complain that 'one sometimes has the impression that between the Moscow House and the district Znanie organisations there is an insurmountable barrier to the extent that several refuse to collaborate with us'.[66] Above all there is little evidence to suggest that these manifold activities made much of a dent in the beliefs of those who continued to hold religious beliefs, or had much success in preventing an apparent growth in religious adherence amongst some sections of the populace.

Whilst much of the anti-religious propaganda discussed above was very general in nature and represented a considerable degree of continuity, there was another type of material which experienced considerable growth during this period, that aimed at 'religious extremists'. Here religious dissenters were portrayed as motivated by greed, pride or the service of foreign masters, though an effort was made to isolate the broad mass of loyal believers from the 'extremists' who sought to sow discord.

The press campaign launched against the Baptist dissenters after 1966 was typical of this approach. In July 1966 *Nauka i religiya* asked 'who are the initiators?', and proceeded to depict them as a 'fanatical religious centre' which had extended inner church squabbles into anti-social and illegal activity. Amongst their crimes were listed the dissemination of slanderous literature, public demonstrations and the organised teaching

---

[66] *Nauka i religiya* 10, 1981, pp. 8–9. The Moscow House was hardly a hotbed of activity in 1985 when I sought to attend two lectures by a relatively senior propagandist. On the first night there was an audience of fifteen, and on the second I found the place locked up.

of religion to children. This article did, however, admit that some contribution had been made to the schism by the 'incorrect practices' of a minority of administrative officials.[67] Other articles accused the Baptists of corrupting the minds of the young, by 'teaching children not to live but to vegetate'.[68] The tone of the attacks was set by CRA chairman Kuroedov who described Baptist leaders as 'mercenary and self-seeking' and as motivated by 'political aims'.[69] By the end of the 1960s a further strand of argument was developed as a growing number of writers attacked the reform Baptists as closely linked to foreign enemies of the Soviet Union.[70] This latter theme tied in with the growing official emphasis of the 1970s on the need to combat 'bourgeois falsification' of Soviet policies in the field of religion and human rights. Numerous books on this theme appeared throughout the 1970s and early 1980s, some concentrating their attention on the activities of foreign religious organisations – research centres, radio stations, bible missions etc. – and others going further in suggesting that foreign intelligence services were playing an active role in stimulating religious activity. Such themes appeared in many works of this period but with authors linked to the KGB enjoying particular prominence.[71]

Though such attacks were often extremely simplistic or absurd – one book asked how publicist Levitin-Krasnov could truly describe himself as Orthodox when he appealed to the leaders of other churches – their very focus on a few individuals reinforced the message that this was a very small minority who deserved everything they got. Such tactics could backfire, as when such articles alerted ordinary believers to people brave (or foolish) enough to challenge the state, but their implicit message that political loyalty would result in a minimum freedom of worship may well have affected some. Such messages were reinforced by occasionally spectacular confessions from religious activists who, like Fr Dmitri Dudko, in June 1980, emphasised that many of their activities had taken on a political colouring and that they had not in fact been arrested for their religious beliefs.[72]

This analysis of dissent as the work of 'extremists' or 'reactionary priests' became ever-more pronounced during the conservative turn that

---

[67] *Nauka i religiya* 7, 1966, pp. 24–5.   [68] *Uchitel'skaya gazeta* 23 Mar. 1966.

[69] *Izvestiya* 30 Aug. 1966.

[70] See Kuroedov's comments in *Izvestiya* 18 Oct. 1969 & the attack on British author Michael Bourdeaux in *Nauka i religiya* 12, 1969, pp. 54–7.

[71] Typical of these was A. Belov & A. Shilkin's *Diversiya bez dynamita* (Moscow, 1972, second edition 1976). Belov was generally reputed to be close to the security police whilst Shilkin was, according to dissident sources, deputy head of the Moscow KGB operations section responsible for religion. See DCCDBR, vol. 1, pp. 10–15.

[72] *Izvestiya* 21 June 1980.

developed in 1979. Lithuanians Catholics, Uniates and Pentecostals were increasingly likely to find themselves depicted as having collaborated with Nazi occupiers during the war or, in the case of the former, as having played a role in the nationalist struggle with Soviet power. In Ukraine a major propaganda campaign launched in the early 1980s to counter revived Uniate activism saw the publication of numerous books and articles detailing the links of the Uniates with a variety of evil forces – bourgeois nationalism, imperialism, Zionism and Maoism.[73] In the case of 'Zionism,' propaganda was followed through with the establishment of an official Anti-Zionist Committee by the Central Committee in 1983, whose plan of work was jointly determined by the Propaganda Department and the KGB.[74]

Though the more extreme attacks were reserved for dissident or banned religious groups, somewhat more reserved critiques began to affect other groups during the early 1980s, notably the Russian Orthodox Church. Developing within the context of Andropov's rise to power and assault on Russian nationalism, it focused in particular on the church's attempt to link its fate to that of the nation. Prominent here was journalist Aleksander Shamaro who in 1982 turned to the question of ancient monuments and the need to check the historicity of many of the stories associated with these places. For Shamaro it was important to note that many of the functions of institutions such as monasteries – as libraries, fortresses, prisons, landowners and income gatherers – had nothing in common with religion. Lyrical descriptions of them as 'music in stone' obscured the fact that the church often sought to use them as 'sermons in stone.'[75] Shamaro was also active in the critique of Orthodox attempts to make propagandist useage of the approaching millennium of Christianity, calling on Soviet scholars to undertake analyses of this event from a materialist viewpoint.[76]

New, non-religious rituals

After 1964 the authorities appear to have taken a more active role in the promotion of new rites, both as an anti-religious measure and as a broader means of political socialisation.[77] Throughout the USSR a series

---

[73] Cf. K. Dmytruk, *Swastikas on Soutanes* (Kiev, 1981); P. A. Petlyakov, *Uniat'skaya tserkov' – orudiye anti-kommunizma i anti-sovetizma* (Lvov, 1982); V. Belyaev, *Ya obvinyayu* (Moscow, 1984).   [74] TsKhSD, f. 89, per. 11, dok. 175 & 195.

[75] A. Shamaro, 'Pamyatniki tserkovnogo zodchestva v ateisticheskom vospitanii' in *Voprosy nauchnogo ateizma*, Vyp.30 (Moscow, 1982), pp. 262–84.

[76] *Nauka i religiya* 7, 1981, pp. 28–33.

[77] See C. Lane, *The Rites of Rulers: Ritual in Industrial Society – The Soviet Case* (Cambridge, 1981); C. Binns, 'Soviet Secular Ritual – Atheist Propaganda or Spiritual Consumerism' *Religion in Communist Lands*, vol. 10, no. 3, Autumn 1982, pp. 298–309.

of commissions on new rites emerged, albeit with differing institutional allegiances – sometimes party, sometimes state.[78] Such commissions were to be found at all levels from republic to district, with the East Kazakhstan oblast alone claiming 135.[79] Composed of party propagandists, academics, cultural workers and teachers, these bodies investigated existing practices, religious and secular, and sought to formulate rituals suitable for socialist society. Most active in this field was Ukraine which developed a special enterprise responsible for new rites. By 1978 the republic had 100 palaces and houses, 400 rite bureaux, 8,500 halls, 1,500 choirs, and 11,150 orchestras available for the performance of new rites.[80]

By the late 1970s the authorities had put considerable effort, at least on paper, into creating a formidable framework of institutions and individuals capable of developing rituals that would not only counter those provided by religion, but which would be attractive in their own right. Though the precise role of ritual was the subject of some debate within the anti-religious establishment, it was increasingly recognised that new rites had a role to play not only in countering religion but in promoting socialist values. The negative and positive elements were clearly brought together in the new wedding rituals introduced in Central Asia, where the officiant publicly reminded those present of the equality of women and their new role in a multinational society.[81]

The promotion of new rites was not without some impact, as official figures for rite participation suggested a decline in the religious and a rise in the secular celebration of key rites of passage. In the Ukraine, for example, involvement in the secular naming of children rose from 47 per cent in 1975 to 64 per cent in 1982, secular weddings from 64 per cent to 82.9 per cent, and funerals from 6 per cent to 49.5 per cent.[82] Problems remained, however, with some critics pointing to the relatively crude and unsophisticated nature of the new rituals. One commentator noted that the dressing up of a new ritual in pseudo-religious form often elicited only laughter from those participating who 'when the show was over' became strangers to each other all over again.[83] Others complained of the

---

[78] In Latvia the commission was responsible to the republican agitprop; in the RSFSR, Estonia and Turkmenistan to the Council of Ministers; in the Ukraine to the Ministry of Culture (1964–9), the Supreme Soviet (1969–78) and to the Council of Ministers (after 1978). Cf. P. P. Kampars & M. N. Zakovich, *Sovetskaya grazhdanskaya obryadnost'* (Moscow, 1967), pp. 228–33; *Pravda* 28 May 1976; *Turkmenskaya iskra* 5 Jan. 1986; *Nauka i religiya* 2, 1969, pp. 36–7, 4, 1974, pp. 112–19, 4, 1975, pp. 13–19, & 2, 1979, pp. 2–9.   [79] *Kazakhstanskaya pravda* 5 Oct. 1980.

[80] On the Ukrainian experience see *Traditsii, obryady, sovremennost'* (Kiev, 1983).

[81] N. Bairamsakhatov, *Novye byt i islam* (Moscow, 1979), p. 43.

[82] *Traditsii, obryady, sovremennost'*, p. 13.

[83] *Molodoi kommunist* 12, 1978, pp. 77–8.

inadequate material base for new rites, with many state agencies unwilling to devote time or funds to their development. As a result civil registration offices were losing out to the churches because the latter provided a more attractive ritual.[84]

Despite these shortcomings, official sources continued to stress the successes achieved in winning people away from religious rites. In practice it is difficult to assess how much of this decline could be attributed to new rites and how much to the continuing 'cost' of public participation in religious rites, though the dramatic rise in religious rite performance in the late 1980s surely raises some questions about the ability of the new rites to lay down deep roots in popular consciousness.[85]

Control

The toning down of more oppressive measures directed against religious bodies, and the need to develop further control mechanisms, was increasingly emphasised in official pronouncements on the religious question. Of course, the fact of state control over or interference in religious life continued to be denied by official spokesmen. As one text put it 'the state does not interfere in the internal activities of religious associations and the church in its turn does not interfere in state affairs'.[86] But even this definition, with its implication of equality between church and state, was not deemed adequate by some writers, with I. Brazhnik arguing that 'the Soviet state is sovereign, its supreme powers an expression of the will of all the workers and giving it broad rights to regulate all spheres of social life. The church in all aspects of its life cannot be excluded from this.'[87] Similar arguments were put forward by V. V. Klochkov, who rejected any definition of separation in terms of the non-interference of the state in the affairs of the church.[88]

In practice the state involved itself intimately in virtually every area of the life of religious organisations, as witnessed by samizdat, official reports and materials that have become available since the collapse of the USSR. Particularly useful in documenting this control was a CRA report 'on church cadres and measures for confining their activities within the limits of the law' produced in the mid-1970s. Dealing exclusively with the Russian Orthodox Church this document prepared by CRA deputy

---

[84] *Komsomol'skaya pravda* 20 Aug. 1982.
[85] The recent rise, could of course, be seen as in part a general reaction to the de facto prohibitions of the past.
[86] *O nauchnom ateizme i ateisticheskom vospitanii* (Moscow, 1974), p. 27.
[87] *Nauka i religiya* 3, 1970, p. 9.
[88] V. V. Klochkov, *Religiya, gosudarstvo, pravo* (Moscow, 1978), p. 245.

chairman V. Furov confirmed the extensive role of the state in overseeing the activities of the Russian Orthodox Church.[89]

In pursuit of control religious elites were a prime target, and the Russian Orthodox Church, with its hierarchical structure, provided considerable opportunities. Here, everyday questions of church life were decided by the Holy Synod, which Furov made clear was:

firmly under the control of the Council. The selection of its permanent members was and remains in the Council's hands ... The patriarch and synod members discuss beforehand with the Council leadership all questions raised in the synod, and they agree and finalise the 'decisions of the Holy Synod'. Exercising permanent control over the activities of the Synod the responsible employees of the Council systematically carry out educational-explanatory work with members of the synod, establish confidential contacts with them, shape their patriotic ideas and attitudes whilst helping them to exert the necessary influence on the whole episcopate.[90]

The CRA also played a key role in the appointment of senior clergy, for example in the 1971 choice of a new Patriarch which we discussed earlier, or in ensuring that 'not one consecration ... takes place without the careful checking of the candidature by the responsible members of the council in close contact with its commissioners and other appropriate interested bodies'.[91]

Amongst the latter bodies was the KGB which, according to documents in recently investigated archives, recruited its own 'agents' from within the ranks of the clergy at all levels. The problems of defining what was meant by 'agent' must be left to a later chapter, but it is clear that to reach a senior position within religious establishments one had to have some dealings with the security police, although each individual dealt with this problem in a different way and those who collaborated did so for different reasons. Nonetheless, in its own reports to the Central Committee, the KGB claimed that its agents amongst the clergy played an influential role in establishing control over the church and in influencing the international religious climate – whether through denunciations of those repressed on religious grounds or, according to the KGB, using the Soviet church delegation to ensure the election of Emilio Castro as general secretary of the World Council of Churches in 1984.[92]

[89] The full text can be found in Keston College archive; the version quoted here was published in *Vestnik RKhD 130* (1979), pp. 275–344.   [90] ibid., p. 277.
[91] ibid., p. 279.
[92] See *Izvestiya* 22 Jan. 1992, and discussion of this issue in chapter 7. The foreign activities of the church were a particular target of KGB operations, with bodies such as the External Church Relations Department of the Moscow Patriarchate riddled with agents in the form of translators, secretaries, chauffeurs, etc. as witnessed by the interview given by a former employee and KGB agent A. Shushpanov in *Argumenty i fakty* 8, 1992.

The authorities also sought to exercise control over the foreign activities of religious groups, with the archives of the Central Committee including annual plans on foreign work produced by the CRA. At a Secretariat meeting attended by Suslov, Kirilenko, Solomentsev and Kuroedov in 1967 one such plan was discussed. After listing the various forthcoming events it stressed the need: 'to broadly utilise contacts ... for propaganda of the success of the Soviet people, the economy and cultural construction, to spread truthful information about religion and the church in the USSR, to strengthen friendship with progressive church circles in the struggle for peace ... '[93]

With CRA and KGB acting – either separately or together – to control senior religious leaders, it became increasingly difficult for the latter to defend fully their institutions. Persistent resistance brought transfer or 'retirement', although the Furov report and other sources indicate that at least some hierarchs within the Orthodox Church sought to find ways to protect the church. For example, in one part of the report there is a division of the hierarchy into three categories: those who were completely loyal and unenthusiastic about increasing the role of religion in society, those who combined loyalty to the state with attempts to expand religious influence, and those who allegedly went beyond the limits of the law in spreading religious influence.[94] Typical of the independent minded bishops was Bishop Khryzostom of Kursk and Belgorod, for a while deputy chairman of the External Church Relations Department of the Russian Orthodox Church, who Furov suggested was using his overt support for the state abroad as a cover for efforts to strengthen religion in his own dioceses.[95]

It was not only the activities of the Russian Orthodox Church that the state sought to place under close control, although the evidence for such activities within other religious groups is less complete. Samizdat sources in Lithuania charged that the republic CRA was involved in a wide variety of activities, from the attempt to impose 'tame bishops' upon the church to the recruitment of informers amongst the clergy. Given what we know about the treatment of the Orthodox Church there is little reason to doubt such claims, although in Lithuania greater grass-roots

[93] TsKhSD, Protocols of the Secretariat, 39, 26 Dec. 1967.
[94] *Vestnik* 130, pp. 277–9.
[95] ibid., pp. 286–8; removed from his post in 1982 Kryzostom was initially transferred from Kursk to Irkutsk, and later sent to Lithuania where, in the late 1980s, he proved a leading Russian supporter of the struggle for Lithuanian independence. When the debate about KGB involvement in the church's life blew up in 1992 he pointed out that virtually every bishop, including himself, had to some degree collaborated with the KGB and urged caution in separating genuine agents from the rest who sought to do their best for the church.

militancy helped to provide the hierarchy with some support for their efforts to resist state demands.[96] In general, where there was a tradition of resistance, religious communities were on occasions able to limit the damage caused by state control. At the 1979 All Union Baptist Congress, for example, the delegates refused to elect to the governing body a candidate presumably agreed beforehand with the CRA[97] – although this might also have stemmed from state efforts to keep potential dissidents within the official fold by giving scope to the more democratic traditions of this particular denomination.

In addition to seeking control over appointments to leading positions within religious groups, the CRA and other bodies were involved in the day to day life of seminaries, monasteries and publishing ventures (where it also acted as censor). For example, entry to seminaries was made extremely difficult with a variety of obstacles – military call-up, refusal of residence permits, threats – being placed in the way of young men who applied. Moreover, religious training institutions were forced to collaborate in this procedure. During 1974 the Catholic seminary in the Lithuanian town of Kaunas sent republican CRA commissioner Tumenas a list of seventeen applicants. After consulting with the KGB and party advisors he crossed off five names according to samizdat sources.[98] Later issues of the *Chronicle of the Lithuanian Catholic Church* report attempts to recruit students as informers, and the expulsion of students who associated with 'reactionary priests'.[99] Further controls over seminaries included the vetting of all staff and textbooks, the obligation of such institutions to give instruction on Soviet legislation relating to religion, and regular visits by atheist lecturers.[100]

As under Khrushchev, the CRA kept extremely detailed records on the activities of religious organisations, including on numbers of places of worship, participants in rites, social profiles of congregations etc. The 1969 report on non-Orthodox congregations includes details on how much each group gave to the Soviet Peace Fund, with figures ranging from 12.7 per cent and 10.1 per cent of their income for the Muslims and Orthodox respectively, to 0.7 per cent from the Lutherans.[101] Substantial information was also available on illegal groups such as the True Orthodox Church and True Orthodox Christians who, according to the CRA, had some 174 groups with 4,200 members at the end of the 1960s.[102] Reports in local archives provide detailed information on local

[96] See virtually any issue of the *Chronicle of the Lithuanian Catholic Church* (*CLCC*).
[97] See Michael Rowe, 'The 1979 Baptist Congress in Moscow', *Religion in Communist Lands*, vol. 8, no. 3, 1980, pp. 192–3.   [98] *CLCC 12* (1974), p. 12.
[99] *CLCC 49* (8 Aug. 1981), p. 45 & *CLCC* 45 (22 Oct. 1980), p. 18.
[100] *Vestnik 130*, pp. 319, & 325–6.   [101] TsKhSD, f. 5, op. 62, ed.kh. 38, p. 53.
[102] ibid., p. 272.

religious communities, the number of rites performed, details about families who had their children baptised, and even denunciations by worthy citizens of priests performing religious rites in private homes.[103]

Control over religious life extended to the local religious community, with even those congregations gaining recognition finding numerous obstacles placed in their way. For example, under the 1929 Law on Religious Associations each community had the right to elect its own executive committee, yet Article 14 of that same law gave registration agencies the right to remove individuals it deemed inappropriate and, in practice, allowed them to impose their own candidates. On occasion this led to the appearance of non-believing executive officers.[104] In similar fashion the state's *de facto* control over the appointment of clergy sometimes led to the imposition of unwanted pastors in individual congregations. During the early 1970s parishioners at the church of St Nicholas in Nikolaev frequently complained about the life style of one of their priests who persisted in assaulting female believers. When his contract with the community came up for renewal the local believers sought to remove him but the CRA commissioner threatened to close the church if they dropped the priest. The attempt of Bishop Bogolep of Kirovograd and Nikolaevsk to remove the erring cleric only resulted in the bishop's own 'retirement'.[105]

This latter example is useful in pointing to the way in which the state sought to utilise religious authorities themselves in controlling and disciplining the more independent minded pastors. During the 1960s and 1970s at least five Orthodox bishops were either transferred to lesser dioceses or 'retired' after expressing critical comments about state policy or seeking to defend the church community against attack, all ostensibly at the behest of the church's leadership.[106] The church was also used against religious dissidents, with the Russian Orthodox Church perhaps most ready, or best known, for playing this role. In 1975 Fr Gleb Yakunin and layman Lev Regelson sent an open letter to the Nairobi meeting of the World Council of Churches detailing the problems facing

---

[103] For example, see documents in State Archive of the Yaroslavl Region (GAYarO), f. 1033, op. 2, d. 86a.

[104] G. P. Gol'st, *Religiya i zakon* (Moscow, 1975), p. 30; the dissident *Chronicle of Current Events 34* (31 Dec. 1974), pp. 54–5 reports on such a case at the St Sergii church in the Uzbek town of Fergana.

[105] *DCCDBR*, vol. 1, p. 88; other cases are documented in pp. 50–71, vol. 4, pp. 434–7, vol. 5, pp. 689–96 & 7311–2, and vol. 7, pp. 866–76.

[106] Archbishop Yermogen of Kaluga, retired in 1967, Bishop Bogolep whose case we have just mentioned, Bishops Pavel of Novosibirsk and Feodosii of Poltava, both transferred to smaller dioceses, and Archbishop Khryzostom of Kursk whom we have already discussed. See J. Ellis, *The Russian Orthodox Church – A Contemporary History* (London, 1986), p. 264.

religious bodies in the USSR. At the instigation of the CRA a campaign was launched to discredit the authors both abroad, where they were criticised by leading Orthodox hierarchs, and at home. In a number of churches the two men were condemned from the pulpit and petitions critical of their activities circulated amongst the faithful. The samizdat report of these activities gives a rather humorous account of such activities in one parish where the priest's attempt to collect signatures was disrupted by an old lady who shouted out 'they're trying to make us join the Catholics', whereupon most of the congregation fled.[107] In some cases it seems that the church leadership sought to avoid outright confrontation by attempting to persuade religious dissidents to cease or renounce their activities,[108] but this was a tactic that influenced few.

Control, then, extended to all aspects of religious life and to varying degrees to all religious communities, although its impact and success is harder to evaluate. Religion at an institutional level was undoubtedly weakened in some respects, as some religious leaders and organisations lost the habit of thinking for themselves. Yet not all succumbed, and some resisted, whether overtly or otherwise. And some religious traditions appeared to find the subservient relationship of church to state more congenial than others. In the case of Islam one has the feeling of a controlled head with little relationship to the mass of religious believers, or any influence on the customs and traditions observed in the impenetrable mahallahs and villages of the Muslim parts of the USSR over which the state's writ sometimes ran only on paper. Elsewhere, as in Lithuania or amongst the Baptists, state efforts to control religion was partially limited by a strong grass-roots militancy which provided, consciously or otherwise, support for a more independent stance on the part of those leaderships, or raised the 'costs' for the state of blatant interference.

Registration – the flexible response

In the face of new challenges the Brezhnev leadership showed signs of rethinking an approach which stressed the need to close places of worship on a large scale, and increasingly developed a more flexible attitude to the question of registration. Initially the rapid closure of places of worship characteristic of the Khrushchev years was replaced by a slow process of

---

[107] AS 2561 (4 Mar. 1976).
[108] As happened in the case of Deacon Rusak, whose appeal to the Vancouver meeting of the WCC in 1983 caused considerable embarrassment. Called in to see his bishop he was promised that he would be able to function as a clergyman if he publicly recanted his activities. *AS 5017* (July 1983).

attrition which deprived communities of registration where it could be done with little fuss, and which made it hard for new communities to gain recognition. But from the mid-1970s certain groups began to meet less resistance to their requests for registration, and this process gathered pace in the second half of the 1970s.[109]

Most official spokesmen of these years repeated the claim that there were around 20,000 registered places of worship,[110] but this figure was grossly overstated, for, as we have already seen, the total number of registered places of worship at the close of the Khrushchev campaign was less than 12,000. If we try and break down the figure by denomination various trends become apparent. Firstly, the Russian Orthodox Church (and the Old Believers) continued to sustain losses. The former saw its total drop from around 7,500 at the time of Khrushchev's fall to under 6,800 by the time Gorbachev came to power, with perhaps two-thirds of losses sustained in the late 1960s and early 1970s, after which the reduction slowed.[111] Occasionally there were new registrations, for example in the period 1977–84 which Kuroedov reported as seeing thirty-three Orthodox parishes registered. The motivations for this slight shift are hard to gauge, though Fr Gleb Yakunin pointed out that the majority of these were close to the Chinese border and were perhaps intended to strengthen stability in these regions by encouraging Russians to stay.[112] Despite this the overall trend remained downward, a fact that should caution us against suggestions that the Russian Orthodox Church – as religious movement, rather than as hierarchical structure – was in some sense favoured during these years. Such 'gains' as were made – new Patriarchal workshops (1980), new Publishing Department buildings (1981), and the decision to hand back the Danilovsky monastery (1983)[113] – do not negate this picture of a symbolic favouring of the central church organisation at the expense of its constituent parts.

Groups whose numbers remained relatively static during these years appear to have included the Armenian Apostolic, the Reformed, the Jews and the Buddhists. Roman Catholics, however, witnessed slight growth from 1,046 registered religious associations at the beginning of 1965 to

[109] Figures for 1 Jan. 1986 used here are taken from *Nauka i religiya* 1, 1992, p. 7.
[110] A. I. Barmenkov, *Svoboda sovesti v SSSR* (Moscow, 1979), p. 174.
[111] *Nauka i religiya*, 1, 1992, 7 gives a figure of 6,745 for the beginning of 1986; V. Garadzha, director of the Institute of Scientific Atheism, reported that the Orthodox lost an average of forty-eight per year in the period 1965–74 and twenty-two per year in 1975–87. *Nauka i religiya* 1, 1989, p. 3.
[112] V. Kuroedov, *Religiya i tserkov v sovetskom obshchestve* (Moscow,1984), 144; for a more detailed discussion of these openings and Yakunin's comments see Ellis, *Russian Orthodox Church*, pp. 21–4.
[113] Reported in *TASS* 11 June 1983. The church had in fact asked for the Donskoi monastery.

1,071 by 1986, with most of the gains in Byelorussia, Siberia or Kazakhstan. From the 1969 CRA report to the Central Committee it is clear that Catholics in Byelorussia raised a variety of problems for the authorities during the 1960s and 1970, directing numerous complaints and requests to officials and often simply ignoring the law and organising religious services with or without permission.[114] In the face of such actions, and from the late 1970s the realisation that the Polish episcopate exercised considerable influence over Byelorussian clergy, the CRA may well have recommended a more flexible attitude to registration as increasingly allowed for by the central authorities.

The religious organisations which benefited most in terms of registration during the Brezhnev years were certain Protestant groups and the Muslims. Amongst the former were the Seventh Day Adventists, whose numbers shot up from 140 in 1964 to 347 in 1986. In many cases new registrations reflected the fact that existing places of worship were simply too small, but should perhaps also be seen as a 'reward' for the total political loyalty of this group and an incentive to discourage those tempted to link up with the more radical True and Free Adventists of the 'underground'. Though the official Adventists were not permitted to open their central organisation, closed during the Khrushchev campaign, a *de facto* centre did emerge with a clearly recognised leader in Mikhail Kulakov.[115]

Another group to make gains as a result of dissent were the Baptists, for whilst the reform Baptists had been subject to considerable repressive activity after 1966, some concessions were made to the community as a whole. More overt forms of state interference appear to have eased after Khrushchev's fall and at the 1969 AUCECB Congress it was reported that some 10,000 individuals had returned to the union. Yet many, especially those with family members in hiding or in labour camps, remained intransigent, and increasingly the authorities dropped the requirement that congregations could only be registered within the Baptist Union, a body some deemed excessively compromised. This proved attractive to a number of congregations which began to register autonomously, causing further splits within the ranks of the *initsiativniki*. From 1965 to 1970 the number of registered Baptist communities rose from 1,663 to 1,936, of whom a small handful were registered autono-

---

[114] TsKhSD, f. 5, op. 62, ed.khr. 38, p. 93 records that Byelorussian Catholics were more active than others in campaigning for the registration of priests and opening of places of worship. In 1969 of 181 letters the CRA received from Catholics, 81 came from this Slavic republic, as opposed to 68 from Ukraine and 19 from Lithuania.
[115] On the position of the official Adventists see M. Sapiets, *True Witness – The Story of the Seventh Day Adventists in the Soviet Union* (Keston, 1990), pp. 253–85.

mously.[116] In some cases autonomous registration proved shortlived because administrative officials proved incapable of refraining from interference. In the town of Dedovsk (Moscow region) the Baptist community gained registration and appointed P. Rumachik as their pastor. In response CRA commissioner Trushin intervened to say that this veteran of the camps was unacceptable and ordered them to cease praying for those imprisoned for their faith. As a result of these and other pressures the Dedovsk community renounced registration.[117] Nonetheless, during the second half of the 1970s and first half of the 1980s around 500 Baptist communities gained registration, some outside of the official union, and by 1986 there were 2,316 registered Baptist associations.[118]

There can be little doubt that the more flexible policy on the registration of Baptist communities was in large part a response to the dissident movement, an attempt to bring them within some form of legal and hence more controllable position. The same appears to have applied to the Pentecostals, who despite persistent harsh treatment and a consistently negative response to their emigration requests, were allowed to register a handful of autonomous communities. The first two were registered in June and October 1969,[119] with others following during the 1970s, and by 1986 a total of 248 had gained registration.

The final category of Christian groups to make gains during this period were the German congregations – Lutherans and Mennonites of various types. As early as 1970 the CRA had been arguing that 'the experience of registration shows that it is better to register than to give communities the possibility of acting without registration or control'. In regard to Mennonite congregations it had called upon its commissioners:

to change most seriously their relationship to active Mennonite associations, deeply study the character of their religious propaganda and work out measures which will bring them under control ... it is necessary in the end to resolve the question of the registration of Mennonite communities or to bring to an end the activities of those who operate beyond the law.[120]

From the mid-1970s this more open attitude to German congregations also reflected the rise of the emigration movement amongst Soviet Germans. In response to this the Central Committee issued a decree in June 1974 'on measures for improving work amongst citizens of the

---

[116] TsKhSD, f. 5, op. 62, ed. 38, p. 194.

[117] *Byulletin (vneocherednoi) soveta rodstvennikov uznikov EKhB v SSSR* (1978), in Keston College archive.

[118] At the 1979 Baptist Congress it was reported that during 1974–8 some 37 congregations had lost registration as against 203 newly recognised, Michael Rowe, 1980, p. 189; when the next congress met in March 1985 it was reported that a further 268 communities had been registered *KNS 224*, 2 May 1984, p. 3.

[119] TsKhSD, f. 5, op. 62, ed.khr. 38, pp. 225–34.   [120] ibid., pp. 244–5.

USSR of German nationality'. This spelt out various ways in which the cultural conditions of Soviet Germans could be improved, and spoke of ensuring that the significant number of German believers had their religious communities placed on a legal footing.[121] For the Lutherans this meant the registration of 129 congregations in the period 1977–83, whilst at least 20 Mennonite communities received recognition outside the Baptist Union.[122]

Dissent and the existence of unofficial pressure on legally recognised religious organisations was not the only cause of flexible registration policies emerging during the 1970s. Soviet Islam found itself under increasing pressure to participate in Moscow's attempts to develop links with the wider Muslim world. In 1968 the only theological training institute to be set up in the Brezhnev years was established in Tashkent, with the specific intent of training Islamic clerics for foreign work. And as this diplomatic initiative grew, so did the tendency of the state to make concessions to the Islamic community at home, with some 69 mosques registered in the period 1977–83.[123] From a 1964 archive figure of 312, the number of registered mosques appears to have risen to 392 by 1985.[124]

Various explanations for this growth can be found. Ratbek Nisanbaev, *kazi* of Kazakhstan suggested that the government permitted this growth in the number of mosques 'because the number of believers in faith is growing rapidly as a result of the high birth rate',[125] although it is hard to see a few dozen openings as meeting the demand of the millions of Soviet 'Muslims'. More important was the need to reinforce the loyalty of those Central Asians who might be seduced by a general Islamic revivalism thought by some to be sweeping the Muslim world; a development brought home and perhaps exaggerated in the minds of Soviet policy makers after 1979 by events in Afghanistan and Iran. But such an argument needs to be treated with care. Many of the Western writers who spoke of an 'Islamic threat' pointed to the role of Sufi orders in promoting Islamic renewal, yet it is noteable that the one area where not a single mosque was opened during these years (and there were only four in the whole republic) was Turkmenistan, traditionally one of the

---

[121] Text in TsKhSD, Protocols of the Secretariat, 129, 26 June 1974; see S. Heitman, 'Jewish, German and Armenian Emigration from the USSR: Parallels and Differences', in R. O. Freedman, ed., *Soviet Jewry in the 1980s – The Politics of Anti-Semitism and Emigration and the Dynamics of Resettlement* (London, 1989), pp. 126–8.

[122] Kuroedov, *Religiya i tserkov*, p. 144; see G. Stricker, 'German Protestants in Tsarist Russia and the Soviet Union', *Religion in Communist Lands*, vol. 15, no. 1, Spring 1987, p. 47 & G. Stricker, 'Mennonites in Russia and the Soviet Union', *Religion in Communist Lands*, vol. 12, no. 3, Winter 1984, pp. 302–5.

[123] Kuroedov, *Religiya i tserkov*, p. 144.   [124] *Pravda vostoka* 8 Jan. 1981.

[125] *Muslims of the Soviet East* 1, 1984, pp. 3–4.

strongholds of Sufism. Here first secretary Gapurov, appointed in 1969, seems to have paid far more attention to anti-religious work than his neighbours and under his guidance a number of noisy campaigns were launched, notably at the continued custom of *kalym* or bride price.[126] If we assume that in purely republican matters he exercised considerable independence then it is likely that the republican CRA commissioner – whose nomenklatura loyalty, as suggested earlier, would be primarily to the Turkmen party rather than his nominal Moscow institutional boss – could ignore commands from Moscow on registrations that were not approved by Gapurov. For this reason mosques were not opened in Turkmenistan, whatever the degree of policy shift in Moscow. In other words, whilst the centre may have encouraged a more flexible attitude to Islamic communities, this was not an area where it chose to impose its views.

If we take the admittedly incomplete figures and evidence presented here a number of conclusions can be drawn. Firstly, it does appear, contrary to received wisdom, that whilst the total number of registered religious associations may have declined during the first decade of the Brezhnev years, by 1986 the figures had risen from a 1964 total of over 11,600 to 12,427. Less clear is whether this trend was a result of a thought-out policy or a largely accidental result of a series of discrete policy responses to problems posed by specific religious communities.

The other general conclusion that can be drawn is that the state's flexible attitude to registration was determined to a considerable extent by the vitality of religious communities expressed in the first place by the existence of dissent within the organisation. In such cases there was some willingness to provide looser requirements for registration, for example, autonomously of the officially recognised denomination, to be followed up by less overt forms of state pressure on those newly legalised communities. That such self-restraint often proved hard for local authorities is witnessed to by samizdat sources which report on communities such as that at Dedovsk which quickly rejected registration. The situation was also complicated by the fact that to some degree in granting registration the first step had to be taken by local authorities and that they varied considerably in their attitudes – hence the very different responses met by 'sectarian' communities. The Central Committee archives, for example, include various reports on letters sent to the Secretariat by local party organs, generally supported by the regional CRA commissioner, seeking the reversal of registration decisions by the

---

[126] See John Anderson, 'Out of the Kitchen, Out of the Temple: Women, Religion and Atheism in the Soviet Union', in S. P. Ramet, ed., *Religious Policy in the Soviet Union* (Cambridge, 1993), pp. 206–28.

central Council for Religious Affairs.[127] And on one occasion, at least according to Kuroedov, the leading opponent of the CRA in a decision to register a church in the Tomsk region was a first secretary by the name of Yegor Ligachev.[128]

There is also evidence of a considerably *ad hoc* attitude. Campaigns for the opening of Russian Orthodox parishes were generally not successful, perhaps because mostly organised by pensioners with little access to domestic or foreign audiences. In Lithuania militant dissenting activities did not succeed in opening Catholic churches, although here the demands were largely for the redress of other grievances. And in Central Asia the registration of mosques from the late 1970s had a largely symbolic function. All of these variations sprang from changing attitudes within the CRA, now prepared or permitted to respond flexibly, and to offer carrots as well as sticks, but also from the evolving nature of centre–republican, centre–local relations in which much depended upon the willingness or otherwise of local officials to implement the more flexible line coming from Moscow.

Repression

The repression of those who failed to confine their religious activities within the narrow limits set down by the law had been a consistent feature of official policy since the revolution, although its intensity and scope had varied over time and according to denomination. Under Brezhnev, discrimination against and harassment of believers continued to a considerable degree, as evidenced not only by samizdat sources but by casual visits to major city churches on Easter Eve where the militia and other bodies sought to prevent the entry of the young or on occasions to disrupt services. Numerous sources document the problems facing believers seeking a secondary education or good professional employment, the brutality many experienced in the army – though this affected many young recruits – the difficulties facing the children of believers in schools which on occasions led to a number being taken from their homes, and the constant breaking up of meetings and fines meted out to some groups. These phenomena are unquantifiable, but are too well documented to need further exploration here.

More overt repression of religious activists also continued after Khrushchev's fall (albeit on a smaller scale), with many still finding their

---

[127] TsKhSD, Postanovlenie TsK KPSS 17 Mar. 1967, in which the Secretariat refuses an appeal from the Karelian obkom to reverse a decision to register a Baptist church in Petrozavodsk; cf. f. 5, op. 75, ed.khr. 270, which discusses the 1978 attempt of Mordovian obkom and government to reverse registration of a Russian Orthodox Church.   [128] *Lyudina i svit* 1, 1992, p. 22.

way into labour camps, places of exile or psychiatric hospitals, and a few being murdered. There were, however, some differences. In the first place repression became more nuanced and less of a blunt instrument. Steps were often taken to persuade critics to cease their 'criminal' activities – whether by offering concessions in the form of a more flexible registration policy, by carrying out prophylactic talks with those involved or by threatening them. Only then came arrest for the most recalcitrant. And even then pressure to recant was often attempted, the most notable success here being the public confession of Fr Dmitri Dudko in mid-1980. A second distinctive feature of this period was that recalcitrant religious leaders were generally disciplined by their own establishments, being transferred or 'retired' rather than subject to arrest. This contrasted with the earlier period, when a number of Orthodox hierarchs found their way into camps, and perhaps reflected a desire not to be seen to be harassing the leadership of recognised churches who were now depicted as totally loyal to the state. Finally, the bulk of repressive activity was now aimed at those explicitly dissenting or involved in 'underground' groups.

Perhaps the best way of measuring repressive trends is to look at the annual arrest rates for our period, as shown in Figure 2.[129] What this chart reveals is that there were peaks in 1966, 1973 and 1980. Following Khrushchev's fall the majority of religious prisoners appear to have been released and during 1965 only a handful were arrested. But from March 1966 a major campaign was launched against the Baptist reformers, heralded in the spring of 1966 by a letter to *Pravda* from two workers who wrote:

in recent times our sectarians have exceeded all limits. They have openly attracted crowds not only in their homes but openly in public places. For example, last July at the Azov station a sectarian group from Rostov-on-Don sang hymns and psalms to the accompaniment of guitars and balalaikas. Passengers were indignant and demanded that they cease their illegal activity. The sect leader, a certain Kulbantsev, responded that the 'initiator' sect did not recognise Soviet laws.[130]

One month later the Presidium of the RSFSR Supreme Soviet issued its resolutions dealing with the interpretation of the articles of the criminal code relating to religion. Over the next nine months the press carried numerous articles hostile to the Baptists, and during the course of 1966

---

[129] Based upon the Keston College card index. Though there are problems with these files – for example, the identification of some political activists as religious prisoners, and the inevitable understatement of totals for less well known groups such as the True Orthodox and the Jehovah's Witnesses – they do give some indication of broad trends. Moreover, they steer clear of the inflated figures provided by some of the more radical East European religious missions.   [130] *Pravda* 19 Feb. 1966.

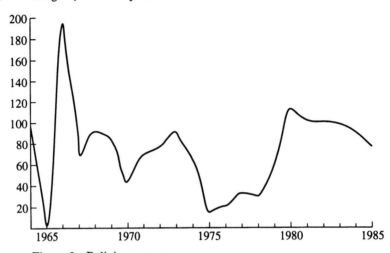

Figure 2   Religious arrests
Source: Keston College individual Card Index

over 180 were arrested. The main aim of this campaign was to curb the activities of the *initsiativniki*, though representatives of other religious groups were also caught under the amended understanding of the Criminal Code.

More generally, those groups simply prohibited by the state continued to face harsher measures, though inconsistently applied, regardless of the changing line on religion. The 1969 CRA report on non-Orthodox denominations contains statistical information on actions taken against various groups, including the True Orthodox, the Jehovah's Witnesses and the Greek Catholics. For example, in Ivano-Frankovsk region alone during 1969 some 12 'Uniate-pokutnyki'[131] were drawn to criminal responsibility (5 for non-fulfilment of military service), and 71 children were taken from their parents and placed in state boarding schools.[132] The same document notes that in 1968–9 some 20 Jehovah's Witnesses refused to perform military service, that 3,000 members of the sect declined to vote, and some 50 were brought before the courts.[133]

Following the 1971 Central Committee resolution which, amongst other things, called for stricter control over observance of the law, a further wave of arrests took place in the early 1970s, reaching a peak in 1973. Though this new assault extended to a broader spread of denominations, the Baptists remained the single largest group. From the

[131] The Pokutnyki (Penitents) were a militant lay group which opposed any compromise with the Soviet system.   [132] TsKhSD, f. 5, op. 62, ed.khr. 38, p. 104.
[133] ibid., pp. 263–71.

1969 CRA report, which notes that some seventy of those sentenced in 1966–7 went straight back to their illegal activities on release,[134] and from a cursory examination of the names of those arrested in the early 1970s, it is clear that harassment of this sort did little to deter the more militant reform Baptists.

During the mid-1970s the arrest rate fell dramatically, in large part a reflection of the detente process and the unwillingness of the state to antagonise those Western states with which it was seeking new relationships. But from 1978 onwards arrests of 'sectarians' in particular picked up again, from late 1979 merging with the general assault on dissent and non-conformity. During the first half of the 1980s the arrest rate for religious activists was averaging roughly 100 each year, and when Gorbachev came to power there were nearly 400 known religious prisoners in the USSR. Of these, 168 were Baptists, 45 Pentecostals, 41 Orthodox, 26 Roman Catholics, 20 Ukrainian Catholics, 20 Jehovah's Witnesses, and a handful were from other groups including Hare Krishnas, Muslims and Adventists. This total almost certainly understated the real figure, for there were unconfirmed reports of many more Jehovah's Witnesses interned for failing to perform military service, Muslims for producing religious literature or organising Koranic schools (and for breach of Soviet family law, though it is difficult to accept these people as religious prisoners), or True Orthodox for burning Soviet passports. Whilst many were imprisoned quite explicitly for religious activities, i.e. under the relevant article of the Criminal Code (142 and 227 in the RSFSR), a significant proportion were sentenced under criminal (generally on false charges such as embezzlement, or speculation) or political articles.[135] What is interesting about these figures is that, with the exception of the 1966 campaign directed specifically at the Baptists, they largely mirror the general pattern of political arrests during the Brezhnev years. In other words they were directed less against religion as such, than against non-conformity in general.

Conclusion

Under Brezhnev the basic hostility of the party-state towards religion remained, as did the paper commitment to an eventual elimination of religion. Propagandists continued to attack religion in an often crude manner, state officials harassed believers and communities, seeking to make their life difficult by extending the state's control over every aspect

---

[134] ibid., pp. 199–217.
[135] Figures based for 1985 on Keston College, *Religious Prisoners in the USSR* (Keston, 1985).

of their life, whilst repressing those who resisted. Even where the centre genuinely sought to moderate excess, the gradual weakening of central control during these years permitted many to act in the tradition of ways learnt from a lengthy heritage of harsh treatment of non-conformity. For all this it is impossible to suggest that religion as institution or ideology was significantly weaker in 1985 than in 1964. For its own reasons the state had permitted the total number of registered religious communities to remain stable, though there had been some losers – notably the Russian Orthodox Church. A substantial proportion of the population retained some commitment to religious ideas, and amongst some sections of the population religion had become fashionable. Moreover, the state had failed to come up with effective responses to the renewed vitality of religion, although religious dissent appeared partially curbed by a resort to repression in the early 1980s. As the need for political and socio-economic reform became increasingly apparent to many within the leadership, it was clear that repression as a means of coping with non-conformity was both unacceptable and inefficient. Indeed, within a few years it was to be realised that the energy and powers of religious communities might well be capable of being harnessed in the interests of the state.

6 Gorbachev and the liberalisation of religious policy

If the Brezhnev years were notable for the absence of a distinctive religious policy, the same could not be said of Gorbachev's time in office. After a hesitant start, a wholesale liberalisation of religious policy began in the winter of 1987–8, and by 1991 it was possible to speak with little qualification of the existence of freedom of conscience within the Soviet Union. As the new approach to the religious question developed in late 1987 and subsequent years, two features of interest to our study emerged. Firstly, the fundamental shift in the nature of Soviet religious policy from a conflictual to a cooperative model. Religion was no longer an enemy to be combatted, but a potential ally to be enlisted in the struggle for reform. And secondly, the relative opening up of the whole process of religious policy making as debates were fought out in the public arena as well as behind closed doors. The process of change is the subject of this chapter, with particular attention devoted to the factors underlying the liberalisation of religious policy and the debates leading up to the adoption of a new All-Union Law on Freedom of Conscience in October 1990.

Gorbachev and the reform impulse

Clearly the impetus for change has to be located within the wider reform process intiated by Mikhail Gorbachev, though the example of the Khrushchev years served to demonstrate that political reform and the liberalisation of religious policy did not necessarily go hand in hand. At one level it could have been argued that change was unnecessary in this area. By 1985 most religious institutions had been brought under a considerable degree of state control, over 400 religious activists were in jail or exile, and the output of the atheist establishment was continuing to rise. But as in other areas of Soviet life there were those even before Gorbachev's accession who had begun to question official verities, and their voices became more insistent with the development of glasnost. Despite continuing references to the declining number of believers and the 'deepening crisis of religion',[1] it had become clear by the early 1980s that many of the conventional analyses of the religious situation were inadequate. Not only were believers still to be found in the Soviet Union, but they formed a considerable proportion of the population. Moreover, there were growing signs that the social composition of the religious community was changing. Some commentators spoke of a 'new type of believer' and noted that amongst those not adhering to a specific faith there was 'much sympathy' for religion.[2]

The opening up of the press under Gorbachev rendered this analysis of the religious situation more explicit. Various authors began to highlight the official tendency to understate religion's vitality and continued attraction to new generations of Soviet citizens. Some linked this renewal to a rejection of the official ideology and the social apathy associated with the years of stagnation. As one put it 'atheism became in certain intellectual circles simply indecent – rather as before the revolution religion was considered equally unacceptable in the ranks of the intelligentsia'.[3] With an increasingly educated body of believers – and, of course, of citizens in general – the party-state had to decide how to proceed. Should it continue to attack religion? If so how was atheist propaganda to be rendered more effective? Or should it seek to develop a new relationship with a phenomenon that showed few signs of 'withering away'?

Gorbachev, religion and the reform process

During Gorbachev's first eighteen months in office there was little sign of change. The press continued to carry material on atheist education and in September 1985 *Pravda* gave considerable space to an article stressing the ongoing need to struggle against religion and all its manifestations.[4] In October 1985 the draft of the new party programme with its injunction to party members to 'overcome religious prejudices' and its rejection of the use of religion 'in a way that harms the interests of society' gave no indication of any fundamental rethinking.[5] And in his speech to the 27th

---

[1] *Aktual'nye voprosy ateisticheskogo vospitaniya na sovremennom etape* (Moscow, 1986), p. 8.
[2] *Nauka i religiya* 4, 1982, p. 19; in an article published in late 1987 CRA chairman Konstantin Kharchev commented on the various changes affecting religious communities, noting the expansion of rite performance in the Moldavian, Tajik, Estonian and Ukrainian republics, as well as in certain Russian provinces. He also noted that whereas in the 1960s and early 1970s most clergymen were 60 or over, today the majority were in the 40–60 age range, whilst 83 per cent of the Orthodox episcopate had a higher education. *Nauka i religiya*, 11, 1987, pp. 21–3.
[3] D. Furman, 'Religiya, ateizm i perestroika', in D. Furman, ed., *Na puti k svobode sovesti* (Moscow, 1989), p. 14.   [4] *Pravda* 13 Sept. 1985.   [5] *Pravda* 21 Oct. 1985.

CPSU Congress the following February, Gorbachev, following the lines set down by Chernenko at the June 1983 Central Committee plenum on ideology, condemned the tendency of some literary and artistic works to 'idealise religious survivals'.[6] At the same time the state continued to maintain close control of religious institutions and well into 1986 was arresting those people who contested official religious policies.

This 'more of the same' approach dominated until late 1986, at which time ambiguous signals began to emerge. In October Yegor Ligachev reminded a group of social scientists of the need to continue the struggle with religion.[7] One month later, Gorbachev, on a stopover in Tashkent en route to India, called for a 'decisive and uncompromising' struggle with religion,[8] though as we shall see, this speech related less to religion as such than to the attempt of the centre to reassert its control over Central Asia. Indeed, the exceptional nature of these remarks was perhaps confirmed in the following months as Gorbachev tentatively unveiled his plans for a broader democratisation of Soviet society, as religious activists were affected by the virtual cessation of political arrests – and by late 1987 roughly a third of all religious prisoners had been released[9] – and as the state began to register, albeit in small numbers, some religious communities.[10]

This same period witnessed a series of unconfirmed rumours about divisions in high places over the religious question. One report suggested that in the spring of 1987 Gorbachev had given permission for parts of the Orthodox Easter liturgy to be broadcast live on Soviet television, only to be countered by Yegor Ligachev who rang the television studios and banned it ten minutes before the programme was due on air.[11] By late 1987 it was clear that the 'moderates' were winning the struggle for some relaxation in official policy, at least with regard to the officially recognised religious communities. Coverage of the forthcoming millennium celebrations became more favourable,[12] religion in general began to receive more objective coverage in the press, and an increasing number of newspaper and journal articles described the persistent abuse of believers' rights. Though more conservative approaches continued to surface, notably in a *Pravda* editorial in early February 1988, which

---

[6] *Pravda* 26 Feb. 1986.   [7] *Pravda* 2 Oct. 1986.
[8] *Pravda vostoka* 25 Nov. 1986.
[9] *Keston News Service* (*KNS*) 287, 2 Nov. 1987 reports that there were 265 religious prisoners, compared with 404 in July 1986.
[10] During the course of 1987 104 religious communities were registered – *Nauka i religiya* 1, 1990, p. 2.   [11] *KNS* 277, 11 June 1987, p. 7.
[12] On changing official attitudes towards the millennium see H. Bell & J. Ellis, 'The Millennium Celebrations of 1988 in the USSR', *Religion in Communist Lands*, vol. 16, no. 4, 1988, pp. 298–328.

reminded communists of the need to combat religion and in particular not to neglect the growing influence of the Russian Orthodox Church,[13] the trend was clearly moving in a more liberal direction.

The changing official line was set forth in *Kommunist* during March 1988. An unsigned article entitled simply 'Socialism and Religion' dealt critically with certain aspects of past religious policies and hinted at change in the future. Whilst insisting on the appropriateness of Lenin's approach to religion and pointing out the incompatability of materialistic and religious world views, it nonetheless acknowledged that there had been mistakes in the past. In the 1930s, especially during collectivisation, many activists had seen the closure of churches and the repression of believers as 'a necessary element of socialist construction in the countryside'; in the 1960s there had been cases where religious communities were unjustly deprived of their registration. Such approaches had not only failed to reduce religiosity, but encouraged the spread of religious fanaticism. Under new conditions there was need for a reassessment of the place of religion in socialist society and a democratisation of the practice of those bodies that dealt with religion.[14]

A more public sign of changing attitudes came in the shape of Gorbachev's meeting with the Orthodox hierarchs at the end of April 1988. Seated at a circular table – rather than the rectangular and implicitly confrontational table generally used in diplomatic meetings – Gorbachev told the assembled hierarchs that religious organisations had been affected by 'the tragic events' of the Stalin years and pointed out that relations between church and state had not always been easy. Though he went on to call for a return to 'Leninist principles' in church–state relations, in effect he strayed considerably from Leninist ideas when he spoke of 'universal norms and customs' which both sides had in common. Once again it was being emphasised, this time from the very top, that in future religious policy was to be based upon cooperation rather than conflict.[15]

One factor influencing the new turn may have been external pressures on the USSR. Although Soviet policy makers had always rejected Western allegations relating to the abuse of believers' rights, the subject had become a recognised part of East–West political discourse as a result of the Helsinki process initiated during the 1970s. And although the reform process was stimulated above all by internal needs, in particular the need to restructure a stagnant economy and revitalise a decaying political system, it was the acceleration of the arms race by the Reagan

---

[13] *Pravda* 2 Feb. 1988.
[14] 'Sotsializm i religiya', in *Kommunist* 4, 1988, pp. 115–23.
[15] *Pravda* 30 Apr. 1988.

administration which exacerbated the economic problems facing the USSR and hastened the recognition of the need for reform. Keeping up with the Americans meant sacrificing yet further consumer interests, a policy seen as containing political risks at home.

In the religious field we have already seen how external pressures from the late 1970s onwards served to stimulate sections of the believing population to resist state pressure or simply to develop their religious life in ways not entirely approved by the state authorities. Official sensitivity, earlier revealed in propaganda attacks on the Vatican and foreign religious organisations, remained high during Gorbachev's first two years in office. Numerous books and articles attacked the use of religion by imperialist agencies;[16] other frequent subjects of attack during this period included Iranian radio stations seeking to influence Soviet Muslims, and Amnesty International for its defence of alleged religious prisoners in the USSR.[17] Yet the question remains as to whether this sensitivity to foreign pressure made a major contribution to change. Or was the major factor here, as in the economic sphere, a product of the growing awareness of the problems facing the Soviet Union internally? After all, it could be argued, and almost certainly was argued by Gorbachev, that attacks on citizens adhering to alternative ideological perspectives were an expensive luxury at a time when the support of the whole population was necessary to get the USSR back on its feet. Foreign pressure may have given the USSR an additional reason to reform its religious policy – after all, reform gained it 'brownie points' in the international arena – but was far from the primary impulse.

At the heart of Gorbachev's strategy for reform lay the building of political 'supports', of appealing for the backing of various groups within society by offering them something that they wanted. Hence the intelligentsia were presented with glasnost', the more advanced managers and workers greater economic autonomy, and the substantial community of believers greater religious freedom. In particular, religious institutions were seen as capable of encouraging their members to be loyal, hard working, peaceful and sober citizens, something that would be further facilitated by expanding their rights. More practically, believers might be able to supplement the efforts of the ailing Soviet welfare system by providing funds and personnel for hospitals, psychiatric institutions and old people's homes. Increasingly the authorities were discovering that in a time of political reform even opium had its uses.

Though official spokesmen did not explicitly spell out such a crudely utilitarian approach, this perception could be found in comments made

[16] For example, N. A. Koval'skii, *Imperializm, religiya, tserkov'* (Moscow, 1986).
[17] *Kommunist Tadzhikistana* 29 Oct. 1987.

by Gorbachev at his April 1988 meeting with Russian Orthodox hierarchs. Here the party leader stressed what he saw as the common commitment of most Soviet citizens, including believers, to the process he had inititiated, and positively evaluated the contribution of the church to the domestic and foreign policies of the state. For this reason the development of better relations had become possible and a process of dialogue begun. Of special note to Gorbachev was the more active participation of the church in official social organisations such as the Children's Fund and the Cultural Fund, and particularly in 'the sphere of morality, where common human values and customs could become our common affair'.[18]

This approach, stressing what was held in common, was quickly taken up by Orthodox leaders at the time of the millennium celebrations. Metropolitan Filaret of Minsk saw parallels between perestroika and the millennium, between the church's 'consolidation of moral, ethical and spiritual forces' and the way in which 'the Soviet Fatherland is gathering its spiritual forces for a sacred aim, the good of the nation'.[19] Two days later Soviet President Andrei Gromyko met participants in the celebrations and welcomed the efforts of the churches: 'in the humanistic efforts currently underway in the country. I am referring especially to the contributions to various voluntary funds whose goal is to preserve peace, protect children, develop culture or restore ancient monuments.'[20] The church's support for perestroika was voiced in a variety of contexts, with Russian Orthodox leaders elected to the new Congress of People's Deputies in 1989 proving most vocal. Metropolitan Aleksii of Leningrad addressing the first meeting of the Congress in June 1989 opened his speech with a panegyric to perestroika, but went on to stress the link between morality and social development. In his view the economic crisis was as much the result of spiritual impoverishment as of narrowly 'economic' factors and he ended with a paragraph reminiscent of Gorbachev's earlier 'support for concessions' approach. 'The church and religious associations are prepared to take part in this process of the moral renewal of our society, and we wait in hope for the speedy adoption of a new law on freedom of conscience which will provide the church with greater possibilities for participation in the social life of our society.'[21] In early 1990 it was again Aleksii who warned the Congress of People's Deputies of the links between rising crime and the failure to inculcate spiritual values amongst young people.[22]

A second expectation was that religious organisations would encourage

[18] *Pravda* 30 Apr. 1988.   [19] *Literaturnaya gazeta* 8 June 1989.
[20] *Pravda* 12 June 1988.   [21] *Izvestiya* 2 June 1989.
[22] *KNS 341*, 11 Jan. 1990, p. 15.

certain, and discourage other, forms of citizen behaviour. In their public exhortations during the late 1980s religious leaders frequently endorsed the state's hopes for sobriety, morality and hard work. In August 1990 the newly elected Patriarch Aleksii II called on bishops and priests to appeal to the people to help bring in the harvest, and suggested that they set an example by deed as well as word.[23] The following spring, in the face of the growing incidence of draft dodging, Central Asian mufti Muhammed Yusuf appealed to all Muslims to perform their military service, something he described as a sacred duty.[24] Muslim leaders continued to perform their traditional role in denouncing officially disapproved practices, such as the payment of *kalym* (bride price), as contrary to Islamic teaching.[25]

Religious leaders were also called in to calm ethnic unrest during this period. Following the large-scale communal violence in Uzbekistan's Fergana valley during the summer of 1989 Muhammed Yusuf was one of those flown into the area with leading party officials to try and calm the situation. In a later interview on Soviet television he claimed that the calls of Muslim leaders had helped to ease the tensions, though at the time *Pravda* noted that 'not everyone had heeded the mufti's call'.[26] At the Central Committee plenum on nationalities questions in September 1989 Gorbachev had noted the complex relationship between religion and nationalism, and that on occasions religious hostility had contributed to ethnic conflict. Yet he stressed that 'we appreciate the peace making activities of the Russian Orthodox Church, Islamic and other religious groups, and we hope that they will use their influence and opportunities to help avert and overcome inter-ethnic conflicts'.[27] Such efforts were encouraged in various parts of the USSR. Armenian Catholicos Vazgen I on a number of occasions issued appeals to Armenians to avoid over-reacting in their attempt to satisfy their legitimate aspirations to regain Nagorno-Karabakh. In the late summer of 1990 Gorbachev appealed personally to Vazgen to use his authority to end the conflicts in the region, though such efforts by this cautious man to follow Moscow's desires only served to isolate him from the increasingly vocal nationalists.[28]

Despite these appeals the impact of the nationality issue on the shaping of religious policy during this period was ambiguous, often pushing it in

[23] *TASS* 16 Aug. 1990.   [24] *Turkmenskaya iskra* 29 Apr. 1991.
[25] *Turkmenskaya iskra* 25 Jan. 1991.
[26] Moscow Television programme on 'Islam and Nationality Relations' broadcast on 25 Apr. 1990; *Pravda* 6 June 1989.   [27] *Pravda* 20 Sept. 1989.
[28] The role of the church in recent events is explored in V. Guroian, 'Faith, Church and Nationalism in Armenia', *Nationalities Papers*, vol. 20, no. 1, Spring 1992, pp. 31–51; and F. Corley, *Armenia and Karabakh – Ancient Faith, Modern War* (London, 1992).

a more conservative direction than might otherwise have prevailed, at least during the earlier period. Under Gorbachev religious organisations in some non-Russian republics had to wait longer than others for substantive concessions or policy changes. In part this stemmed from Gorbachev's much commented upon insensitivity to the national question. At the 27th Party Congress, whilst subjecting many areas of Soviet life to a critical eye, he returned to safe Brezhnevite platitudes about nationalities policy as 'an outstanding achievement of socialism' and spoke of a 'qualitatively new social and international community'.[29] And it is significant that of Gorbachev's few negative comments on the religious question, most were issued in the context of an attack on nationalism and its various byproducts.

It is from this perspective that we should read Gorbachev's first public pronouncement on the religious issue, made during the brief visit to Tashkent in November 1986. Central Asia had been the subject of an anti-corruption campaign since Andropov's brief tenure of office, and this had been renewed under Gorbachev. Amongst its targets were a wide range of 'negative phenomena', including report padding, bribery, speculation, nepotism and clientelism, feudal relations towards women and 'religious survivals'. During the course of 1986 the region's press carried a large number of articles attacking religion.[30] This campaign in Central Asia appears to have gathered pace towards the autumn, with many regional bosses using the rhetoric of earlier days:

Nationalism is seeking for itself a religious front. It is necessary to admit that individual citizens succumb to this hostile propaganda as a result of ideological sabotage against the republic's (Tajikistan) population and the unscrupulous manipulation of its national and religious feelings, and as a result of the weakening of ideological and educational work.[31]

It was in this context that Gorbachev visited Tashkent and called for a 'decisive and uncompromising struggle with religion'.[32] Though the full text of this speech is not available, it is clear that here was a call for an attack on religion in a very specific context, and not for a more generalised campaign. Though its focus reflected official concerns of the 1980s with Islam, and though it was reinforced by an unpublished Central Committee decree on combatting Islam issued in August 1986,[33] Gorbachev's prime target was the localism that had to some extent taken

[29] *Pravda* 26 Feb. 1986.   [30] *Pravda vostoka* 31 Jan. 1986.
[31] *Kommunist Tadzhikistana* 31 Aug. 1986.   [32] *Pravda vostoka* 25 Nov. 1986.
[33] This decree of 18 August 1986 was repealed by a 1990 decree issued by the Central Committee on the grounds that the religious situation had changed in those areas traditionally confessing Islam, as had the party line on religion. Centre for the Preservation of Contemporary Documents, (TsKhSD), f. 89, per. 11, dok. 5.

day-to-day running of the regions out of central control under Brezhnev.
And it is arguable that it was in part this suspicion of the religious-
national link that delayed the liberalisation of religious policy in the
Muslim regions until some time after it was begun elsewhere.

In Lithuania the religious-national link appears to have had an
ambiguous impact upon the development of liberalisation. In some areas
it acted as a break, with the release of leading clerical activists from camps
not taking place until 1988 – compared with early 1987 for most
prominent Russian Orthodox dissenters. And even after change did
manage to impact upon religion, the central leadership remained wary
especially as the secessionist movement came to dominate Lithuanian
politics during the late 1980s. Thus it is perhaps not surprising to find
Gorbachev denouncing the politicisation of the Catholic Church in
Lithuania at the end of 1989,[34] despite the radical rethinking of the
religious question that had taken place by then. Nonetheless, the context
was very different from that pertaining in Central Asia. In Lithuania the
vast majority of the clergy had sought to resist state encroachments on
religious life, and once the reform process began to affect the republic
they increasingly took matters into their own hands. More problematic
was the situation in areas where religion and nationalism came together
and served to block liberalisation as happened in Ukraine. We shall
discuss this case later, but it is worth noting that here the fear of the
contagion of nationalism affecting the second most important Soviet
republic played a major role in impeding the progress of religious
liberalisation.

Whilst the liberalisation of religious policy may have been motivated
by a desire to widen the basis of support for reform, the impact of support
from religious leaderships on the behaviour of the average believer is
hard to assess. Whilst religious institutions increasingly enjoyed a high
degree of public trust – with one poll showing that they had the trust or
support of 37% of the population by March 1990, as opposed to the
CPSU's 16%[35] – it is far from clear that hard work was encouraged or
ethnic tension diminished by the appeals of religious leaders. Moreover,
as perestroika developed it became apparent that just as the state could
use religion for its own ends, so too could its nationalist and radical
critics.

---

[34] *Pravda* 26 Dec. 1989. Gorbachev was speaking at a Central Committee plenum to
discuss the split in the Lithuanian party.   [35] *Moscow News*, 13 May 1990.

The impact of glasnost

Though there may have been factors favouring liberalisation, further encouragement came from a society that was given a voice by that very programme of change. In the religious field as elsewhere we see an official encouragement of criticism in the interests of reform taking on a life of its own and in time going beyond the limits decreed or desired by the political leadership. Thus in the shaping of a new policy an important role was played by the wider society which increased the pressure on the authorities to maintain the reform momentum. In particular, glasnost' permitted certain sections of the artistic community, the increasingly free media and traditionally cautious religious elites to promote an extension of freedom of conscience.

Glasnost, especially as it developed after the Chernobyl disaster in April 1986, made it possible to turn a critical eye on the state's treatment of religion. Whereas the scholarly critique of the religious situation reached a minority, that developed in the pages of the liberal press in the period 1986–8 reached millions. In January 1987 *Moskovskie novosti* published an article detailing the tribulations of the Orthodox community in the town of Oktyabr'sky where the local authorities were placing obstructions in the path of those seeking to register a new religious community.[36] This remained a lone example until the early summer of 1987 when the quantity of such articles multiplied and their tone became more critical. In July *Literaturnaya gazeta* described a case in the Chuvash autonomous republic where, depite permission to build a new church, the Orthodox community was persistently obstructed by local officials in their efforts to begin construction work.[37] One month later *Moscow News* correspondent Aleksandr Nezhny, the journalist at the forefront of press exposure of abuses, described the problems facing believers in the town of Kirov who had been left with only one church by the Khrushchev campaign.[38] By late 1987 and early 1988 many of these complaints were being taken up by officials of the Council for Religious Affairs, the very body many suggested was responsible for these same abuses of believers' rights.[39]

[36] *Moscow News* 25 Jan. 1987.
[37] *Literaturnaya gazeta* 15 July 1987; at some point in 1988, and possibly in response to this article, the RSFSR CRA discussed the question of 'the course of perestroika in the work of the Chuvash CRA commissioner' and called upon him to restructure his own style of work with religious communities and 'to normalise religious circumstance' in his region. State Archive of the Yaroslav Region (GAYarO), f. 1033, op. 1, d. 100, pp. 42–8.   [38] *Moscow News* 16 Aug. 1987.
[39] Cf. Academician Dmitri Likhachev's suggestion that 'in the recent past the CRA did intervene, and very actively, in the life of the church', in *Literaturnaya gazeta* 9 Sept. 1987.

Though many articles focused on similar abuses, gradually the critique began to broaden out. For example, an article which appeared in *Sovetskaya Belorussiya* in late December 1987 not only detailed examples of discrimination against believers, but went on to suggest that there may be grounds for cooperation between believers and atheists – 'after all, we have a great deal in common, such as the desire to see the Fatherland strong and prosperous, and her people purer, kinder and wiser'.[40] And whereas the early articles stressed the isolated nature of such abuses by local authorities or insensitive bureaucrats, by early 1988 it was increasingly acknowledged that such instances were 'unfortunately not yet rare... they result from the fact that certain executive committee workers think that the legislation on religious cults is one way and only affects religious believers, and moreover, that its function is solely restrictive and prohibitive. This is a mistaken view.'[41]

This evolving and more systematic critique of state policy was raised most clearly in an article which appeared just a week before Gorbachev met the Russian Orthodox hierarchs. Returning to the case of the Kirov believers he had discussed the previous August, Aleksandr Nezhny noted that their immediate complaint had not been met following his article, and cited his own dealings with the local authorities which suggested that their change of heart had been grudging. Above all, Nezhny argued, these authorities appeared to assume that they played by different rules from other people, that there were two democracies and two moralities, 'one for the authorities and one for the ordinary people'. Though his earlier article had focused on one community, he had since received further letters from believers facing similar difficulties – in Brest, Leningrad, Donetsk, Chernigov, Novgorod, Gorky, Sverdlovsk, Kiev and many other regions. At first, 'I was unable to find a suitable explanation for the motives behind the behaviour of certain local bodies of power.' But this led him to raise more fundamental questions, for 'the church was separated from the state 70 years ago, and since then has always had to ask the state's permission to form a community or open another house of worship'. During much of this time religion had experienced wave after wave of assaults which swept away churches and individuals. And it was this approach to the religious question which had imprinted itself upon the minds of those who dealt with religion. Clearly the time had come for a major rethink, one which in Nezhny's view could best be handled by an independent commission attached to the Supreme Soviet and including believers in its ranks.[42]

---

[40] *Sovetskaya Belorussiya* 26 Dec. 1987.
[41] *Sovetskaya Rossiya* 3 Feb. 1988. The author was V. I. Garadzha, director of the party's Institute of Scientific Atheism.   [42] *Moscow News* 24 Apr. 1988.

Glasnost also gave religious institutions new opportunities to influence the changing situation by participating in public debate. Having been rendered rather suspicious and cautious by their considerable experience of dealing with the Soviet state, religious bodies were slow to respond in the early years of perestroika. Up until 1988 religious dissidents had continued to protest official religious policies, as well as the apparent compliance of religious authorities in the face of pressure. In May 1987, for example, a group of nine Orthodox believers (including Fr Gleb Yakunin) signed an open letter addressed to Gorbachev speaking approvingly of the changes which he had initiated and suggesting ways in which reform might be expanded to affect religion. In particular they called for a radical revision of the laws on religion so as to remove all discrimination against believers. Above all they stressed open discussion of change so that 'atheists and believers could freely express their opinions about the legislation'. They ended:

We want to believe in the reality of the forthcoming reconstruction (perestroika). The process of democratisation which is taking place in our country is by its very essence indivisible. The Russian Orthodox Church cannot be excluded from it. Only then will the participation of believers in the process of renovation which has begun in our society, and in the social, cultural and spiritual life of the people be of value.[43]

By December 1988 the boundary between dissent and permitted criticism had been crossed by Fr Gleb Yakunin, one of the authors of this appeal, who was able to push his case for legal change in the pages of *Ogonyok* where this time his co-signatories included such luminaries of perestroika as Tatyana Zaslavskaya, Sergei Zalygin and Sergei Averintsev.[44]

For many religious leaders, themselves formed under communist party rule and accustomed to playing by the system's rules, responding to change was as difficult as for any other Soviet bureaucrat. They remained unsure as to how serious the reform programme was to be and, in some cases, feared that their own positions would be undermined by reform. Statements and interviews initially followed traditional paths. In November 1985 Patriarch Pimen issued a statement expressing full support for the Soviet position in the forthcoming Geneva summit;[45] one month later Metropolitan Filaret of Kiev told a Moscow press conference that Soviet believers enjoyed total freedom of conscience.[46] As late as November 1987 Patriarch Pimen was to be found issuing a message on the seventieth anniversary of the Russian revolution, which depicted the history of church–state relations in the USSR in glowing colours, and

---

[43] Summarised in *KNS 277*, 11 June 1987, pp. 2–5.   [44] *Ogonyok* 50, 1988, p. 5.
[45] *KNS 235*, 28 Nov. 1985, pp. 3–4.   [46] *Izvestiya* 10 Dec. 1985.

which ignored even the horrors of the 1930s which by then were being openly discussed in the Soviet press.[47]

By this time, however, some religious representatives were beginning to raise more controversial issues and discuss church–state relations in a more critical vein, albeit still rather cautiously. In the summer of 1986 the new rector of the Leningrad Theological Academy, Nikolai Gundyaev, gave an interview in which he spoke of a new tolerance to religion developing, of churches opening in a number of areas, and of the younger generation coming into the church – noting that 70% of Leningrad seminary and academy students came from secular or atheist families. More surprisingly, in the context of a discussion of the banned Ukrainian Catholic Church, he suggested that the forcible destruction of religious communities was not perhaps the best approach to ecumenism. Although at this early stage there were only hints as to areas where change was necessary, the Leningrad rector's advocacy role was clear in his suggestion that the forthcoming millennium celebrations should provide an opportunity for a reassessment of the church's role in Soviet society.[48]

The first member of the Orthodox Church's ruling group to tackle the question openly was Aleksii, future patriarch but then Metropolitan of Tallinn and Estonia, and until 1986 chief administrator of the Moscow Patriarchate. In December 1985 he had written privately to Gorbachev suggesting that separation of church and state need not prevent collaboration between them in dealing with some of the problems facing society. Three months later this letter was discussed by the Central Committee Secretariat which then issued a decree stressing that the church should limit itself to the satisfaction of believers' religious needs and should not interfere in the political arena.[49] In September 1987 Aleksii, now heading the Leningrad diocese, gave an interview which brought ongoing problems in church–state relations out into the open:

It is sad when sometimes at local level, and running counter to the basic principles of socialism... believers are treated with a certain suspicion... When atheist articles are written in an unfriendly tone and give quite unreliable information, this does not contribute to the creation of a healthy atmosphere for dialogue.

He went on to single out for criticism certain features of the 1929 Law on Religious Associations which he said reflected the needs of a different period.[50]

From this point onwards religious spokesmen began to appear in the press with increasing frequency and gradually their critique of official attitudes towards religious policy became more extensive, although not

---

[47] *KNS 285*, 3 Dec. 1987, pp. 8–9.   [48] *KNS 256*, 7 Aug. 1986, pp. 4–5.
[49] *Izvestiya* 2 Mar. 1993.   [50] *Moscow News* 20 Sept. 1987.

until 1990 or even later did some speak with complete frankness of the past. Lining up with official perspectives on what was and was not permitted by glasnost, church spokesmen stressed the need for creative dialogue in finding answers to common problems. Adventist leader Mikhail Kulakov noted the growing role of the clergy and religious activists in public discussions of dilemmas facing the USSR, yet pointed out that despite the changes it was not that long ago (1986) that his daughter graduated from school with a report that quite unnecessarily pointed out that she shared her parents' religious convictions.[51] Simultaneously there were signs that some within the elite were willing to use clerical voices to support their own analysis of the problems facing society. *Pravda*, for example, published a letter from Archbishop Mikhail of Vologda and Veliki Ustyug attacking much of what passed as youth culture, particularly pop music, and stressing the need to pass on more healthy folk traditions.[52]

As the millennium celebrations took place and faded into memory, the press carried an increasing number of articles on religion, the abuses of the past, and on the need for reform, all of which contibuted to the discussion of change that we shall deal with below. And as we shall also note, just as glasnost provided a new platform from which religious bodies could argue their case, democratisation was to take this a stage further by permitting the election of religious leaders to the new parliamentary bodies that were to play some role in the framing of policy documents which implemented the new policy turn.

Controversies

This liberalisation of religious policy aroused considerable public debate focusing attention on issues such as the celebration of the Christian millennium, the relationship between religion and morality, the place of religion and atheism in Soviet society, and the reform of legislation affecting religious communities.

When Gorbachev came to power there were two significant religious anniversaries approaching: the 600th anniversary of the conversion of Lithuania due in 1987 and the millennium of the adoption of Christianity by Vladimir of Kiev in 988. The former was not the subject of much central discussion, and in the event the celebrations were muted by Soviet unwillingess to allow Pope John Paul II to participate and the fact that by June 1987 liberalisation had not really taken hold. The latter, however, was the subject of considerable public discussion and eventually of a well publicised state and church celebration.

[51] *Moscow News* 2, 1988.   [52] *Pravda* 21 Dec. 1987.

During the 1970s the Russian Orthodox Church had devoted considerable attention in its limited publications and public addresses to the connection between Orthodoxy and Russian history and culture. Anniversaries such as that of Kulikovo field in 1980 were celebrated in terms of the church's contribution to Russian victory, and much was made of the Orthodox tradition in art and literature. In part a genuine expression of Russian patriotism, one can also see these campaigns as a tactic designed to link the church to the nation and thus preserve it from any new all out attack. This use of Russian nationalism, though supported by many Russian writers and historians, was strongly attacked by some within the ideological sector of the party. During the early 1980s this critique found a specific target in the millennium of Christianity in Rus' due in 1988.[53] This negative view of the millennium continued into Gorbachev's first year in office. In September 1985 *Pravda* warned that both domestic churchmen and foreign powers might use the millennium to stir up political unrest.[54] Various writers stressed the political motives underlying Prince Vladimir's acceptance of Christianity,[55] whilst Alexandr Yakovlev attacked attempts 'to depict Christianity as "the mother" of Russian culture'.[56]

Nonetheless, it became clear by late 1986 that the party-state had recognised the impossibility of ignoring this anniversary and was seeking ways to make the best of it. Twelve months later attitudes towards the millennium as expressed in the media became increasingly favourable. Particularly prominent here was Academician Dmitri Likhachev who stressed the church's role in forming Russian spiritual culture, but stressed that Christianity's prime significance was ethical not political or ideological. Hence, whilst praising Orthodoxy's contribution to Russian culture he emphasised the negative element of the acceptance of Christianity – its unification of church and state.[57]

In April 1988 this growing acceptance of the millennium and its religious significance was given further prominence in an *Izvestiya* interview with Patriarch Pimen. Here the head of the Russian Orthodox Church stressed the broad religious, historical and cultural significance

[53] See N. Gordienko, *Kreshchenie Rusi – fakty protiv legend i mifov* (Leningrad, 1983).
[54] *Pravda* 13 Sept. 1985.
[55] In September 1986 central television showed a programme entitled 'The Tenth Century in the History of Rus''. Here Gordienko and two other leading atheists stressed that Vladimir had chosen Christianity because it enabled him to set up a centralised state based on the domination of some people by others, and held out to the masses future happiness in the afterlife in return of quiescence in the present. Reported in *KNS 262* 30 Oct. 1986, p. 10.
[56] A. N. Yakovlev, 'Dostizhenie kachestvenno novogo sostoyaniya sovetskogo obshchestva i obshchestvennye nauki', *Vestnik akademii nauk SSSR*, 6, 1987, p. 69.
[57] *Ogonyok* 10, 1988, *p.* 12.

of Vladimir's acceptance of Christianity which enabled the country to take its rightful place in 'the world wide historical process'[58] – shades here of Gorbachev's talk of perestroika as rejoining the Soviet Union to European civilisation. The final seal of approval came a few weeks later when Gorbachev met the Orthodox hierarchs and spoke of the millennium as 'a significant milestone' in Russian history.[59] Critiques of the church's interpretation of the millennium continued to be published, with N. Gordienko, for example, suggesting that the church rather than creating Russian culture had done much to destroy the genuine pre-Christian heritage in its struggle with paganism.[60] But by then the battle had been lost, and the 'liberal' approach was dominant.[61]

Another key issue raised under Gorbachev was the question of the relationship of religion to more general human values. In his controversial novel *Plakha* (The Scaffold) Chingiz Aitmatov had put forward the idea that in some sense 'religion' was essential to human existence regardless of the truth of its claims. His hero whilst clearly believing religion to be a delusion, nonetheless argues that we need a god to live morally. Symbolically this former seminarian who struggles to right the social ills of contemporary Soviet society ends by being crucified after refusing to deny the existence of god.[62] A seemingly more utilitarian approach was taken by the poet Yevgeni Yevtushenko who called for the free publication of religious literature, especially the scriptures of the various traditions, as a means of enabling the Soviet people to make sense of their cultural heritage.[63] One could also note the growing use of religious language and symbolism in the literary and artistic works of those who sought to expand the boundaries of glasnost'. Typical of this was the growing use of words such as 'repentance' – notably in Abuladze's film of that title – or 'charity', a concept which writer Daniil Granin noted had been erased from Soviet consciousness and practice by its associations with religion.[64]

This more open attitude to religious themes met with resistance from the ideological and anti-religious establishment. Aitmatov's *Plakha* was an early subject of attack. In July 1986 veteran atheist I. Kryvelev noted

---

[58] *Izvestiya* 4 Sept. 1988.   [59] *Pravda* 30 Apr. 1988.

[60] *Leningradskaya pravda* 1 June 1988; see a review of the literature on the millennium by Yu. Kryanev & T. Pavlova in *Kommunist*, 12, 1989, pp. 124–7.

[61] On this debate see Bell & Ellis, 'The Millennium Celebrations'; M. Bourdeaux, *Gorbachev, Glasnost and the Gospel* (London, 1990), chapter 3.

[62] See the discussion of this and other works in Mary Seton-Watson, 'Religious Themes in Recent Soviet Literature', *Religion in Communist Lands*, vol. 16, no. 2, Summer 1988, pp. 117–25, and I. Maryniak, 'Truthseekers, Godbuilders or Culture Vultures: Some Supplementary Remarks on Religious Perspectives in Modern Soviet Literature', *Religion in Communist Lands*, vol. 16, no. 3, Winter 1988, pp. 227–36.

[63] *Komsomol'skaya pravda* 10 Dec. 1986.   [64] *Literaturnaya gazeta* 18 Mar. 1987.

the subtle resurrection in Soviet literature of the old claim that without religion there could be no morality. Singling out favourable references to the Bible in various works he suggests 'read the Bible. If you do so, what you will find is preaching of the most unbridled bloodshed ... the biblical precepts serve present day Israeli soldiers as important material for the extermination of the Arabs.' Defenders of the Bible might turn to the New Testament, but this was little better for it accepted all the precepts of the old, and was much more threatening in its talk of torments beyond the grave. To religious morality Kryvelev countered the atheist tradition which provided a non-religious morality based upon 'conscientiousness, justice and spirituality in the best and loftiest sense of these words'.[65] Two months later his position was backed up by a *Pravda* editorial on atheism which attacked those artistic works which 'prettify church life and rituals', which attempt to identify religious and socialist morality, and which were guilty of the sin of reviving 'god-seeking' ideas long ago condemned by Lenin.[66]

Over the next few months *Komsomol'skaya pravda* carried an ongoing debate on this issue with the critics of 'god-seeking' and 'god-building' making much of the running. In March 1987 the paper carried a review of readers' letters in which many were said to have been critical of those writers who ignored the reactionary essence of religion. One correspondent rejected Yevtushenko's appeal to publish the Bible on the grounds of what it had done to Polish youth. Another rejected the view that non-resistance was at the heart of Christianity, and suggested that the early Christians actually went to the lions (and quite rightly?) for disobedience to the state. Yet not all were critical. A Leningrad artist who was not religious nonetheless suggested that it was better, 'to turn to the past including the religious past, in order to return to present generations those permanent values without which a human being becomes a self-satisfied beast ... it is not god-seeking that represents a real threat, but the triumph of boorishness and consumerism ...'[67] One month later the youth paper returned to the fray with an article by T. Tazhurina, a teacher at Moscow University, entitled 'Just how is religion useful?' She noted that over the last fifteen to twenty years certain intellectual circles had developed a taste for religious issues, something reinforced by the stagnation of the late 1970s and early 1980s. In this atmosphere Marxism had become a scapegoat, as many stressed the importance of a plurality of philosophies. Yet this she suggested could only be a transitional phase, 'to be followed by the predominance of a single world

[65] *Komsomol'skaya pravda* 30 July 1986.   [66] *Pravda* 28 Sept. 1986.
[67] *Komsomol'skaya pravda* 12 Mar. 1987.

view'. 'God building' only undermined the ideological firmness of the Soviet building and 'it is time to remove the halo of civic boldness from attempts to propagate religious ideas in Soviet culture'.[68] Once again, however, this attempt to stem the tide was proving belated and within twelve months the political leadership had made it clear that old ways of dealing with religion had been rejected and that debates over the relationship between religion and morality were a natural part of the socialist pluralism of ideas.

Debates over the millennium and morality were part of a much wider argument that emerged in the late 1980s over the role of religion and atheism in a restructured Soviet society. In turn this ongoing discussion ran parallel with the bureaucratic struggles over a new law on religion which we deal with in the next section. For the resolution of the question of religion's role related closely to the issue of what rights should be granted or denied to religious institutions and communities.

In late 1987 V. I. Garadzha, director of the Central Committee's Institute of Scientific Atheism, published an article calling for the application of the new thinking to the sphere of religion and atheism. Rejecting the administrative approach to the religious question and the attempt to 'finish off' religion, he argued that the time had come to end the idea of opposing believers to atheists. Following the standard rhetoric of the 1970s, he stressed that most believers were loyal, hardworking citizens, but he went much further in arguing that in the struggle for the restructuring of 'social and moral values' the two sides might 'be able to find a common language'.[69] Similar language was used by Gorbachev in his April 1988 meeting with the Orthodox hierarchs, where he spoke of believers and atheists as joining together in 'the common great cause of restructuring and renewal of socialism'.[70]

At a round table discussion organised by the Central Committee's Academy of Social Sciences in late 1988 Archbishop Kirill of Smolensk and Vyazma spoke forthrightly about some of the problems facing believers. In particular he pointed to the difficulties facing those who wanted to go into higher education or enter the teaching profession, and especially those wishing to enter a seminary. Such actions contributed to the public hypocrisy so readily condemned nowadays, leading those attaining high positions in society to disguise their belief or refrain from church attendance in their own towns. If until recently it was only the elderly who went to church it was not because of their 'low level of consciousness', but because 'they had nothing to lose'. Alongside discrimination was the utilisation of ideological stereotyping that pushed

[68] *Komsomol'skaya pravda* 10 Apr. 1987.   [69] *Nauka i religiya* 12, 1987, pp. 10–12.
[70] *Pravda* 30 Apr. 1988.

believers into a second class status, and which dismissed religion as a 'bourgeois survival'.[71]

At first conservative elements within the party seem not to have taken much notice of the changing face of church–state relations, perhaps being preoccupied with struggles on other fronts, but also perhaps seeing the shift as essentially tactical in nature and as open to reversal. In 1989, however, resistance was to harden, with attempts to stifle efforts at developing a genuinely liberal law on freedom of conscience and growing criticism of the new liberalism creeping into the press. The latter fightback was in part stimulated by an article entitled 'rethinking' which appeared in *Nauka i religiya* in January 1989. Here V. I. Garadzha, ostensibly chief guardian of party orthodoxy, questioned many of the traditional tenets of Soviet atheism as hitherto conceived.

Starting from the premise that it was the stereotypical, dogmatic style of the past that was hindering a true re-evaluation of atheist work, Garadzha suggested that overcoming such an approach was the primary task facing the party. In particular he was concerned to reject the simplistic 'one track' theory of development towards socialism, with its corollary that removing exploitation and conflict within society will automatically lead to a 'crisis' of religion and its rapid extinction as a social phenomenon. This was not just a theoretical oversimplification, but had a practical impact upon society:

In a very real way the victory of socialism means for believers a destruction of their faith. In that case why should they work conscientiously, why should they be involved in a society that hastens the coming of 'atheist socialism'?

It is clear that...setting up 'good atheists' against 'bad believers' has in practice undermined social unity in the struggle for the ideas of socialism and communism, thus demobilising and alienating significant sections of society.

This view of believers and religion as 'harmful' to society led to the administrative excesses of the 1930s and early 1960s. Equally it was a view based upon false premises, because the harm was seen in its role as 'bourgeois ideology', though religion predated the 'bourgeois' by many centuries. More importantly it ignored the real position of religion in the social sphere, underestimating the contribution of religion to liberation struggles in Latin America or to campaigns for peace in the West. For Garadzha, it was impossible to go on describing such activities as in some sense hostile to socialism. After all could one really say that:

some of the moral precepts preached from the pulpit contradict those which we are trying to instill into the Soviet people? Ministers of the church together with atheists are engaged in the fight with drunkenness and drug addiction, alcoholism and crime, and against the dislocation of moral values.

[71] *Nauka i religiya* 6, 1989, pp. 6–8.

Given this shared approach, the time had come for a far more constructive dialogue between believers and atheists, a discussion based on honest debate and which would not cover up the 'deep contradictions' between the two world views.[72]

This re-evaluation of the role of religion in Soviet society brought forth considerable criticism. A construction worker from the Chernigov region attacked Garadzha for reinforcing the common view that the decline in religious belief had caused the moral decline of society, and noted the high crime rates in 'religious' America.[73] A pensioner from Alma Ata basically agreed with his approach but wondered to what extent atheists and believers could truly have common aims – or were communist society and the kingdom of God on earth 'one and the same'?[74] A number of writers questioned Garadzha's suggestion that neither believers nor atheists had a monopoly on truth. If a person doesn't believe her convictions to be true how can she defend them? Such an approach was clearly at odds with the approach taken by Lenin who posited two clearly opposing ideologies, only one of which could be true.[75] The leading Leningrad atheist N. Gordienko attacked Garadzha's caricature of Soviet atheism, and suggested that it was far less dogmatic than he portrayed. More importantly, he asked the question never fully answered by the spokespersons of perestroika, i.e. what did they actually mean by 'universal human values'?[76]

Other publications voiced the growing suspicion felt by many party activists about the greater prominence being given to religion in public life. Journalist N. Kozhanov reported that many party activists felt that to retreat in this area was to abandon Marxism.[77] A Marxism–Leninism lecturer from Voronezh, attacked the regular preaching of the clergy in the press and on television, a development he saw as aimed at the restoration of the pre-revolutionary position of the church.[78] Such views reflected the unease felt by many party ideological workers who had much to lose from the ending or playing down of state atheism. And as we shall see this attack on the new thinking on religion, however muted, reflected a concern within the party apparatus about the implications of change in this area. It was during this very period that the draft law on religion became bogged down in the party bureaucracy and that the would-be radical Kharchev was replaced as Chairman of the Council for Religious Affairs by the more conservative Yuri Khristoradnov. Although the latter publicly proclaimed his commitment to the new

[72] *Nauka i religiya* 1, 1989, pp. 2–5.   [73] *Nauka i religiya* 6, 1989, p. 19.
[74] ibid.   [75] *Nauka i religiya* 8, 1989, p. 9.   [76] ibid., pp. 6–7.
[77] *Pravda* 15 Apr. 1989.   [78] *Zhurnalist* 4, 1989, *pp.* 9–14.

equality of believers and atheists,[79] under his direction the CRA appeared to obstruct an 'excessive' liberalisation of the law capable of guaranteeing this new relationship.

Shaping a new law on freedom of conscience

Towards a new law: the debate

Throughout the Khrushchev and Brezhnev years the restrictive nature of Soviet legislation on religion had been a major focus of the critique of state policies offered by religious dissidents. In particular they pointed to the denial of juridical personality entailed in Lenin's separation decree, the inequality of believers and atheists implicit in Article 52 of the 1977 constitution, and the extremely narrow interpretation of the amended 1929 Law on Religious Associations which in effect restricted religious freedom to worship in the small number of registered religious communities. From 1987 onwards this critique was increasingly echoed in the pages of the Soviet press, in language that often differed little from that of the former dissidents. By 1988 the call for a new law on religion was being taken up by legal specialists and even by officials of the Council for Religious Affairs, and the process of drafting a new law had already been set in motion.

I have dealt elsewhere with the early stages of the debate leading up to the adoption of the new law,[80] and here will simply outline the main landmarks in the public discussion of the law. Prominent in this was Konstantin Kharchev, a man with no experience in the religious field, appointed to head the CRA in late 1984. By his own admission his initial attitude towards religion was traditional and hostile, yet over the next five years, whether for reasons of principle or opportunism, he was to become a leading, if not always politically astute, promoter of reform in the religious sphere. Early interviews stuck to the official line that problems in church–state relations stemmed largely from the abuses of local officials and argued that what was needed was less radical change than the 'perfection' of existing legislation. Nonetheless, there were signs that his thinking was beginning to stray outside orthodox parameters when in an interview with *Izvestiya* published in early 1988 he gave a list of activities permitted to religious communities, and included the right of parents to invite ministers of religion to give religious instruction to their children, something prohibited in practice since the late 1920s. In the same

---

[79] *Pravitel'stvenny vestnik* 20, 1989.
[80] J. Anderson, 'Drafting a Soviet Law on Freedom of Conscience', *Soviet Jewish Affairs*, vol. 19, no. 1, pp. 19–33.

interview he noted that in the last year alone he had received 3,000 complaints from believers, mostly concerning the refusal of local officials to register their communities.[81] Four months later he was to be found speaking of the 'petty regulation' of the 1929 law which 'strove to be aware of every step and every activity of the church and thus deprive it of any independence'.[82] And at a meeting of RSFSR CRA commissioners held in Kuibyshev in June 1987 Kharchev stressed that registration should be automatic unless the religious community in question had grossly violated the law.[83]

By mid-1988 it was clear that changes in the following areas were under consideration: the granting of the unambiguous right of juridical personality to religious communities, permission for the church to become involved in public life and carry out charitable activities, some expansion of rights *vis-à-vis* religious education of children, a loosening of the registration requirement, and the possible development of some alternative to military service.[84] By the end of that year many writers went much further, with two Interior Ministry jurists suggesting that the registration requirement be scrapped and that activities covered by Article 142 and 227 of the RSFSR Criminal Code be decriminalised.[85] Around the same time O. Osipov suggested that the simplest thing would be to do away with the Law on Religious Associations. Thousands of believers were ignoring its provisions, not because they were anti-Soviet but because the law did not provide an adequate basis for freedom of conscience – 'when law and life contradict one another it is not life but law which must change'.[86]

Not all were happy with this attempt to reinterpret or revise the law. L. F. Kolonitsky argued that on the whole the present law provided adequate guarantees for the exercise of freedom of conscience.[87] In March 1988 V. V. Klochkov, whose 'conservative' attitude to law and religion we discussed in a previous chapter, made a similar claim:

Ignoring generally recognised principles of freedom of conscience, bourgeois and clerical reactionaries describe as a violation of this freedom in the USSR the forfeiture of the church's opportunity to participate in the political, economic

---

[81] *Izvestiya* 27 Jan. 1988.   [82] *Ogonyok*, 21, 1988, pp. 26–8.

[83] GAYarO, f. 1033, op. 1, d. 100. Others speakers revealed some uncertainty as to what perestroika meant for religion, with emphases on a liberal interpetation of the law, criticism of the widespread abuses by local officials, but also evidence of a continuing aspiration to control religious organisations.

[84] See the speech CRA legal secretary T. Belokobyl'skaya gave at the Moscow Theological Academy in late 1987 reported in *Russkaya mysl'* 18 Mar. 1988.

[85] F. M. Rudinsky & M. A. Shapiro, 'Pravosoznanie grazhdan v sfere realizatsii svobody sovesti i praktika ee osushchestvleniya', *Sovetskoe gosudarstvo i pravo* 12, 1988, pp. 22–31.   [86] *Nauka i religiya* 12, 1988, pp. 14–15.

[87] *Sovetskaya Rossiya* 5 Apr. 1988.

and cultural life of society ... Yet neither bourgeois theory, nor the laws of the capitalist lands, nor international legal acts view such participation as a necessary element of freedom of conscience. According to these international instruments, the churches have only one function, the 'satisfaction of the religious needs of citizens', and this is provided for in Soviet laws.[88]

Undeterred by Gorbachev's subsequent meeting with the hierarchs and the new official line on religion, Klochkov returned to the fray in September, attacking the one sided interpretation of the 1929 law that was becoming dominant and defending the restrictions on the religious education of children.[89]

By this time, he was too late so far as public discourse was concerned. In a December 1988 interview, Kharchev had dismissed the 1929 legislation out of hand as a 'typical Stalinist document', and suggested further radical changes in the legal regulation of religious life. He could see no reason why parents should not be able to take their children to synagogues, mosques or churches for religious instruction, and argued that the present understanding of 'registration as permission' should be dropped – it was clearly absurd that a group of friends at prayer required permission while a group of comrades gathered for a sing-song did not.[90]

The drafting process

Though discussion of new laws had occurred at various points since Khrushchev's fall, notably in the mid-1960s and from the late 1970s onwards, it was not until 1987 that the CPSU Central Committee commissioned the Council for Religious Affairs to produce a new draft law on freedom of conscience.[91] The CRA in turn appears to have forwarded a request to the Institute of State and Law of the USSR Academy of Sciences to produce such a document,[92] which was then returned to the special commission attached to the Council. This commission included representatives of the CRA, the KGB, the Procuracy, and the Ministries of the Interior, Justice and Foreign Affairs.[93] At various stages the CRA appears to have consulted religious leaders, but they were not included on the commission drafting the law.[94]

---

[88] V. V. Klochkov, 'Svoboda veroispovedeniya v SSSR i burzhuazno-propagandistskie vymysly i deistvitelnost', *Sotsialisticheskaya zakonnost'*, 3, 1988, pp. 26–29.

[89] *Izvestiya* 17 Sept. 1988.   [90] *Ogonyok* 50, 1988, pp. 2–5.   [91] ibid., p. 5.

[92] *New Times* 40, 1988, pp. 24–6.

[93] According to Kharchev interviewed after his fall in *Ogonyok* 44, 1989, p. 11.

[94] Fedor Burlatsky, head of the Soviet Public Commission for International Cooperation on Humanitarian Problems and Human Rights, commented in January 1989 that this absence of believers exacerbated the problems caused by the first draft because it reflected essentially a bureaucratic mentality. *Radio Liberty Research Report on the USSR* 4, 1989, 27 Jan. 1989, p. 28.

This initial stage of the shaping of a new law took place behind closed doors, but from January 1989 discussion of legal change increasingly came out into the open. With at least one draft law circulating in typescript by the end of 1988, the CRA in February 1989 organised a meeting of 'the Public Scientific Consultative Commission attached to the Council for Religious Affairs' at which church leaders were given an introduction to the official draft.[95] Simultaneously the legal journal *Sovetskoe gosudarstvo i pravo* published a draft and commentary prepared by lawyer Yuri Rozenbaum.[96]

The official draft[97] opened with a general preamble promising equal rights to all citizens regardless of belief, but broadened the understanding of freedom of conscience by adding 'the right to propagate religious or atheistic views'. Though the draft clearly stated the right of religious communities to juridical personality, it did not remove the much hated registration requirement. At the local level religious societies (i.e. individual congregations) were to be set up by ten or more adult citizens (twenty in the old law) who had to apply for registration to the local soviet, which had to reply within the month. Should the soviet refuse, the believers could appeal to the 'state organ of the USSR for religious affairs' (Articles 10–11). Rozenbaum's draft and commentary suggested that there should be a further right of appeal to the courts. The draft law included a series of articles effectively removing the bans contained in Article 17 of the 1929 Law on Religious Associations – for example on charitable activities. The religious education of adults was allowed for 'at home or in the religious society' (Article 7) and parents or guardians were given the right 'to ensure the religious and moral education and teaching of their children in accordance with their own convictions' (Article 3). Also permitted were religious rites in private homes, hospitals and places of correction – although the latter two still required permission from the relevant administrations, something often denied in previous times. It also left unclear the question as to whether such rites would have to be performed by priests, pastors, mullahs of registered congregations, or whether a dying person could call in a Ukrainian Catholic (still banned at this point), an unofficial mullah or other unregistered clerics. Finally the CRA draft made provision for the implementation of the legislation on freedom of conscience. The CRA version spoke rather vaguely of the 'state organ for religious affairs' whilst Rozenbaum preferred to leave

[95] *Izvestiya* 16 Feb. 1989.
[96] Yu. Rozenbaum, 'K razrabotke proekta zakona SSSR svobode sovesti', in *Sovetskoe gosudarstvo i pravo* 2, 1989, pp. 91–8.
[97] The text used here is one that reached Keston College in England a few days after the meeting reported in *Izvestiya* and contained in the KC Archive.

monitoring largely to local soviets and legal organs, although suggesting that a new state committee on religious affairs should be set up and attached to the Presidium of the Supreme Soviet. This was more in line with the suggestion of Kharchev in his December 1988 interview, which spoke of transforming the CRA from an organ of administration into an organ of peoples power.[98] From the viewpoint of believers the draft was a vast improvement on existing legislation, but remained ambiguous on many points. The registration requirement was not relaxed to the degree hoped for by many religious groups, whose confidence in the law was not helped by the fact that final decision making power rested in the hands of bodies that had in the past abused their authority. Nonetheless, the underlying principle that henceforth everything not prohibited was permitted was welcomed by many.

In response to this draft both the Russian Orthodox Church and a group of religious activists produced their own versions of what the law should look like. The former tended to amend the state draft at the margins, for example explicitly stressing the equality of all world-views, religious or otherwise, or adding to the prohibition of teaching religion in schools a similar ban on the teaching of atheism. Amongst other things the Orthodox argued that the church should have the same rights as any other social organisation, that the right to set up charitable and educational associations should be explicitly granted, and that minors should be free to participate in religious life. Though accepting the principle of registration, the Orthodox draft followed Rozenbaum in favouring a right of appeal to the courts. The draft produced by the activists went further in extending the rights of religious organisations, in guaranteeing their involvement in public life and access to the media, in allowing for conscientious objection to military service, but also by moving into more controversial territory in arguing for the return of all church property and possessions confiscated since 1917.[99]

Neither of these drafts was published in the media, a sign perhaps of the ongoing political sensitivity of the religious question. Over the next few months the press continued to publish discussion of what should be included in a new law on religion,[100] but the legal draft itself disappeared into the corridors of the bureaucracy. In theory, as Kharchev was later to point out, the draft should have proceeded from the CRA's special commission to the Supreme Soviet;[101] in practice, it was forwarded to the

[98] *Ogonyok* 50, 1988, p. 5.
[99] Texts in KC Archive. I have discussed these drafts in more detail in *KNS 324*, 27 Apr. 1989, pp. 23–4.
[100] For example, see discussion and comments in *Nauka i religiya* 2, 1989, pp. 6–8.
[101] *Ogonyok* 44, 1989, p. 11.

Central Committee's Ideological Commission. A brief press report on the meeting of the Commission on 5 May 1989 noted that its members had discussed the draft sent to it, noted its improvement of legal guarantees of religious freedom, but at the same time suggested that 'the draft requires further elaboration, after which it would be published in the press for wide discussion, and finally examined in the USSR Supreme Soviet'.[102] A later report in the Central Committee bulletin merely noted that commission members had made various suggestions, and then forwarded the draft to the Politburo.[103] In fact, following the Ideological Commission's meeting the draft disappeared for the best part of a year and, according to Fedor Burlatsky, this was just one of a series of draft laws affecting human rights which 'disappeared' at this time.[104] The reasons for this blockage were in part connected to wider political struggles within the Kremlin, but they also stemmed from two other developments in 1989 – the so called 'Kharchev affair' and, more importantly, debates over how far reform should extend.

The Kharchev affair

In June 1989, shortly after the swallowing up of the legislative draft by the apparat, Konstantin Kharchev was removed as head of the Council for Religious Affairs and replaced by Yuri Khristoradnov, a conservative bureaucrat unlikely to devote much effort to pushing for change, especially if that involved going against the Central Committee and KGB.[105] Shortly after his sacking Kharchev gave an interview to Aleksandr Nezhny in which he set out his understanding of the reasons for his fall.[106] Subsequent statements by Politburo ideology chief Vadim Medvedev[107] and Aleksandr Degtyarev, deputy head of the Ideology Department[108] provided alternative explanations.

From these sources one can piece together Kharchev's various 'sins', which included – according to his own account – the development of a genuine commitment to the defence of believers' rights. This brought him into conflict with Yegor Ligachev who strongly opposed the CRA chairman's proposal to open new churches in Moscow – 'let them build

[102] *Pravda* 8 May 1989.   [103] *Izvestiya TsK KPSS* 6, 1989, p. 77.
[104] *Izvestiya* 10 Oct. 1989.
[105] For more detail see John Dunlop, 'Kharchev Affair Sheds New Light on Severe Controls on Religion in USSR', in *Radio Liberty, Report on the USSR*, 23 Feb. 1990, pp. 6–9; Jane Ellis, 'Some Reflections about Religious Policy Under Kharchev', in S. Ramet, ed., *Religious Policy in the Soviet Union* (Cambridge, 1993), pp. 84–104.
[106] *Ogonyok* 44, 1989, pp. 9–12.
[107] *Argumenty i fakty* 46, 1989, 18–24 Nov. 1989, p. 2.
[108] *Ogonyok* 48, 1989, pp. 28–9.

churches in Poland, but we won't'.[109] Kharchev had also sought to expose and neutralise the role of the KGB and Central Committee in controlling religious life through the CRA. In late 1988 Kharchev claims prime minister N. Ryzhkov issued a resolution reducing the number of deputy chairman of the CRA from three to one. If implemented this would have had the effect, amongst other things, of removing Yevgeni Milovanov, a KGB officer under the command of the religious section of the KGB's Fifth Directorate. Simultaneously Kharchev's more relaxed attitude to the possible legal recognition of the Hare Krishnas and the Uniates did not go down well with many party officials, in particular with Central Committee Secretary Vadim Medvedev and Ideology Department head Aleksandr Kapto.[110] Finally, the mercurial Kharchev managed to upset many religious leaders by his often tactless, clumsy style. According to Degtyarev it was after the Orthodox Holy Synod had approached the Supreme Soviet with a request for Kharchev's removal that the errant CRA chairman was sacked, a fact this Central Committee official reports rather wistfully, pointing out that the church had succeeded where the apparat had failed. Whilst Kharchev's own accounts do mention conflicts with the church, his prime focus is on his clashes with the Central Committee and 'the neigbours', i.e. the KGB, in trying to push through a more genuinely liberal law on freedom of conscience and to reduce the state's role in religious matters.[111]

Though Kharchev attracted the wrath of Ligachev, Medvedev and Kapto, their failure to remove him suggests that Gorbachev himself may have played a key role in protecting the CRA chairman from his critics. Equally, the removal of that support, perhaps faciliated by Kharchev's rather heavy-handed approach in his dealings with the Russian Orthodox Church leadership, came in mid-1989 when Gorbachev was meeting increasing resistance from within the party following the fright given to the apparat by the recent elections. Whilst the Kharchev affair may with hindsight appear a side show, it does illustrate the involvement of senior political leaders in religious affairs. It also ensured that during 1989 attention was largely focused on personnel matters whilst the draft law on freedom of conscience disappeared into the bureaucratic maw.

---

[109] Ligachev was not mentioned in the printed version of Kharchev's interview and was identified as responsible for these words by Aleksandr Nezhny in a conversation with Radio Liberty's London correspondent. *KNS 339*, 30 Nov. 1989.
[110] See Fr Gleb Yakunin's comments whilst on a visit to the USA. *News Network International* 14 Aug. 1989, pp. 6–8.   [111] ibid.

How far to go

If the Kharchev affair was symptomatic of the apparat's temporary success in slowing down reform of the law, a more substantive issue was the question of how far liberalisation should go. In particular, should recognition be granted to religious communities hitherto deemed beyond the pale – with debate focusing largely on the Ukrainian Catholic issue, although, as the Kharchev interview indicated, the question of the Hare Krishna movement came up in his clashes with the Central Committee. Though the last Hare Krishna prisoners were not released until December 1988 the state's attitude towards this group, which had been so harshly treated in the early 1980s, began to soften in the middle of that year. In August the Moscow community was granted registration and, though they faced continued problems over the next two years or more, their fate was clearly not at the centre of church–state relations.[112]

Far more politically charged was the question of the Greek Catholic Church, located primarily in Western Ukraine. Involving a wide range of actors – the Kremlin, the KGB, the CRA, the Moscow Patriarchate, the Ukrainian authorities, the Ukrainian Catholics and the Vatican – this was one of the most difficult religious problems facing the Gorbachev leadership. Up until 1988, if not later, the Ukrainian authorities had kept a tight rein on manifestations of nationalist activity in the republic, but increasingly even this traditionally tightly controlled republic was feeling the pressure of nationalism. In such conditions Kiev saw problems in allowing greater freedom to a religious group so closely linked to nationalist strivings, particularly in the Western regions. Equally, the Kremlin found itself in a dilemma, unable to justify the denial of religious freedom to a large religious community, yet under pressure from a hostile Russian Orthodox Church which stood to lose a substantial proportion of its parishes should this church be legalised. Up until mid-1988 the problem was kept under control, but after the millennium celebrations it was brought out into the open by the Catholics themselves, coming to a head at about the same time that central discussion of a new law on freedom of religion stalled.

Our discussion here can only focus on a few key developments in 1988–9 which led to a partial resolution of the issue.[113] During 1987, 2

---

[112] See O. Antic, 'The Spread of Modern Cults in the USSR', in Ramet, *Religious Policy in the Soviet Union*, esp. pp. 260–8.

[113] For more detail see S. Keleher, 'Catholic Ostpolitik and the legalisation of the Ukrainian Greek Catholic Church' (unpublished conference paper); B. Bociurkiw, 'The Ukrainian Catholic Church in the USSR under Gorbachev', *Problems of Communism*, Nov.–Dec. 1990, pp. 1–19; M. Tataryn, 'The Reemergence of the

Ukrainian Catholic bishops, 22 priests, 36 religious and 174 lay persons had issued an open letter to John Paul II in which they spoke of their intent to come out of the underground.[114] Over the next two years, as more and more Catholics 'went public', it became increasingly difficult to avoid discussing the issue, though it was carefully kept out of sight during the June 1988 millennium celebrations. Yet during that summer the Uniate question was being raised at Orthodox–Catholic discussions and in Kiev the authorities were holding secret talks with bishops of this allegedly non-existent church. Despite these tentative discussions, the official line remained that this was a non-problem. The Russian Orthodox Church, the party with much to lose from legalisation, continued to claim that the vast majority of west Ukrainian believers were Orthodox. The state for its part, in the person of Konstantin Kharchev, maintained the line that the church entered into union with the Orthodox of their own free will and that if there was a problem it was between churches, and not for the state to resolve.[115] The denial of the Greek Catholics' existence, however, became increasingly difficult to maintain in conditions of glasnost'. One survey carried out by the Central Committee's Institute of Scientific Atheism in the Ternopol oblast reportedly found that some 20 % of the population identified themselves as Greek Catholics, despite the absence of registered places of worship.[116] Moreover, the actions of the state increasingly undermined this official view, for by 1988 negotiations and discussions were taking place in a variety of arenas. During the millennium celebrations in June 1988 Ukrainian Catholic bishops were able to travel to Moscow to meet Vatican representatives. For many activists this was but the first step, and some expressed unease or fear that the Vatican might share the state's view that this was a matter to be settled between churches. From their perspective it was the government that had banned the church in 1946, and thus it was up to Moscow to takes steps towards legalisation. Nonetheless, this visit marked a step forward, for whilst in Moscow, a delegation of Ukrainian Catholics was also received by the CRA which, in effect, made a *de facto* and partial recognition of their existence.[117] Though they were not received by Kharchev, it may well be that his authority lay behind the meeting, for by this time his own position appears to have been undergoing change. By the end of the year indeed, one CRA official

Ukrainian (Greek) Catholic Church in the USSR', in Ramet, *Religious Policy in the Soviet Union*, pp. 292–318.
[114] Tataryn, 'The Reemergence of the Ukrainian (Greek) Catholic Church', p. 297.
[115] *KNS 295*, 3 Mar. 1988, pp. 19–20.
[116] Reported by *Ukrayinsky visnyk* and quoted in *KNS 297*, 31 Mar. 1988, pp. 7–8.
[117] *KNS 304*, 7 July 1988, p. 16.

expressly stated that the Ukrainian Catholic Church had the right to exist just as any other religious community, but admitted that the question was 'highly charged politically'. But like other official spokesmen he argued that this was a matter that had to be resolved by the churches concerned, in particular the Russian Orthodox Church and the Vatican.[118]

Throughout late 1988 and early 1989 the state publicly continued to portray this as essentially an inter-church squabble, and to depict its own role as essentially mediatory. But, in Ukraine, concern over the issue was clear in the willingness of the authorities hastily to register hundreds of new Orthodox congregations, in an effort to preempt Uniate 'recruitment' of those believers alienated by persistent denial of registration. For their part the Ukrainian Catholics appealed to the Russian Orthodox Church for mutual forgiveness, after all both had suffered under Stalinism, and to direct its fire on state bodies. The pace with which democratisation developed aided them here, for it became increasingly possible to draw attention to their plight in the public arena. In part they adopted traditional methods, holding open air masses and pilgrimages attended by many thousands.[119]

In May 1989 they took their case to Moscow. With the newly elected Congress of People's Deputies about to convene, a group of Ukrainian Catholics organised hunger strikes in Moscow's Arbat and lobbied delegates on route to the sessions. Their case was advanced when *Moscow News* took up their cause, reporting on the hunger strike and demonstrations and allowing genuine debate of the issues. At the end of July the same paper published an article by Metropolitan Filaret of Kiev and Galicia in which he repeated traditional claims about the voluntary liquidation of the Ukrainian Catholic Church in 1946–9, the links of the church with the Nazi occupiers, and the stimulation of the issue by 'Uniate and nationalist centres abroad'. Denying that they had experienced persecution, Filaret stated that the Ukrainian Catholics were free to worship in the Ukraine whether in Orthodox or Roman Catholic parishes. Alongside Filaret's attack *Moscow News* published a response from Sergei Filatov of the Academy of Sciences' USA and Canada Institute which demolished the various arguments deployed by Filaret, pointing to the role of the NKVD in the suppression of the Uniates. Denying that they were but a few, Filatov quoted Western estimates to suggest that there might be as many as 4 million adherents of this church, and noted the existence of a strong organisation comprising at least 5 bishops and 200 priests. He ended by suggesting that the Uniate Church would have to be legalised eventually, and that it might be better for the

[118] *KNS 311*, 27 Oct. 1988, p. 11.   [119] Reported in *KNS 334*, 21 Sept. 1989, p. 5.

Orthodox to accept this so as not to have their own Galileo to haunt them in the future.[120]

Earlier the issue had been raised in the pages of *Sovetskaya kul'tura* which published an undelivered speech to the Congress of People's Deputies by Sergei Averintsev (himself an Orthodox layman) which, in dealing with the religious question, suggested that the ban on Uniatism 'does not promote the dignity of our state' nor was it in accord with the long-term interests of the Russian Orthodox Church.[121] Such attitudes were not viewed kindly by the latter which reportedly as late as August 1989 attempted to persuade the Pope to direct Ukrainian Catholics to make a choice between Latin-rite Catholicism and Orthodoxy.[122]

All of these developments placed the issue on the public agenda and made some form of resolution essential, a need reinforced by the approach of Gorbachev's visit to the Vatican, due in December. Even at this late stage, however, those wishing to liberalise in this area faced considerable difficulties, with resistance coming from within the party at central and republican level, as well as from the Russian Orthodox Church. Conservatives in the Soviet Politburo were well represented by Volodymyr Shcherbitsky, first secretary of the Ukrainian party. Though willing to go along with the increasing registration of Russian Orthodox parishes in his republic during late 1988, he drew the line at the Uniates. Addressing a republican party plenum in October he attacked 'religious extremism' and attempts to raise new demands 'under the cover of democratisation'. During the summer of 1989, as the issue came to a head, the Ukrainian party remained wary, expressing its concerns at a plenum of the Soviet Central Committee. Leading the attack was Ivano-Frankovsk first secretary I. G. Posterenko who noted that:

the recent reactivisation of representatives of Uniatism seeking the legalisation of the Ukrainian Catholic church, which compromised itself in the eyes of the Ukrainian people, has aroused particular concern. Here it is worth noting the statements and newspaper articles indicating the reactionary nature of the Uniate movement and its alliance with nationalism, and which explain that the so-called Uniate question is no more than a cover for nationalism.[123]

Such attacks, however, were undermined by growing divisions within the Ukrainian leadership and events in the western regions. By the summer of 1989 Ukrainian Catholic communities were beginning to occupy ruined or closed churches, and individual parishes of the Russian Orthodox Church had started to go over to them. In many areas local

[120] *Moscow News* 31, 1989, 30 July 1989, p. 15.
[121] *Sovetskaya kul'tura* 15 June 1989.   [122] Keleher, 'Catholic Ostpolitik', p. 26.
[123] *Pravda* 21 July 1989.

authorities were turning a blind eye to these developments, emboldened perhaps after the 'resignation' of First Secretary Shcherbitsky in September. The focal point of these developments was Lvov where 150,000 took part in mass demonstrations on 17 September, and where town mayor Bogdan Kotyk sought Kiev's consent to allow the demonstration to go ahead. In October the priest of the Orthodox Transfiguration Church in Lvov and his entire congregation went over to the Uniates. Though the Orthodox claimed that this had been a violent seizure of their property, mayor Kotyk told Kiev radio that there had been an orderly transfer at the behest of the majority.[124]

As Gorbachev's visit to Rome drew close a decision could not be delayed. The precise details of Vatican–Kremlin diplomacy remain shrouded in secrecy, but it is clear that the Ukrainian issue was discussed and that the Pope took an absolutist stand on Uniate legalisation. By this stage, in any case, the process of democratisation and the impossibility of repression meant that the question had to be dealt with and that legalisation must come in some shape or form. In practice the first announcement came several days prior to the Rome meeting when Lvov CRA commissioner Yury Reshchetylo read out a declaration that Greek Catholics had the right to register their parishes. This announcement was made to the wider world on 1 December when the chairman of the Ukrainian CRA issued a statement restoring legal rights to the Greek Catholic Church and granted it equal rights with other churches and religious organisations. The statement called for the resolution of clashes over property to be conducted in accordance with the law and established procedures, and left the choice to existing parishes as to which church they wished to join.[125] Though there remained ambiguities over whether this decision implied recognition of the Ukrainian Catholics as a church – as opposed to individual parishes – whether the decision extended beyond Western Ukraine, and over questions of property, this statement marked the state's acceptance that it could no longer sustain a ban on a religious group with considerable support, whatever the views of other religious groups or sections of the party apparatus. By the end of the year over 600 parishes had applied to register and over 200 priests had come over from the Russian Orthodox Church.[126] From the beginning of 1990 the Uniate issue became increasingly one between churches rather than between church and state, although the state continued to play an ambiguous role right up to the collapse of the USSR. Equally im-

---

[124] *KNS 334*, 21 Sept. 1989, p. 5, & *338*, 16 Nov. 1989, p. 8.
[125] On this see Keleher, 'Catholic Ostpolitik', pp. 34–6; *KNS 340*, 14 Dec. 1989, pp. 17–18.
[126] Tataryn, 'The Reemergence of the Ukrainian (Greek) Catholic Church', p. 305.

portantly, the resolution of this issue, however many problems remained, at least partially cleared the way for further progress in drafting the new law on freedom of conscience.

Adopting the new law

In early 1990 the press once more began to carry articles and discussion columns devoted to the question of the new law, with considerable prominence being given to the views of religious activists. Various issues were raised by the clergy, including the need for religious organisations at all levels to be given legal status, the right to social involvement and charitable activity, and the question of religious education.[127] These calls for liberalisation of the law were backed up by opinion polls which showed that a vast majority of the population wanted religious groups to be given more rights, including the right to publish and set up Sunday schools.[128]

In April 1990 the process moved forward once more, as the Presidium of the Council of Ministers met and decided to pass the law to the Supreme Soviet.[129] Though not yet published, the draft accepted by the Soviet government was analysed and found wanting by Yuri Rozenbaum in the pages of *Izvestiya* a few days later. In his view it was good that the draft ended previous restrictions, but he was critical of the fact that the vast majority of the law was devoted to regulation of religious life rather than freedom of conscience. Might it not be better, he argued, for religion to be covered by a general law on social organisations rather than treated specially, for this way fewer opportunities might be open to the state to renew its interference in religious life.[130]

In May the draft law was discussed further at a meeting sponsored by Burlatsky's Public Commission on Humanitarian Issues and Human Rights, and religious leaders present were somewhat critical.[131] The reasons became apparent from various interviews given by Orthodox hierarchs in the following months. Archbishop Kirill told *Moscow News* that despite all their submissions on the various drafts, the current document under discussion moved further than ever from the church's position. In particular, it failed to guarantee equality for believers and atheists, did not properly define ownership and legal rights, was unclear on the religious education of children, and still did not give sufficiently

---

[127] These three are the central points raised by Archbishop Kirill in a dialogue published by *Kommunist* 2, 1990, pp. 69–80.

[128] Reported on Moscow Radio on 19 Feb. 1990 and quoted in *KNS 345*, 8 Mar. 1990, p. 12.   [129] Reported in *Izvestiya* 12 Apr. 1990.

[130] *Izvestiya* 15 Apr. 1990.   [131] *Izvestiya* 17 May 1990.

clear definition of the competence of state bodies on religious affairs.[132] Significant public support for change came from Boris Yel'tsin in a press conference at the end of May, where he stressed the need for equality for believers and atheists, and suggested that many properties could be handed back to the church. He also supported alternative services for conscientious objectors.[133] Whilst this debate went on, 17 May 1990 saw the first parliamentary discussion of the draft law in the Commission for Nationalities Policy of the Council of Nationalities of the USSR Supreme Soviet. On 30 May the draft was given a first reading in the Supreme Soviet and six days later was published in the press.[134] The new draft granted legal status to parishes and religious organisations, permitted private or church based religious education, allowed ownership of property, removed all the old restrictions on publishing and charity, and abolished discriminatory tax rates on church employees. According to deputy Ilya Zaslavsky, the most controversial question in committee discussion was religious education, and for that reason the draft offered two options. The main document specified a secular education system, with religious instruction being permitted in private homes or on church premises, but an optional amendment explicitly banned religious education from general schools.[135]

The summer was given over to public debate, with the church – most notably in the person of the newly elected Patriarch Aleksii II – expressing criticism of certain features of the draft, in particular the section on religious education.[136] Other issues raised in the press included the return of confiscated church property,[137] and the failure to provide for registration of religious denominations or organisations as a whole, as opposed to individual congregations.[138]

After taking into account some 1500 suggestions the drafting committee produced a new draft, although it could not agree on the question of extra-curricular religious education in schools. Eventually, on 26 September, the bill was given a second reading and passed by 341 votes, against 1 abstention and 1 rejection, and the law then passed on for detailed clause by clause discussion. On 1 October clause by clause voting brought agreement on most issues, although the deputies voted against religious education in school premises at the request of parents.

[132] *Moscow News* 6–13 May 1990.
[133] *BBC Summary of World Broadcasts*, *SU/0780/B1–10*. From a press conference on Soviet TV on 30 May 1990.   [134] *Izvestiya* 5 June 1990.
[135] *KNS 352*, 14 June 1990, p. 5.
[136] See the Patriarch's interview with *Izvestiya* 16 June 1990, and his speech to the Supreme Soviet on 26 Sept. reprinted in *Zhurnal Moskovskoi Patriarkhii* 1, 1991, pp. 56–8.   [137] *Izvestiya* 27 June 1990.
[138] Patriarch Aleksii, reported in *KNS 358*, 13 Sept. 1990, p. 12.

But when the final decision was made the proposal for a specific ban on such activites was also omitted, thus leaving the issue open to the discretion of individual school authorities.[139] That resolved, the law was finally passed that evening and published in the press on 9 October, coming into effect immediately.[140]

The new dispensation

A changing reality

Well before the introduction of the new law on freedom of conscience there had been a perceptible change in the atmosphere surrounding religious organisations. In the first place, the portrayal of religion in the press altered radically, with a growing number of articles detailing the abuses that religious communities had experienced for many years, and the emergence of a far more favourable, even respectful attitude towards religion. The millennium celebrations in summer 1988 were reported extensively by the media as were the various openings of religious institutions that began to gather pace in that year. By the summer of 1989 religious broadcasts were appearing in Lithuania,[141] and within a few months the first religious sermon – admittedly a rather innocuous homily from Metropolitan Pitirim of Volokolamsk – had been broadcast on Moscow TV.[142] By the winter of 1990–1 religious broadcasts, phone-ins and faith healing sessions were common occurrences, and in April 1991 the first Orthodox radio station, *Radonezh*, commenced its activities.[143]

Clerical prominence was not limited to the media, for black-robed and bearded figures were increasingly found in the public arena, from schools to elected bodies. In early 1989 Metropolitan Pitirim was able to address students at Moscow's Higher Party School on his vision of the church's role in society.[144] More importantly, in March 1989 a number of religious leaders were 'elected' to the new Congress of People's Deputies created by Gorbachev's constitutional reforms (with Metropolitan Vladimir of Rostov and Novocherkassk serving as a member of the electoral commission). Of those elected Patriarch Pimen (nominated by the Soviet Peace Committee), Metropolitans Aleksii (Soviet Charity Fund) and Pitirim (Soviet Culture Fund) were part of the group of 750 deputies nominated by 'social organisations' and thus did not have to face the electorate. Central Asian mufti Muhammed Yusuf, Allahshukur Pasha Zade, chairman of the Muslim Board of Transcaucasia, and Catholicos

[139] *Izvestiya* 1 Oct. 1990.   [140] *Izvestiya* 9 Oct. 1990.
[141] *KNS 330*, 20 July 1989, p. 7.   [142] *Moscow News* 22 Oct. 1989.
[143] *Khristianskie novosti* 19, 28 Apr. 1991, p. 392.
[144] *KNS 322*, 20 Mar. 1989, p. 16.

Vazgen of the Armenian Church were also elected, as was Moldavian priest Fr Petr Buburuz, the only cleric to face a serious electoral contest. Metropolitan Aleksii of Leningrad and Novgorod published his election platform in the press, arguing that 'a genuine renaissance of our society is inconceivable without the inclusion of the Christian element' and committing himself to campaign for a humanising of the legal system, a resolution of the nationality issue, and the preservation of the nation's moral and physical health.[145]

As the atmosphere changed so did the attitudes and practices of religious communities. The new law on religion may have got bogged down in the corridors of power in 1988–9, but this did not hinder many religious communities from claiming the rights they expected to be forthcoming. Whilst their leaders often remained cautious, individual congregations started to develop pastoral work, young people's circles, Sunday schools and charitable activities, all still prohibited under existing legislation. Kiev Baptist congregations held mass baptisms in public during 1988,[146] whilst their co-believers in Tashkent were advertising concerts and question and answer sessions by the end of the year.[147] This detachment from the state was evident in a lecture given by Lithuanian Cardinal Vincentas Sladkevicius in August 1988 where he simply informed the state authorities that the church would no longer seek their approval for any appointment within the church and announced that from then on all parish priests would conduct catechism classes for children and young people.[148] For their part the authorities increasingly turned a blind eye to such actions, although this varied from region to region.

Nonetheless, concrete changes were gradually introduced from 1987 on. From the beginning of that year the arrest of religious activists, with the exception of conscientious objectors and Koranic teachers in Central Asia, virtually came to an end, and religious prisoners began to be released. From a figure of some 400 when Gorbachev came to power, the total had fallen to 260 by the end of 1987, and under 100 by early 1989.[149]

The state's attitude to registration also changed. In 1987 104 communities were registered, with a further 1,610 in 1988 – of the latter 1,244 were Russian Orthodox, 72 Georgian Orthodox, 71 Roman

---

[145] *Meditsinskaya gazeta* 12 Feb. 1989, quoted in Oxana Antic, 'Candidates in Cassocks for USSR People's Deputies', in *Radio Liberty Report on the USSR* 17 Mar. 1989, pp. 13–14.

[146] *KNS 302*, 9 June 1988, p. 16, on the Kievan congregations and their celebrations during the millennium period.   [147] According to one western visitor.

[148] Reported in *KNS 313*, 17 Nov. 1989, pp. 18–20.

[149] *KNS 321*, 1 Mar. 1989, pp. 19–20. Of these most were Muslims or Jehovah's Witnesses.

Catholic, 48 Muslim and 36 Pentecostal.[150] By early 1990 CRA chairman
Yuri Khristoradnov could report that 4,500 religious organisations had
been registered since the onset of perestroika.[151] Nearly three-quarters of
new registrations were in Ukraine, where the total of registered
communities rose from 5,689 in 1988 to 9,994 in 1991.[152] By the
beginning of the latter year the total number of registered religious
associations in the USSR had risen from a 1986 total of 12,427 to
21,284.[153] Even traditionally banned groups such as the Uniates,
Jehovah's Witnesses, and Hare Krishnas were now able to register. In
addition to new places of worship there were dozens of new training
centres, monasteries and convents, and charitable and other institutions
run by religious bodies.[154]

As the number of places of worship increased so too did participation
in religious rites. In the town of Yaroslavl Orthodox baptisms rose by
nearly a third in the first half of 1987 – as opposed to the region's villages
where numbers remained stable – a development explained by the local
CRA commissioner in terms of the appearance of hierarchs on television
and the dropping of the requirement that those wishing to have their
children baptised produce their passports and in effect register baptism
with the authorities.[155]

These changes did not go uncontested and many local authorities
continued to harass religious communities or obstruct registration. In
1988 alone the CRA reversed eighty-three decisions of local bodies to
refuse registration to religious communities, a trend more than confirmed
by cases reported in the religious and secular press of this period. Some
of these became national scandals, as in the case of the Orthodox believers
of Ivanovo where the refusal of the local authorities to hand over a church
to the community, despite the CRA's ruling in the believers' favour, and
the subsequent hunger strikes by elderly women, was taken up by the
liberal press and the Moscow intelligentsia. This story ran through much
of 1989 until eventually the local authorities had to cave in.[156] But
increasingly official resistance to registration faltered. In Dneprodzerzhinsk believers campaigned during 1988 for the opening of the St
Nicholas Cathedral closed under Khrushchev. City mayor I. Brazhnik[157]

---

[150] *Moscow News* 9 Aug. 1989.
[151] Speaking whilst on a visit to Scandinavia and reported in *KNS 347*, 5 Apr. 1990, p. 12.
[152] *Lyudina i svit* 5, 1991, p. 51.   [153] *Nauka i religiya*, 1, 1992, p. 7.
[154] A glance through the pages of *Keston News Service* (until its demise in mid-1991), the
bulletin *Khristianskie novosti* and the secular press will yield numerous examples.
[155] GAYarO, f. 1033, op. 1, d. 100, p. 78.
[156] Cf. *Ogonyok* 1, 1989 & 28, 1989, and *Izvestiya* 14 Aug. 1989. See Hedrick Smith, *The
New Russians* (London, 1990), pp. 421–7.
[157] Possibly the same I. Brazhnik who we noted taking a harsh anti-religious line during
the Khrushchev and Brezhnev years. See pp. 20–1, 121.

was adamant that it would not be opened under any circumstances, but was opposed by A. Primak, a local party secretary, who argued that 'since there are believers in the city they have the right to satisfy their spiritual needs'.[158] Yet such obstruction did not end completely, and as late as May 1991 Bishop Palladi of Izhevsk and Udmurtiya addressed a letter to Russian president Boris Yel'tsin in which he noted the continued obstacles being placed in the way of registration by the local CRA commissioner.[159]

The late 1980s saw the gradual relaxation of state controls over the importation, production and censorship of religious books. By 1989 over 2 million copies of the Bible or New Testament had been imported, with permission granted for a further 15 million plus by 1995.[160] Two years later the need for permission to import was no longer necessary, although state controls over paper supply often served to limit domestic printing. Despite official hiccups, other religious groups – notably Muslims and Hare Krishnas – were able to receive religious literature sent by foreign sympathisers.

The state also relented on the issue of emigration by the much persecuted Pentecostals from 1988 onwards, with some 2,000 permitted to leave in that year and the same number within the first three months of 1989.[161] Though the door remained open, the need to leave began to lessen as the reality of the changes in religious policy began to be appreciated by believers who increasingly felt free to practise and spread their faith within the Soviet Union.

Alongside these changes affecting the day-to-day life of religious communities, new opportunities were arising for them to become involved in charitable activities. As Mervyn Matthews has pointed out, by the second half of the 1980s it had become clear that the Soviet welfare system was being placed under growing strain by the economic crisis, the ever increasing number of pensioners, and the likely growth of poverty under the impact of economic reform. As Gorbachev's programme developed the possibilities for independent initiative in this area became greater, and were stimulated by a discussion in the press of the whole question of charity.[162] Central here was Daniil Granin's oft quoted March 1987 article 'On Charity' in which the Leningrad writer noted that the word *miloserdiye* (charity, mercy) with its religious connotations,

[158] *News from Ukraine* Apr. 1988, no. 18.   [159] *Russkaya mysl'* 10 May 1991.
[160] *KNS 327*, 22 June 1989.
[161] *KNS 322*, 30 Mar. 1989, p. 8; F. Corley, 'Religious Believers and the New Soviet Emigration', *Religion in Communist Lands*, vol. 16, no. 1, pp. 78–80.
[162] M. Matthews, 'Perestroika and the Rebirth of Charity', in A. Jones, W. Connor & D. Powell, eds., *Soviet Social Problems* (Harvard, 1991), pp. 154–71.

had virtually disappeared from the public vocabulary, and that the people had lost almost any sense of compassion.[163]

In the religious sphere the problem was that under the 1929 Law on Religious Associations charitable activity was forbidden to religious organisations. By 1988 this prohibition was being increasingly questioned, with the Voronezh CRA commissioner noting that in practice the churches were allowed (if not compelled) to contribute thousands of roubles to the Peace Fund or Chernobyl Fund despite the legal ban. This was an anomaly which should be resolved by either banning all contributions or changing the law so as to allow religious groups more scope in this area.[164] The problems of the latter approach were spelt out by CRA chairman Konstantin Kharchev in a private briefing at the Higher Party School in Moscow where he noted the shortage of personnel in hospitals – 20,000 in Moscow alone – and the applications of churchmen to engage in charitable activities. Yet, he asked, if believers work in the hospitals how will it reflect on communism when a patient goes to his death knowing that after seventy years of socialism the state was still unable to provide a bed pan?[165]

As church initiatives in this area began to gather pace and the state temporised, limiting its permissions to financial donations, some in the church began to demand a greater role. Interviewed in March 1988 the rector of the Leningrad Orthodox Theological Academy, Archpriest Vladimir Sorokin, noted the continued obstacles to charitable activity and the ambiguous attitude of the state:

I fear formalism in charity. Some clergymen were invited to the offices of the Lenin Children's Fund. It seemed that once again only money, donations were expected of us. But the church is not a bank. Our money is in the believers' pockets. And they want more than just to transfer money to some account – they dream of helping the nearest hospital, a nearby childen's home or home for the elderly ... True charity lies in concrete deeds. Would it really be bad if alongside the state hospital there were one operated by believers?[166]

In practice, by late 1988, religious involvement in charitable activity was taking place in various parts of the country. In Moscow Orthodox parishioners were carrying our orderly work in one hospital, priests were visiting the sick, and members of the Baptist church were helping out at the Kashchenko Psychiatric Hospital. A further stimulus to such actions was the Armenian earthquake of December 1988 which produced thousands of roubles from believers' pockets, brought volunteers to the region and opened the Soviet Union to sisters from Mother Teresa's

[163] *Literaturnaya gazeta* 18 Mar. 1987. [164] *Nauka i religiya* 2, 1988, pp. 25–6.
[165] *Russkaya mysl'* 20 May 1988. [166] *Meditsinskaya gazeta* 30 Mar. 1988.

Missionaries of Charity. In the Islamic regions of the USSR visitors reported the reappearance of the alms stall in local bazaars, and in July 1989 *Izvestiya* carried the first report on formal Muslim involvement in charitable work.[167]

There remained problems. The two small homes opened by Mother Teresa in Moscow faced considerable obstruction from local authorities in their efforts to carry out basic repairs.[168] Religious leaders reported that it was still hard to find volunteers from congregations with little experience of pastoral care. Metropolitan Vladimir of Rostov noted that 'a few believers, coming into contact with living reality, with the difficult and because of that even more necessary service to mankind, could not endure it and left'.[169] And one commentator warned of the dangers of viewing the church's role in purely instrumental terms, arguing that religion's prime role was to promote true values within society and that it was from this task that charitable activity should spring.[170] Nonetheless the work of religious organisations in this area continued to expand and be recognised by the state. Sometimes the two sides collaborated, as in the spring of 1990 when the Moscow Patriarchate and the Health Ministry signed an agreement to set up clinics for alcoholics and drug addicts.[171] Numerous initiatives followed, from the activities of the evangelical Central Asian Christian Mission, through the work of the revived Orthodox Brotherhoods, to the soup kitchens set up by Christian Democrats and others in various cities. In many cases religious leaders were appointed to sit on various public charitable commissions.[172] However utilitarian the attitude of the authorities in promoting this development, charitable activity was seen by most believers as a natural outgrowth of their faith and a duty they would have chosen to perform in conditions of religious freedom.

Guaranteeing religious freedom

Though the 1990 Law on Freedom of Conscience and Religious Associations defined the new legal status of religious organisations in Soviet society, a series of other decisions also contributed to their new position. By 1990 the Communist Party had in effect dropped its overt hostility towards religion, a change of attitude reflected in the new party statute adopted by the 28th party congress in July 1990. Dropping the

---

[167] *Izvestiya* 2 July 1989.
[168] *Moscow News* 8 Oct. 1989.
[169] *Izvestiya* 29 Apr. 1989.
[170] *Literaturnaya gazeta* 10 Jan. 1990.
[171] *Izvestiya* 19 June 1990.
[172] For example, the deputy kazi of the Turkmen Muslims became a member of the Council of Humanitarian Assistance of the Turkmen People. *Turkmenskaya iskra* 21 May 1991.

old requirement that party members 'struggle resolutely against...
religious prejudices and survivals of the past',[173] the new statute merely
enjoined party members to 'propagandise the ideas of the party'.[174]

As the party dropped or lessened its hostility towards religion, state
bodies began to shed some of their less publicised discriminatory
practices. Belief was no longer an obstacle to advancement in many
professions. Various non-legal practices, such as the requirement for
parents to register their passports before baptising their children were
quietly dropped during 1987.[175] In 1989 the Council for Religious Affairs
announced that the much criticised, unpublished instructions and
decrees that it had issued betwen 1961 and 1983 were to be abrogated as
incompatible with the principle of a law governed state.[176]

Various other laws adopted at the end of the decade had some impact
upon the legal status of religious bodies. In some cases believers found
the change unacceptable, as in the case of the 1988 cooperative law which
banned such bodies from producing religious items for profit. Others
were more favourable. The 'Fundamentals of Legislation of the USSR
and the Union Republics on Land' adopted in February 1990 granted
permanent tenure to various bodies, including religious organisations,
'for the purposes of agriculture and forestry'.[177] In the 1920s some
religious communities had successfully run religious collective farms but
these had eventually been closed down and apart from a few monastic
allotments, religious farming had ceased to exist. Under the new law such
experiments could be restarted, and by 1990 the Seventh Day Adventists
were already running an agricultural training course.[178] Five days later a
new law on property granted religious organisations the right to own
buildings or other facilities 'essential to their activities',[179] a provision
which at that time contradicted both the 1918 decree on separation of
church and state and the existing law on religious associations.

It was in this changing legal context that the 'Law of the USSR on
Freedom of Conscience and Religious Organisations' was published in
October 1990. Article 1 defined the purpose of the law:

This law guarantees the rights of citizens to decide and express their attitude
towards religion, to convictions corresponding to this and to the unhindered
confession of a religion and the performance of religious rites, and also to equality

---

[173] The party statute of 1961 which uses this phrase can be found in M. Matthews, ed.,
   Soviet Government – A Selection of official Documents on Internal Policy (London,
   1974), pp. 188–206.   [174] *Pravda* 18 July 1990.
[175] During a six-month stay in Moscow during 1987 I noted one church which had a notice
   to this effect at the beginning of my stay but which had removed it by the end.
[176] *Moscow News* 9 Apr. 1989.   [177] *Izvestiya* 7 Mar. 1990.
[178] W. Sawatsky, 'Protestantism in the USSR', in Ramet, *Religion Policy in the Soviet
   Union*, p. 342.   [179] *Izvestiya* 10 Mar. 1990.

and protection of the rights of citizens regardless of their attitude towards religion, and it regulates the relations connected with the activities of religious organisations.

The opening section of the law, entitled 'General Provisions' stressed the rights of all citizens to express and spread their convictions, to rear their children or wards in accordance with their personal attitudes, and the equality of all regardless of religious belief. This opening section also dealt with the separation of 'church (religious organisations)' and state. To this end it stressed that the state would not assign to any religious organisation any privilege or the discharge of state functions, although it dropped the draft's prohibition on religious ceremonies being performed at state occasions. Under Article 5 the state was also to abstain from the funding of religious or atheist activity. The same clause allowed religious organisations to participate in public life and to make use of the mass media, but expressly forbade religious organisations – as opposed to individuals – from participating in political parties or providing funding for such parties. Finally, Article 6 dealt with the vexed question of religious education, opting for a secular school system and the allowing of unhindered religious education of all citizens outside of the state schools.

Section II and III of the draft dealt in some depth with the place of religious organisations, giving legal recognition to bodies other than the local religious associations described in the old law (Articles 7–11). Under the new law the registration requirement was maintained, but it was not necessary to the setting up of religious organisations, only to their recognition as legal entities (Articles 8 & 13). Decisions on registration were left in the hands of the local authorities, but a right of appeal to the courts was included (Articles 14–15). A variety of forms of religious property was envisaged – leased from the state, given by the state or simply purchased. Donations and money given for charitable purposes was to be tax free, but the profits of economic activities were to be subject to taxation (Articles 18, 19, 23).

Section IV removed many of the restrictions on religious activity contained in the notorious Article 17 of the 1929 Law. Religious organisations were given broad rights to undertake charitable activity, set up international links on their own, publish and produce their own religious literature, and perform religious rites in a variety of places – from the private apartment to the prison. Servicemen were permitted to attend religious services during their own free time with no hindrance from commanding officers (Article 21). Protection was also afforded to places of pilgrimage and other holy places recognised as such by individual religious groups. All those working for religious organisations were granted the same contractual protection and pension rights as other citizens (Section V). Article 29 of the new law dealt with 'the state bodies for religious affairs' which were to be formed by the Council of Ministers at union and republican level. This was to be 'an informational, consultative and expert centre', developing contacts with religious bodies, keeping a data bank on those located within the USSR, promoting good relations between those of all faiths, and utilising the services of religious and other experts to oversee their work. Finally, Article 31 put forward the radical principle that in the event of a conflict between the new law and the Soviet Union's international treaty obligations, the latter were to prevail.[180]

Though the law was treated by many as a step forward, some expressed reservations on certain points.[181] In part these stemmed from the fact that the law was ahead of other necessary changes – for example, there was a statement about the agreement of the law with the USSR constitution, yet the latter's Article 52 still effectively prohibited the propagation of religious views now allowed by the law. In certain respects the registration requirement was still deemed unsatisfactory by many insofar as it left the decision in the hands of the same local soviets which had often refused it in the past. There was also a feeling amongst many believers that the ambiguity about religious education in schools laid the door open for arbitrary decisions by individual school directors. Instead they proposed a clause that would allow such education, but on a voluntary basis and with the approval of parents. Underlying all these complaints was the point made by Fr Vyacheslav Polosin, chairman of the Russian Parliament's Committee on Freedom of Conscience and Charity, that the union law moved beyond general principles to detailed central regulation at a time when such matters were increasingly being taken over by individual republics.[182] And it was perhaps ironic that by the time the much awaited law appeared in late 1990, its contents had already been rendered irrelevant by the *de facto* creation of freedom of conscience from below and by the passing of republican laws which gave religious organisations yet more rights.[183] Within a year the law was to be

---

[180] *Izvestiya* 9 Oct. 1990.
[181] See the commentary on the law by Giovanni Codevilla in *Religion in Communist Lands*, vol. 19, nos. 1–2, Summer 1991, pp. 130–45.
[182] *Nauka i religiya* 2, 1991, pp. 2–3.
[183] Perhaps inevitably the Baltic states led the way, with the Latvian parliament adopting a law on alternatives to military service in early 1989, the Estonian government announcing the end of punitive taxation on clergy in September of that year, and the Lithuanian parliament amending the constitution to provide for the independence and legal status of the church in November. The Lithuanian parliament also passed revised legislation on religious organisations which provided greater scope for religious

rendered redundant by the collapse of the Soviet Union and the effective ending of a distinctive central religious policy.

Conclusion

Our concern in this chapter has been with the evolution of Soviet religious policy from one of overt hostility towards religion to a more cooperative relationship in which religious organisations were often viewed as potential partners in the process of reforming the USSR. During the late 1980s the political elite began to realise, however reluctantly in some cases, that seventy years of attacks on religion had failed to remove it from society. Indeed, by the late 1970s there was increasing evidence that religious ideas remained entrenched within the popular consciousness, and that at least some religious communities were enjoying a degree of revitalisation. In such circumstances it was perhaps inevitable that a new leadership committed to the renewal and humanisation of the Soviet Union should address the religious question. And as the reform process gathered pace many of the new forces given life by change in turn contributed to pushing religious liberalisation further. A central role here was played by the media, which analysed the problems facing believers as well as giving them space to argue for greater freedom. Such activities were supported at the grass roots level by the increasing boldness of religious communities creating ever more space within which to operate, often in ways that until late 1990 went beyond the parameters established by law.

Simultaneously the process by which official policies evolved became more open, as political and bureaucratic conflicts were brought out into the open by the media and, on occasion, by officials willing to 'leak'. Resistance to change lingered amongst ideological and control agencies but became increasingly difficult to maintain as the reform process developed. Moreover, many 'conservatives' developed ambiguous attitudes towards the religious question, as the potential alliance later developing between old style communists and some groups of Russian nationalists began to take shape towards the end of the decade. For this reason, and despite grudging comments about the 'excesses' of religious liberalisation heard from Ligachev and others, the growing anti-reform lobby of the late 1980s does not appear to have pushed for a renewed assault on religion.

education in schools than that envisaged by the Soviet law to be adopted in October 1990. Given that the RSFSR law passed in late 1990 also effectively permitted religious education in state schools, on a voluntary basis, a situation had arisen by the end of that year in which All-Union law conflicted in part with that of various republics.

By the end of 1990 then the Soviet state had in effect dropped its long tradition of assault on religious values and institutions and provided a legal framework within which religious groups could exercise freedom of conscience. Almost immediately this framework was undermined by republican laws and the collapse of the USSR, though as we shall see in chapter 7 not all the assumptions and models of religion–state relations developed during the Soviet period were to disappear as easily as did the 1990 law.

7   Religion, state and politics into the 1990s

The collapse of the Soviet Union in late 1991 completed the fragmentation of religious policy, and left religious groups in fifteen different states each with their own ideas on how to handle religion. Religious communities faced a new set of problems as they sought to come to terms with their pasts, with political and social pluralism, and with the challenges of operating in a freer environment. Whilst religion–state problems remained in some areas, there were also a growing number of inter-religious conflicts often closely linked to nationality tensions coming to the fore. And in the political arena religious bodies had to decide how best to use their resources and influence in a situation where many appealed to them for support. This chapter explores how, in the transition from Soviet republics to independent states, with varying degrees of success religious groups came to a new *modus vivendi* with the political authorities.

Religion's response to change

Internal reform

For many years religious activists had charged that the leadership of religious organisations compromised too much with the state authorities. After 1985 such claims were magnified, particularly when cautious leaders responded slowly to the possibilities provided by perestroika. Reform movements sprang up within a number of religious communities often, though not always, initiated by former dissidents. In Latvia, for example, the 'Rebirth and Renewal' movement succeeded in unseating the Lutheran establishment at a general synod in early 1989, and the new leadership promptly entered the political arena by calling for the 'annulment of the Molotov–Ribbentrop pact, self-determination and Latvian independence'.[1]

---

[1] M. Sapiets, 'The Baltic Churches and the National Revival', *Religion in Communist Lands*, vol. 18, no. 2, Summer 1990, p. 156.

During the late 1980s pressures were also building up within the Islamic community. In February 1989 demonstrators in Tashkent called for the resignation of the Central Asian mufti, Shamsuddin ibn Babakhan, accused of an un-Islamic life style. The Uzbek authorities acted quickly to meet the protestors' demands. Twenty-five representatives from the crowd were received by the Uzbek prime minister, and shortly thereafter the mufti 'resigned'. On 15 March a *kurultai* (congress) of Central Asian and Kazakh Muslims selected a new mufti, Muhammed Yusuf.[2]

The Central Asian example proved contagious, for in May of the same year Muslims marched through the town of Makhachkala, capital of the North Caucasian region of Daghestan, calling for the removal of their mufti on the grounds that he had failed to defend the interests and rights of believers and had abused his position for personal gain. Whilst demanding his resignation and trial, they also appealed for the registration of more mosques in the region.[3] Their demand was not initially met, but in January 1990 a conference was offered a choice of three candidates to replace the existing mufti and elected B. Isaev. Yet this demand which started as a call for the purification of Islam and the replacement of leaders deemed to have been excessively close to the state, had other ramifications. The election of a new leader did not bring peace, demonstrations continued and it became apparent during 1990 that many of these related to power struggles within the North Caucasian Religious Board. These were based to a considerable degree on national differences, with Chechens, Ingush and others each seeking to create their own administrative structures.[4] This incident also seems to have exacerbated the authorities' fears concerning the possibility of Muslims in different parts of the USSR linking up and fomenting trouble. At a meeting of North Caucasian CRA commissioners and religious leaders in April 1990, one official noted that amongst those who had led the May events had been Abas Kebekov whose brother had studied under a well-known Central Asian fundamentalist teacher in the Andizhan region of Uzbekistan.[5]

Dissatisfaction with the various Islamic administrations set up by the Soviet state continued to grow during the early 1990s. Over the summer of 1992 the Muslim Board for the European and Siberian regions of the

[2] *Pravda Vostoka* 5 Feb. 1989; 14–17 Mar. 1989; *Sunday Times* 7 Feb. 1989; *Moscow News* 9 Apr. 1989.

[3] Copies of various documents relating to this dispute were circulated to all RSFSR CRA commissioners. This account is based upon documents in the State Archive of the Yaroslavl Region (GAYarO), f. 1033, op. 1, d. 104 & d. 106.

[4] Cf. *Izvestiya* 22 July 1989 & 10 Mar. 1990.

[5] GAYarO, f. 1033, op. 1, d. 106, p. 44.

Commonwealth of Independent States began to fall apart, as Muslim activists in the Tatar and Bashkir republics sought to create their own religious leaderships. According to mufti Talgat Tadzhuddin, these efforts involved less than 10 per cent of Muslim communities in his region and were led by young radicals associated with the nationalist movements in the two republics.[6] These years also witnessed attempts to remove the new Central Asian mufti Muhammed Yusuf on the grounds that he, like his predecessor, had been too close to the KGB, too willing to carry out the wishes of the state, and that he had sold copies of the Koran freely donated by Saudi Arabia.[7] In April 1993 he was demoted to the post of first deputy mufti subordinate to Muktarkhan Abdullaev, a man apparently selected in the time honoured way with the support of the state authorities[8] – though by now the muftiate's brief extended only to Uzbekistan and Turkmenistan.

Within the Russian Orthodox Church calls for internal reform were largely the work of former dissidents such as Fr Gleb Yakunin in the early stages of perestroika. Nonetheless, many within the Orthodox establishment recognised that the church was not entirely ready to respond to the new situation. At the beginning of 1990 Archbishop Kirill of Smolensk, one of the more dynamic young hierarchs, told *Literaturnaya gazeta* that the church was as much in need of reform as society, and went on: 'Our Church has much to do in order not to fall behind as it has sometimes done in the past... I know that there is a view that our hierarchy is making little effort to bring perestroika into the church. This is not so...' And he described the ways the church was seeking to expand theological education, to restore churches, and to develop charitable activity, although recognising that both material and human resources were often lacking.[9]

Yet two years later the ambiguous role of the hierarchy in previous years and the need for reform were brought up in the context of the controversies surrounding allegations that some church leaders had served the KGB. Following the abortive coup attempt in August 1991 a Russian parliamentary commission was set up to investigate the work of the security agencies, with deputy and priest Gleb Yakunin assigned to work on material relating to religion. Interviewed in January 1992 he noted various ways in which the secret police had sought to establish control over religious life and revealed the KGB codenames of various church leaders described as 'agents' by the authorities. Typical of the

---

[6] *Nezavisimaya gazeta* 2 Sept. 1992 & 22 Feb. 1992; *Moskovskie novosti* 6 Sept. 1992.
[7] *Komsomol'skaya pravda* 9 July 1991; *Pravda vostoka* 11 July 1991; *Economist* 21 Jan. 1991.   [8] *Radio Liberty Supplement*, 20, 1993, p. 6.
[9] *Literaturnaya gazeta* 3 Jan. 1990.

documents quoted by Yakunin was one which spoke of 'agent Potemkin who took part in the central committee meeting of the World Council of Churches (1987)... he acquired information about the situation in the headquarters of this organisation, on the forthcoming changes in the leadership of its subdivisions'. Frequently mentioned in this and other reports were agents 'Abbot', 'Adamant' and 'Antonov',[10] men who were soon identified as Metropolitans Pitirim of Volokolamsk, Yuvenali of Krutitsy and Kolomna and Filaret of Kiev and Galicia.[11]

The church leadership initially remained silent on the matter, but it was not one that could be brushed under the carpet. A group of Metropolitan Pitirim's parishioners wrote to *Nedelya* noting that in the old days all religious life was under KGB control and everyone having contacts with foreigners had to write reports. Did this give anyone the right to turn upon church leaders?[12] A more weighty response came from former Politburo member Aleksandr Yakovlev who suggested that sensationalised witch-hunting hardly served the cause of true church reform.[13] From within the church Patriarchal adviser, Deacon Andrei Kuraev noted that under the old system the hierarchs had no choice but to compromise with the state and that this did not make them 'agents'. More importantly he raised the question of the veracity of the reports, and noted the tendency of the KGB to exaggerate its success in recruiting agents. For example, he himself had been sent abroad as a theological student, but he had no idea of whether he was listed as an 'agent', and was not at any stage asked to write reports.[14]

This question of what was actually meant by 'agents' remained problematic, particularly given that the relevant and surviving documents were not available to more than a few individuals. After all, virtually everyone the KGB had dealings with was given a codename – from active collaborators to dissidents. This issue was taken up by the independent minded Archbishop Khryzostom of Vilnius and Lithuania, himself not always popular with the authorities during the 1970s. Despite his maverick stance and conflicts with the state, Khryzostom said that he had maintained contacts with the KGB over eighteen years, and these had only ceased two years earlier. Throughout these years he had filed reports on foreign trips and his contacts with foreigners. This he did deliberately, in order to use his position to build up the church and thus, despite being the possessor of a KGB codename ('Restorer'), Khryzostom maintained that he was never an informer. He did not doubt that

[10] Cf. *Argumenty i fakty* 1, 1992, *Megapolis express* 3, 1992, & *Izvestiya* 22 Jan. 1992. The final report was published in *Khristianskii vestnik*, 1992, no. 9 (November).
[11] *Ogonyok* 4, 1992, pp. 2–3.   [12] *Nedelya* 9, 1992.   [13] *Izvestiya* 22 Feb. 1992.
[14] *Moscow News* 10, 1992, 8 Mar. 1992.

there were KGB agents within the ranks of the church – and he named 'the police officer and atheist' Metropolitan Mefodi of Voronezh – but argued that the matter had to be treated more soberly than hitherto and without the throwing of unsubstantiated charges.[15]

Behind the scenes the church sought to prevent further revelations. In early February Patriarch Aleksii went to see Ruslan Khasbulatov, speaker of the Russian parliament, and reportedly asked him to limit or halt the parliamentary commission's enquiry.[16] Shortly afterwards the commission's work was indeed brought to a halt, although this may have been a case of the church leadership shooting itself in the foot because by that time work on Orthodox collaboration had been completed and that on other religious groups hardly started. In consequence it appeared to the public as if it was primarily the Orthodox who had been thus compromised with the KGB – though revelations about other groups had been published.[17]

More formally, the church took up the issue of KGB involvement in the church at a Council of Bishops held in early April 1992. Arguing against those hierarchs who wanted to drop the matter Metropolitan Kirill proposed the formation of a church commission to discuss the whole issue and produce a reasoned report based upon solid evidence.[18] The creation of the commission appeared to illustrate the Russian Orthodox Church's growing awareness of the need for a review of past activities and some form of internal cleansing if it were to retain credibility in a new era, yet in practice it appears to have met infrequently and by mid-1993 had produced no results.

Inter-religious conflict

The attempt to maintain credibility was not helped by the growing incidence of inter-religious conflict in the early 1990s. Tensions between religious groups, like those between nations, had to some extent been frozen by communist rule, with the possibilities for overt hostility limited, except when it suited the authorities. But the freeze was essentially a product of state socialism, i.e. it worked only partially, and the policies pursued by the state often contributed towards the long-term exacerbation of inter-religious conflict.

Within the Russian Orthodox Church tensions stemmed in part from the appearance on Russian soil of the *emigré* church which attracted the support of some believers disillusioned with what they saw as the

---

[15] *Russkaya mysl'* 24 Apr. 1992.   [16] *Moscow News* 9 Feb. 1992.
[17] See *Nevskoe vremya* 26 Feb. 1992, where St Petersburg rabbi Levitis is alleged to have been a KGB agent.   [18] *Nezavisimaya gazeta* 7 Apr. 1992.

compromises of the Patriarchal church. From 1990 onwards, particularly in those areas where church leaders proved slow to move with the times, a number of parishes defected to the Russian Orthodox Church in Exile.[19] The response of the Moscow Patriarchate was inevitably hostile. Interviewed in November 1990 Patriarch Aleksii was scathing about the overseas church's attempt to poach fellow Orthodox parishes and criticised the creation of a 'theological-political inspectorate from abroad checking whether we were believing in the right way, praying in an Orthodox fashion, or whether church life was virtuous'. He suggested that their critique of his church was essentially political, not theological, unless they believed support for the monarchy to be a necessary tenet of Orthodoxy.[20] The Church in Exile responded with attacks on the Patriarchate's compromises with the state, its failure to canonise the 'new martyrs' (including Tsar Nicholas II and his family), and its commitment to what they saw as the heresy of ecumenism.[21]

By mid-1991 the 'Free Russian Orthodox Church' (the name used in Russia) had won over at least forty priests from the Patriarchate, as well as a small number from the formerly underground True Orthodox Church, though most of the latter refused to accept the leadership of the church abroad – from May 1991 they were able to register their own denominational statute with the RSFSR Ministry of Justice.[22]

The issue of the Church Abroad's activities rumbled on throughout 1991, exacerbated somewhat by the rather partial attitude of many official bodies and the somewhat ambiguous attitude of the Moscow Patriarchate at the time of the August coup – whilst 'Free' church priests joined Fr Yakunin and others on the barricades, many of the bishops temporised before coming out against the Emergency Committee. After the coup it became increasingly possible to register parishes of the Church Abroad, though tensions between the two jurisdictions remained. Typical of this was a case that developed in Kuibyshev during the summer of 1991, where the two sides battled over the church of John the Baptist. Here, as elsewhere, the Patriarchal church quickly found support from the local authorities, people who, in the words of journalist Aleksandr Nezhny, had replaced their earlier persecuting attitude with one that separated churches into 'our' and 'enemy' churches. An attempt to resolve the situation was undertaken by Russian deputy Valentina Linkova, chairperson of the Russian parliament's subcommittee on believers' rights, but she too took the line that 'our' church had to be defended against one

---

[19] *Literaturnaya gazeta* 28 Nov. 1991.   [20] *Literaturnaya gazeta* 28 Nov. 1990.
[21] See the rather partisan account of the issue in V. Moss, 'The Free Russian Orthodox Church', in *RL Report on the USSR* 1 Nov. 1991, pp. 8–12.
[22] *Keston News Service 379*, 11 July 1991, p. 8.

she claimed was sponsored by the CIA. Nezhny pointed out that even Boris Yel'tsin appeared to take the view that one side should be preferred against the other, a stance the critical journalist felt inappropriate for the leader of a multi-ethnic, multi-denominational federation.[23]

Following the collapse of the USSR conflicts between the two churches have persisted over issues such as 'ecumenism' – denounced as a sin by the *emigré* church – and the question of to whom churches should be returned. For the Church Abroad the Moscow Patriarchate was fatally compromised and its leaders needed not only to repent but to resign; from the perspective of the Moscow church their critics had no right to condemn men who acted as they felt best in difficult conditions nor, as we shall see, to identify religious orthodoxy with certain political positions. At the time of writing there are few signs of reconciliation, despite the return of at least one parish to Patriarchal jurisdiction[24] and the efforts of a few individuals on each side who felt that the cause of the church was not helped by fighting old battles.

During the late 1980s inter-religious conflict was often closely related to the nationality question and nowhere was this clearer than in Ukraine, where the state's refusal to recognise the existence of national churches served to place the dominant Russian Orthodox Church in unholy alliance with the communist authorities and give them an unfortunate stake in continuing suppression, in particular of the Ukrainian Catholic Church. As already noted, by late 1989 it had become possible for Ukrainian Catholic churches to register with the state authorities, but ongoing difficulties over property and the transfer to the Ukrainian Catholic Church of many hitherto Orthodox communities raised the temperature in the winter of 1989–90.

In January 1990 Metropolitan Aleksii of Leningrad alleged that violence was being used by the Uniates to regain churches, an allegation repeated by Orthodox hierarchs at various meetings and in the press.[25] One month later a group of Orthodox hierarchs led by Metropolitan Filaret of Kiev met parliamentary speaker Anatoly Lukyanov. Here the bishops repeated claims of violence directed against Orthodox parishes, in particular noting the growing tendency of local officials and the CRA to sanction the transfer of property to the Uniates. Still playing the loyalty card Metropolitan Filaret of Kiev noted that over the years the hierarchs had done everything to be useful to the Soviet fatherland, yet now the authorities were taking the side of their opponents. And in a clever aside Metropolitan Vladimir of Rostov and Novocherkassk

---

[23] *Moscow News* 28 July 1991.   [24] *Izvestiya* 5 Mar. 1993.
[25] See Metropolitan Kirill in *Literaturnaya gazeta* 3 Jan. 1990.

pointed out that in fact it was state property that the Uniates were seizing, as all church land was merely leased to the church.[26] In truth the Orthodox hierarchs had much to worry about, for by the spring of 1990 the Ukrainian Catholics had received over 350 former Orthodox priests, whilst by early 1991 the newly registered Church had 1,677 registered parishes in the three western regions of Ukraine, as against 461 Russian Orthodox.[27]

Despite the public hostility, contacts were maintained with the two churches, assisted by the Council for Religious Affairs and the Vatican, holding regular meetings to attempt to resolve their differences, especially those relating to property and the full state recognition of the Ukrainian Catholics as a religious denomination (as opposed to the recognition of individual parishes). Though the talks broke down on various occasions, there were signs that publicly at least the Orthodox were prepared to seek a compromise. Interviewed shortly after his election, Patriarch Aleksii accepted that charges of violence may have been exaggerated and suggested that it should be up to individual parishioners to decide which church they wanted to join. But this should be done in an orderly and legal fashion.[28] Though tensions and conflict remained, by 1991 the issue was becoming less significant, as the Ukraine passed its own law on freedom of conscience and in May granted the Ukrainian Catholic Church full legal recognition as an independent denomination.[29]

Potentially the most serious inter-religious conflict, because of its relationship to Ukrainian-Russian tensions in early 1992, was in part connected to the activities of a single personality – Metropolitan Filaret of Kiev, Patriarchal Exarch of Ukraine. For over two decades this ambitious hierarch had been one of the most political subservient of all Orthodox hierarchs, a man whose denunciations of religious dissidents and the Ukrainian Catholic Church often surpassed in vehemence the rhetoric of republican ideologists. In early 1992, during the extensive press coverage given to so-called KGB bishops, it was revealed that Filaret was one of the three senior hierarchs mentioned in the KGB reports, his codename being 'Antonov'. His position was not helped by simultaneous revelations about his autocratic treatment of those below him or the fact that this monk committed to celibacy kept a family.[30]

Initially the Russian Orthodox Church chose to do nothing, but in late March–early April the issue came to a head in another context at a synod of bishops meeting in Moscow. On the agenda, apart from the question

[26] TsKhSD, f. 89, per. 8, dok. 41, pp. 1–16.   [27] *KNS 371*, 21 Mar. 1991.
[28] *Izvestiya* 16 June 1990.   [29] *KNS 378*, 27 June 1991, p. 5.
[30] *Ogonyok* 4, 1992, pp. 2–3.

of KGB links to the church, was the question of granting the Ukrainian Orthodox Church full canonical independence – administrative independence had been given to Ukrainian and Byelorussian churches in 1990.[31] After considerable debate, in which the Ukrainian bishops themselves proved divided, it was agreed that whilst financial independence could be affirmed, full autocephaly required the decision of a Local Council of the whole Church.[32] During the course of this meeting Filaret agreed to resign as head of the Ukrainian Orthodox Church, but once back in Kiev renounced his decision and suggested that it had been made under pressure from the Russian episcopate. Subsequently the Ukrainian leadership, in the shape of Nikolai Kolesnik, chairman of the Ukrainian Council for Religious Affairs, and President Leonid Kravchuk, made clear their support for Filaret.[33] And at this point the whole church issue became entangled with the difficult relationship between Russia and Ukraine, something which ensured extensive coverage in the press.

The conflict rumbled on through May, with the Moscow Patriarchate threatening Filaret with a church court and then convening a council of Ukrainian bishops at the end of the month at which sixteen of the eighteen bishops voted to depose him and elect Metropolitan Vladimir of Rostov and Novocherkassk as head of the Ukrainian Orthodox Church.[34] Both Filaret and republican CRA chairman Kolesnikov refused to recognise this decision.[35] The former began to gather his supporters and increasingly to speak of the need to create a new independent Ukrainian Orthodox Church. Eventually, at the end of June, a council in Kiev brought together Filaret's adherents with some members of the Ukrainian Autocephalous Orthodox Church (UAOC). This church created after the Russian revolution and destroyed under Stalin, had survived in emigration until 1989 when it was revived within Ukraine. Though Filaret had previously expressed considerable hostility towards the UAOC – and any manifestation of Ukrainian religious independence[36] – at various times describing its emigre head Patriarch Mstyslav as a 'Hitlerite' and 'false patriarch', in his new guise as Ukrainian patriot some form of collaboration seemed appropriate. At the June 1992 gathering Metropolitan Filaret took up Leonid Kravchuk's comment

[31] *Zhurnal Moskovskoi Patriarkhii* 2, 1991, p. 2.
[32] *Moscow News* 5 Apr. 1992; *Izvestiya* 8 Apr. 1992.
[33] *Moscow News* 3 May 1992.   [34] *Nezavisimaya gazeta* 29 May 1992.
[35] *Nezavisimaya gazeta* 30 May 1992 & 4 June 1992.
[36] According to Dmitri Pospielovsky, during the mid-1980s the future Patriarch Aleksii had proposed granting the Ukrainian Church greater autonomy and had been opposed by Filaret with the full support of republican party leader Shcherbitsky. *Nezavisimaya gazeta* 15 July 1992.

that 'an independent state should have an independent church',[37] and as
a result of this meeting was born the Independent United Ukrainian
Orthodox Church (IUUOC), replacing the Autocephalous Church and
ostensibly headed by the nonagenarian Mstyslav and his deputy Filaret.
But Mstyslav denied his support for this body[38] and in December 1992
wrote to the Ukrainian authorities calling for the reregistration of the
Ukrainian Autocephalous Church statute.[39]

An important feature of these developments was the immediate
and public support for the new church coming from the Ukrainian
authorities, who appeared to be seeking a solution whereby the
Ukrainian Catholic Church became the state church in Western Ukraine
and an autonomous Orthodox Church the state church in the eastern
region. Even before the unified council the Presidium of the Ukrainian
Supreme Soviet had issued a statement which refused to recognise the
deposition of Filaret as head of the Ukrainian Orthodox Church.[40] And
on 23 June a group of parliamentary deputies had set up a committee to
defend the rights of Ukrainian Orthodox believers. Once Filaret's council
had taken the decision to unite the two groups, the speaker of the
Ukrainian parliament sent a further congratulatory greeting, suggesting
that the creation of a new church would prevent religious war in Ukraine.
Yet conflict, unseemly and often taking a violent turn, quickly developed
as adherents of rival churches attempted to take disputed properties.[41]
And by mid-1993 the existence of three rival churches meant that
attempts to create a genuinely national Orthodox church appeared no
closer.[42]

Ukraine was by no means the only republic where religion and national
politics were closely inter-related. In Moldova tensions became apparent
in the latter half of 1992 as divisions within the Orthodox Church became
entangled with national politics. During September of that year a small
group of Moldovan priests critical of the 'Russian imperialism' of
Metropolitan Vladimir of Chisinau and Moldova, set up the brotherhood
of Stephen the Great, whose aim was the creation of a unified Moldovan
church within a reunited Romanian–Moldovan state. One month later
this group joined the 'Christian Alliance for Reunion with Romania', a
political coalition unhappy with president Mircea Snegur's perceived
back-peddling on reunification. Around the same time the Moscow

---

[37] A comment made at various times by Kravchuk, including in an interview with Radio
Mayak on 24 Aug. 1992. *BBC Summary of World Broadcasts SWB/1470 B/6*.
[38] See the accounts in *Nezavisimaya gazeta* 27 June 1992 & 30 June 1992; and Mstyslav's
comments in the same paper on 18 Nov. 1992.
[39] *Nezavisimaya gazeta* 25 Mar. 1993.   [40] *Literaturnaya gazeta* 1 July 1992.
[41] See Patriarch Aleksii's account of such incidents in a letter to Leonid Kravchuk.
Megapolis ekspress 26 Aug. 1992.   [42] *Moskovskie novosti* 6 June 1993.

Patriarchate sought to counter nationalist agitation by granting the church full administrative independence, whilst retaining canonical jurisdiction over the Moldovan diocese.[43] This was not sufficient to prevent a few clerics campaigning for the restoration of the Bessarabian metropolitanate and, more importantly, seeking the support of the Romanian Orthodox Church for their actions. This was forthcoming in December, with Romanian Patriarch Teoctist appointing Metropolitan Patru to head a Bessarabian diocese based in Balti (Bel'tsy).[44]

Initially the Moldovan government sought to steer a middle course, with president Snegur making plain his preference for a national church independent of both Moscow and Bucharest, possibly under the jurisdiction of Constantinople.[45] But once it became plain that the existing church structure had the support of the vast majority of priests, the government, as represented by the minister of culture and cults Ioan Ungureanu, refused to register the statute of the Bessarabian Church. In an interview published in early 1993 Metropolitan Vladimir praised what he described as an 'Orthodox government', recognised its desire to create a national church, but pointed out that so long as Moldova remained an independent country the question of unification with the Romanian church was not open to discussion.[46]

Religion and the state

Ongoing problems

By late 1991 many of the traditional problems of religion–state relations in the Soviet Union had been resolved. None of the fifteen independent republics retained any official commitment to anti-religious activity, the closure of places of worship against the will of believers had ceased, and religious activists were no longer arrested. To a considerable degree the new states abstained from the crasser forms of interference in the daily life of religious communities, though the disposition to intervene remained strong amongst many administrative agencies and officials. Moreover, there remained tensions between religious institutions and the state, often relating to questions of property. Some religious communities demanded back all the land and buildings confiscated under Soviet rule, although they could not hope to maintain such properties without substantial financial aid. Problems also arose as contending

---

[43] *Russkaya mysl'* 13 Nov. 1992.   [44] *Nezavisimaya gazeta* 24 Dec. 1992.
[45] See Felix Corley, 'Moldovan Orthodox Church Split', talk written for the BBC World Service, 23 Jan. 1993.   [46] *Russkaya mysl'* 8 Jan. 1993.

religious groups appealed to the state for control over ruined or long disused buildings.

In the Russian republic a draft law on the property of religious organisations produced in early 1991 returned all property and attached land nationalised under the 1918 separation decree, except 'unique historical, cultural and architectural monuments under state protection and used by state or social organisations for scientific or cultural-educational purposes', with religious organisations allowed to seek permission to use the latter.[47] Difficulties remained, however, with the Russian Orthodox Church at various times coming into conflict with bodies such as the Sergiev Posad (Zagorsk) museums – situated within the monastery grounds – and a crematorium business situated in Moscow's Donskoi monastery.[48]

A second area where tensions remained related to the administrative regulation of religious life. Up until 1990 this function had been performed largely by the KGB and the Council for Religious Affairs. In mid-1990 the newly elected Russian parliament's Committee on Freedom of Conscience had abolished the Russian CRA, whilst the October 1990 USSR Law on Freedom of Conscience had envisaged the transformation of the Council into an 'informational, consultative and expert centre'.[49] Yet in practice the central Council maintained its offices and for some time at least sought to exercise some influence over religious life. After the August 1991 coup the situation changed somewhat, with the abolition of the 4th Department (i.e. religious section) of the KGB's Directorate for the Protection of Constitutional Order, and the disbanding of the CRA at the end of the year.[50]

Ongoing tensions between religious bodies and the state were exacerbated by the perception that many officials continued to assume that religious life was in need of regulation. In Russia the official within the Justice Ministry heading the department responsible for registering religious comunities was former CRA employee A. I. Kudryatsev;[51] in Armenia the Council for Religious Affairs attached to the Council of Ministers continued to function from the same office and with the same officials.[52] In St Petersburg the mayor's office established a Department for Relations with Religious Organisations in December 1991. Described as consultative, the new body was situated in the former buildings of the CRA, took over its files, and was headed by a former employee of that agency. Though there was no intrinsic reason why such a body should act

[47] *Russkaya mysl'* 19 Apr. 1991.
[48] *Moskovskie novosti* 26 July 1992 & 16 Aug. 1992.   [49] *Izvestiya* 9 Oct. 1990.
[50] *Izvestiya* 13 Sept. 1991.   [51] *Russkaya mysl'* 5 Feb. 1993.
[52] S. Brook: *Claws of the Crab – Georgia and Armenia in Crisis* (London, 1993), p. 236.

in a prohibitive fashion, some churches in the region reported growing problems with local officials after its creation.[53]

Fears of a revival of state control over religious organisations were further stimulated when it became known that in November 1992 Ruslan Khasbulatov had approved the creation of an Expert Consultative Commission attached to the Russian Supreme Soviet's Commission on Freedom of Conscience and Charitable Activity.[54] The official tasks of this body were to monitor the development of religious life, to keep data on religious organisations and to advise state bodies on religious matters, but it had no executive powers. Headed by Yuri Rozenbaum, its membership included nine other 'experts' on religion – including members of the former atheist establishment – representatives of the Ministry of Security (the renamed KGB), of the Russian Security Council and the State Committee on Nationality Policy, and representatives of nine religious communities. The presence of representatives of the old anti-religious agencies and the security services aroused the suspicion of many religious activists, who saw in this body an attempt to revive the CRA.[55]

Towards state religions?

Whilst grumbling about state control continued in religious circles, greater public controversy arose over the suspicion that religious groups were seeking or had achieved a favoured status within some of the successor states. In February 1992 *Ogonyok* carried an article in which Dmitri Bykov recalled:

In my time each school year opened with either a Leninist lesson or a lesson on courage. In the first case from the school director, in the second from a veteran ...We then gave thanks for our happy childhood... The oldest pioneer leader reverently laid flowers before Lenin's bust.

As God is my witness I can see no progress. Every school year must now begin with a prayer of thanksgiving for the children's happiness. Prayers are offered up for Russia and Russian success, and happiness in personal life. The former pioneer leaders make obeisance before an icon.

And he went on to criticise the excessive prominence given to religion in many spheres of public life, arguing that this process was not only contrary to true pluralism, but also to the interests of Orthodoxy which saw itself being transformed from religion into ideology.[56]

---

[53] See *Nevskoe vremya* 1 Jan. 1992; *Russkaya mysl'* 17 Apr. 1992; I have a copy of the new department's statute.

[54] This decree of the Presidium of the Supreme Soviet was issued on 23 Nov. 1992, but not published. A copy is in my possession.   [55] *Nezavisimaya gazeta* 4 Feb. 1993.

[56] *Ogonyok* 6, 1992, pp. 8–9.

From the late 1980s religious leaders had indeed been far more visible, attending public functions alongside political leaders, being elected to the new parliamentary bodies, and even helping to legitimate newly elected politicans. In many of the republics and then successor states religious holidays were turned into national holidays, and democrats and nationalists alike were keen to be seen participating in major religious festivals. And during the last days of the USSR there was increasing criticism of the favoured treatment accorded to the Russian Orthodox Church with Muslim leaders expressing particular concern.[57]

Yet as the Soviet Union fell apart it was not only in Russia that there emerged evidence of the authorities being prepared to favour particular churches, as in Ukraine, or to grant religious groups special privileges. Uzbekistan, for example, has proved willing to ban proselytism,[58] and accept Islam as a *de facto* state religion whilst ensuring that it remains firmly under state control by appointing all leading religious officials. In some republics clerics were drawn into political life, as deputies and members of political parties, and in Georgia President Gamsakhurdia appointed a priest as prefect of the Axalcixe region – a typically provocative move as this was a predominantly Muslim area.[59] In Moldova, the government minister responsible for religious affairs openly supported granting the Orthodox Church a special status as the national church, proudly pointing out that within Europe only his country and Greece had prohibited religious proselytism.[60] And in July 1993 the traditionally Buddhist republic of Kalmykia formally proclaimed Buddhism and Christianity state religions.[61]

During the early 1990s a growing number of writers attacked what they perceived as the 'clericalisation' of Russian life,[62] though the leadership of the church denied that it either possessed or sought such a role. Patriarch Aleksii suggested that there could be no return to the pre-revolutionary position: 'The time of "ruling" or state religions has gone. The symphony of church and state cannot be restored: both state and society have moved too far from a religious basis. Principles other than theocratic lie at the foundations of a contemporary democratic multi-national state.'[63]

This did not, however, preclude attempts on the part of the church to

[57] *Pravda* 3 Dec. 1991.   [58] *Nezavisimaya gazeta* 2 Dec. 1992.
[59] *Moscow News* 2 June 1991; S. F. Jones, 'Georgia – A Failed Democratic Transition', in I. Bremmer & R. Taras, ed., *Nations and Politics in the Soviet Successor States* (Cambridge, 1993), p. 304.   [60] *Russkaya mysl'* 13 Nov. 1992.
[61] *Osteuropaiches Christentum* 30 July 1993, p. 50.
[62] *Nezavisimaya gazeta* 28 Jan. 1993.
[63] *Nedelya* 2, 1992, see similar positions developed by the Patriarch in interviews with *Glasnost'* 18–24 June 1992 & *Rossiskie vesti* 19 June 1992.

utilise its close relations with the Russian authorities to its own ends, as happened in early 1992 when the Patriarch persuaded Ruslan Khasbulatov to bring to an end parliamentary investigations into KGB links with the church,[64] or at the end of the same year when he reportedly asked the Russian parliament to ban the activities of non-Orthodox missionaries on Russian territory.[65] Moreover, many within the Russian Orthodox Church felt it perfectly legitimate to seek a greater role in society and one which placed limits on the social and cultural pluralism developing in the 1990s. Fr Mikhail Ardov attacked the press's obsession with sexuality, prostitution and crime and called for the introduction of 'a moral and wise censorship', as opposed to a totalitarian one, to curb pornography.[66] Moreover, one survey carried out in 1989–91 revealed that the majority of those polled believed that only those who believed in God should be given state posts, whilst 15 per cent believed that Orthodox believers should be given advantages within the new Russia.[67]

In the Russian federation the question of Orthodoxy's response to the new pluralism was clearly tied in with its efforts, real or imagined, to acquire once more the status of established or dominant religion. Freedom of conscience created space for religious groups to compete for influence, and the Moscow Patriarchate increasingly felt ill at ease in this new situation. Initial concern focused on relations with the Vatican after Rome's decision in 1991 to create administrative structures for Roman Catholics in the USSR, in particular the establishment of two dioceses in Byelorussia and the appointment of apostolic administrators for Moscow, Novosibirsk and Karaganda. According to the Vatican the Kremlin had been informed of these changes, though permission had not been sought. CRA deputy chairman M. Ivolgin, however, refused to recognise the authority of the Moscow appointee Archbishop Tadeusz Kondrusiewicz on the grounds that Moscow had not been consulted.[68]

The response of the Russian Orthodox Church was to charge that this was part of a wider Catholic plan aimed at the conversion of Russia, though in June 1992 the Vatican's Pontifical Commission for Russia issued an instruction to Catholics in the CIS to observe 'their ecumenical responsibilities' in the region so as to avoid suspicion of proselytism.[69] This did not, however, satisfy the Orthodox who felt that they were a church embattled, and were increasingly fearful of losing parishes to a variety of other denominations. The waters were muddied further by

[64] *Moscow News* 9 Feb. 1992.   [65] *The Tablet* 23 Jan. 1993, p. 96.
[66] *Nezavisimaya gazeta* 25 Apr. 1992.   [67] *Moskovskie novosti* 11 Aug. 1991.
[68] *KNS 377*, 13 June 1991, pp. 7–8.
[69] *Nezavisimaya gazeta* 4 Aug. 1992; the English text of this document can be found in *Catholic International* 15–31 Oct. 1992, pp. 888–93.

Russian politicians of more 'patriotic' bent who used the issue as a means of attacking the Yel'tsin government and the liberal-dominated Ministry of Foreign Affairs for their dealings with the Vatican.[70]

The questions of religious pluralism came to a head yet again in the first half of 1993 as religious leaders, in particular those of the Russian Orthodox Church, expressed concern at the activities of foreign evangelists and missionaries in Russia. In April Patriarch Aleksii reportedly wrote to press and information minister Mikhail Poltoranin calling for some limitations on the production of religious material. One month later he called for a moratorium on religious propaganda.[71] Metropolitan Kirill pointed to the unregulated nature of the religious market place and the fact the Russia permitted foreigners unrestricted opportunities that would not be available in many European democracies.[72] In June some of these concerns were taken up by presidential adviser Sergei Stankevich who noted that various former Soviet republics had in fact banned proselytism and suggested that there was a need to ban religious groups which enjoyed advantages as a result of their 'full purses' or which were totalitarian in nature. He did, however, make explicit his belief that amongst those religious groups traditional to Russia should be included Catholics, Baptists, Muslims and Jews, as well as the Orthodox.[73]

On 14 July 1993 the Russian parliament passed amendments to the law on freedom of conscience, one of which proposed the banning of foreign religious organisations unless they were invited by domestic religious communities and accredited with the state authorities. Supporting the amended law were the parliamentary commission on freedom of commission (all of whose members with the exception of Fr Gleb Yakunin having voted in favour), mufti Talgat Tadzhuddin, and Patriarch Aleksii who, on the morning of the debate, wrote to speaker Ruslan Khasbulatov stressing the Orthodox Church's support for religious liberty but arguing that choice 'must not be imposed from outside'. Catholic and Protestant spokespersons were less happy. One agreed that the activities of foreign organisations gave cause for concern but felt that 'the state police truncheon' was not the best way of dealing with this.[74] Many felt that the amended law in effect served to privilege the Orthodox.[75] Yuri Rozenbaum, head of the consultative council which many feared might pose a new threat to religious freedom, also opposed the law, arguing that it contradicted various international conventions to which Russia was party and that it was reminiscent of the state's struggle with heresy in the Middle Ages. He also noted that accreditation of

[70] *Glasnost'* 26 Mar. 1992.   [71] *Moskovskie novosti* 4 July 1993.
[72] *Nezavisimaya gazeta* 5 June 1993.   [73] *Nezavisimaya gazeta* 17 June 1993.
[74] *BBC SWB/1745 B/1* (July 1993).   [75] *Moskovskie novosti* 25 July 1993.

religious bodies was to be 'in accord with the interests of the state and social harmony' and wondered how this was to be understood.[76]

Extensive criticisms of the law delayed implementation, for President Yel'tsin sent it back to parliament for reconsideration on the grounds that in several respects it was poorly drafted and possibly incompatible with international agreements. Parliament in turn noted the president's lament about the poor spiritual state of Russia but used it to defend their original intentions, and accepted a revised law which retained the prohibition on the activities of foreign missionaries (Article 21). Simultaneously, the law appeared to give certain advantages – such as free air time – to 'the traditional confessions of the Russian federation' (Article 8). Catholic and Protestant critics persisted in their critique of the potentially discriminatory nature of this law which failed properly to define which were 'indigenous' religions.[77] Ignoring these objections the parliament proceeded to pass the amended law whilst beseiged by Yel'tsin's forces in late September but, passed after the Supreme Soviet's dissolution, the law effectively fell with the defeated parliamentarians.

Though the Russian Orthodox Church denied any aspirations to restore its pre-revolutionary position as a state church, it was clear by mid-1993 that in certain respects it had acquired a privileged position. Its leaders enjoyed an access to the political elite not shared by other religious groups, although there is little evidence that its influence extended beyond the religious sphere. More importantly, in mid-1993 its desire to limit the activities of foreign religious groups brought it into the political arena where it found itself in alliance with the anti-Western inclinations of many within the Russian elite. In the light of subsequent events, and despite the church's attempt at mediation in early October, its previous appeal to such forces may have undermined its credibility, especially when it appeared that the mediation effort initiated by the church served as a cover for some opponents of Yel'tsin to organise more forceful measures of political struggle. Yet whilst this may have served to reinforce the Russian Orthodox Church's wariness of political factions, it is unlikely to stop it utilising its centuries long association with the Russian state to its own advantage in the long term.

Religion and politics in a new era

From the time of the revolution clerics explicitly and religious activists implictly had been banned from the political arena by the effective legal limitation of religious activity to worship in the few registered churches,

---

[76] *Nezavisimaya gazeta* 23 July 1993.
[77] A letter dating 30 Aug. 1993 from leaders of the evangelical denominations.

mosques or synagogues. This situation was to change radically under Mikhail Gorbachev and after. As part of the democratisation process a new draft electoral law published in October 1988 permitted the nomination of religious activists as candidates for election to the new quasi-parliamentary bodies then being constructed.[78] Though religious bodies were to remain on the fringes of public life, over the next four years representatives of the various religions, in particular the Russian Orthodox Church, were to become much more visible within the political arena.

During the first elections to the Congress of People's Deputies a number of religious activists were nominated by social organisation or elected to the new parliamentary body, although at this stage most were chosen from existing religious elites. One year later elections to republican parliaments and local soviets produced a wider spread of religious candidates with some 192 Orthodox, 55 Muslim and 10 Lutheran clerics elected.[79] Whilst Mikhail Gorbachev may have seen this opening up of the public arena to religious institutions in terms of building supports within society, whether through church backing for perestroika, the calming of ethnic tensions, or the provision of additional personnel for an ailing welfare system, it soon became clear that religion could also be used to promote ends at variance with Gorbachevian notions of reform.

In republics such as Lithuania, Latvia and Tajikistan campaigns for religious freedom were often closely linked to emerging nationalist movements. In Ukraine the renewed campaign for the legalisation of the Ukrainian Catholic Church provided a major starting point for the emergence of nationalist activity in that most pivotal of republics. And this church, along with the Ukrainian Autocephalous Orthodox Church, was to call quite explicit for its flock to vote for Ukrainian sovereignty in the March 1991 referendum – and in the three western regions of the republic over 85 per cent did so.[80]

Democratic opponents of Gorbachev also looked to the religious constituency for support. Standing for election to the Russian parliament in the spring of 1990 Boris Yel'tsin included greater rights for religious bodies in his election programme.[81] Increasingly opposition politicians sought to demonstrate their respect for religion, holding frequent meetings with religious leaders and appearing at key religious festivals,

---

[78] *Izvestiya* 23 Oct. 1988.   [79] *Nauka i religiya* 6, 1991, p. 3.
[80] Cf. R. Solchanyk, 'Ukraine, Belorussia and Moldavia – Imperial Integration, Russification and the Struggle for National Survival', in L. Hajda & M. Beissinger, eds., *The Nationalities Factor in Soviet Politics and Society* (Harvard, 1990), pp. 175–203; *KNS 372*, 4 Apr. 1991, pp. 3–4.   [81] *Sovetskii molodezh* 6 Feb. 1990.

(i.e. Russian Orthodox celebrations). In June 1990 Yel'tsin was one of the first to pay his respects to the newly elected Patriarch Aleksii II, travelling to Leningrad on 17 June for the reconsecration of St Isaac's Cathedral. Interviewed about the event, the Russian president noted that it was 'a tribute to what is being done for the morality and purification of the people ... the state should work side by side with the church for the sake of spiritual values'.[82] This overt attempt to identify with religion was criticised by some church spokesmen. Archpriest Sorokin, rector of the Leningrad Theological Academy saw the Russian president's attendance at a televised Easter service in 1991 as an attempt to gain the votes of believers in the forthcoming presidential elections. He went on, 'I'm not against Yel'tsin. I just think he is typical of the two facedness in our society.' Noting that Yel'tsin failed to cross himself throughout the service, Sorokin said he preferred Gorbachev's position – not going to church because he was a communist.[83]

At the time of the collapse of the Soviet Union, then, religion and politics were beginning to interact and, whilst politicians of all hues sought to use religion for their own ends, some religious activists were developing a wider vision. In particular, a small minority set about developing religious based political parties or attempted to link religious values to specific political programmes.

Islam and politics: the Islamic renaissance party in Tajikistan

After the collapse of the Soviet Union the possible rise of 'fundamentalism' in the former Muslim republics became a topic of considerable concern amongst journalists and security specialists. This in part reflected the general ignorance of the region, an often simplistic understanding of recent developments in the Muslim world, and the desire to find a new bogey to replace communism. But it also had its roots in academic writings on Central Asia, where a debate had raged from the late 1970s as to whether or not there was an 'Islamic threat' to the Soviet Union.[84]

By the late 1980s the possibility of Islamic political activity had been increased by the general reform process. Islamic identities may have been weakened by Soviet rule but remained in place, often strengthened by

---

[82] *KNS 353*, 28 June 1990, pp. 3–4.   [83] *KNS 375*, 16 May 1991, pp. 7–8.
[84] A. Bennigsen & M. Broxup *The Islamic Threat to the Soviet State* (London, 1983); A. McAuley, 'Nation and Nationalism in Central Asia', in C. Keeble, ed., *The Soviet State – The Domestic Roots of Soviet Foreign Policy* (London, 1985), pp. 42–56; A. Taheri, *Crescent in a Red Sky – The Future of Islam in the Soviet Union* (London, 1989).

almost universal observance of Muslim rites of passage. They were given further scope by the rediscovery of the past taking place even before Gorbachev came to power. And from 1989, when the liberalisation of religious policy began to have an impact on Central Asia and other 'Muslim' areas, some religious activists began to organise movements and parties aiming to strengthen Islamic influence on the daily life of the region. On occasions this took the form of attempts to 'purify' the existing Islamic establishment, as in the attempts to replace religious leaderships in Central Asia, the North Caucasus and in Russia. Religion also enjoyed a higher profile in public life from 1990 as political elites in Central Asia took great pains to show respect for religion, whether through turning key feast days into public holidays, being seen with Islamic leaders, or permitting their appearance in the media. Yet simultaneously they made it plain that this was a religion to be used for the good of the state, something evident in the backing they often gave to official religious leaderships under pressure from reformers.

During 1989–90 various unofficial Islamic organisations emerged, of which the most significant in political terms was the Islamic Renaissance Party (IRP). In early June 1990 some 200 Muslims from various parts of the USSR met in Astrakhan to set up the IRP. The gathering selected a council of *ulema* (scholars, theologians) to lead the organisation, and proclaimed their commitment to revitalising Islamic life within the USSR. In particular they advocated religious freedom for all, reform by peaceful means, a restructuring of the economy taking greater account of the environment, and the public recognition of what they saw as womens' primary role of homebuilding and child rearing.[85] More significant in the light of later events was the establishment of a Tajik branch of the IRP at a conference held in October 1990 just outside Dushanbe.

By early 1991 the IRP claimed 30,000 members in three regional organisations – for Central Asia (dominated by Tajiks), for the Caucasus (dominated by the inhabitants of the north Caucasus) and for European Russia and Siberia (mainly Tatar).[86] None had been able to register as political parties at this stage, though the organising committee had been registered in Moscow. Sensitive to the bad press that Islam had received, one of the IRP's Tajik leaders Davlat Usman rejected the perceived linkage of Islam to aggression, and stressed the IRP's aims as primarily

---

[85] M. Atkin, 'Islamic Assertiveness and the Waning of the Old Order', *Nationalities Papers*, vol. 20, no. 1, Spring 1992, pp. 63–4; in an interview with BBC television in the summer of 1992 the chairman of the Tajik branch of the IRP Mohammed Sharif Himmat Zoda spoke of providing women with work suitable to the dignity and sanctity of motherhood, and suggested that they might start by covering their heads.

[86] *Postfactum* 6, 1991, special issue on Islamic question.

concerned with the regeneration of faith after seventy years of anti-religious attacks.[87] A similar line was taken by Valiakhmed Sadur, formerly a researcher at the CPSU's Institute of Scientific Atheism and now Moscow press spokesman for the IRP. He described the party's concern as the revitalisation of Islam and the protection of the interests of Soviet Muslims, something the official clergy had conspicuously failed to do. He denied any intent to create separate Muslim states, and argued that the IRP was firmly committed to pursuing change through constitutional and peaceful means. Pushed on the question of women's rights, he argued that whilst the role of women was primarily located in the home, there was nothing in Islam to prevent them taking advantage of educational opportunities.[88]

Yet within the IRP there were those who took a more radical stance. A report appearing in *Nezavisimaya gazeta* in May of that year noticed that some IRP activists, headed by G. Dzhemal, were pushing for the creation of Islamic republics in Central Asia and the Caucasus, and that these were willing to exacerbate religious and ethnic conflicts in order to pursue their aims – though little evidence was provided for the latter claim.[89] Amongst the by-products of this approach were the development of links with the Russian 'patriots'. Islamic activism received increasingly favourable coverage in conservative papers such as *Den'* and *Glasnost'*, and on issues such as Russia's response to the Gulf War both sides adopted a critical attitude towards the Western allies.[90] Asked about this connection in May 1992 Valiakhmed Sadur pointed out that Islamicists and patriots alike shared a rejection of a slavish following of the Western path of development.[91]

Regardless of debates within the IRP, their attempts at making political progress were persistently obstructed by the unreformed political leaderships of Central Asia. In Tajikistan, where they were strongest, the government refused to grant them registration, claiming that the IRP was an unconstitutional party likely to stir up inter-ethnic conflict. They also met with initial hostility from the official Islamic establishment. In Tajikistan *kazi* Abkhar Toradzhon advised his clergy to maintain strict political neutrality and concentrate their efforts on the moral and spiritual improvement of the people.[92] Other Central Asian

---

[87] *Komsomolets Tadzhikistana* 21 Nov. 1990.

[88] *Izvestiya* 8 Jan. 1991; some of the ideas agitating the IRP can be found in their paper *Al'-Vakhdat* (Unity) published in a Russian edition from January 1991.

[89] *Nezavisimaya gazeta* 8 May 1992.

[90] See the interview with Moscow imam Sheikh Ravilem Gainutdinov in *Glasnost'* 8, 1992.

[91] *Nezavisimaya gazeta* 21 May 1992. See Dzhemal's article on Eurasia in *Den'* 20–26 Sept. 1992.   [92] *KNS 362*, 8 Nov. 1990, pp. 6–7.

leaders took a similar line,[93] though this began to change in 1992. In Uzbekistan Muhammed Yusuf spoke in 1992 of trying to restore Sharia law in the newly independent state and of bringing the general level of Uzbek religiosity up to the standard of that prevailing in the Fergana valley – a traditional centre of Uzbek religious enthusiasm and a part of Uzbekistan increasingly run by militant Islamic forces.[94]

In Tajikistan *kazi* Abkhar Toradzhon, a member of the republican parliament, became ever more outspoken in defence of Muslim rights, arguing for the public observance of religious holidays and the switching of the day of rest to Friday.[95] By the end of that year he had turned down an opportunity to stand in the Tajik presidential elections, but was beginning to work more closely with the Islamic and democratic opposition to President Nabiev. Though the IRP was not allowed to field a candidate in the presidential elections of November 1991, the democratic candidate supported by the party received some 34 per cent of the vote in a region where most leaders continued to receive near unanimous support in largely symbolic elections. From this position the opposition to President Nabiev felt able to make increasing demands for change and true representation, and in March–April 1992 staged massive demonstrations in Dushanbe and other cities. Counter demonstrations by government supporters increased the tension, and in early May lives were lost as government troops fired on demonstrators. In the ensuing days Nabiev was forced to flee the capital and then agree to a coalition government in which the opposition held a third of the posts and IRP deputy leader Davlat Usman was appointed a deputy premier.[96] By this stage IRP leaders and the official clergy led by Toradzhon were working together to try to reduce tension and restore orderly government capable of dealing with the serious economic difficulties facing this poorest of former Soviet republics. But by the end of the summer tensions within the newly independent state had led to the forced resignation of Nabiev, followed by deterioration into civil war.

Many of the tensions emerging in Tajikistan in 1992 stemmed as much from regional and clan differences as from ideological divides, though

---

[93] For example, Central Asian mufti Mohammed Yusuf told a central newpaper that Muslims did not need parties, for: 'Islam itself is a political party of 14 centuries standing with the Koran as its rules and the Sunnah as its programme. But then our faith is above political parties' (*Komosomol'skaya pravda* 8 Dec. 1990). And even in late 1991 Kazakh kazi Ratbek Nisanbaev could be found suggesting, perhaps with good reason, that a pan-Islamic or pan-Turkic party could only cause harm in his multi-ethnic republic (*Izvestiya* 13 Nov. 1991).

[94] Interviewed by the BBC in the spring of 1992.

[95] *Komsomol'skaya pravda* 23 Mar. 1991.

[96] B. Brown, 'Whither Tajikistan?', *RFE/RL Report on the USSR* 12 June 1992.

Tajikistan

here I can provide little more than the briefest of summaries.[97] For most of the Soviet period the republic had been dominated by the political elites of the economically dominant Leninabad region in the north of the country (see map). Under perestroika the new possibilities for political organisation had stimulated the creation of a series of political movements, including the IRP, often based upon the hitherto politically underrepresented parts of the country such as the Kurgan-Tyube region and the Gorno-Badakhshan Autonomous region. But when these groups sought to participate in the political order in 1992 and then ousted President Nabiev, the Leninabad elites formed a coalition with groups in the Kulyab region.[98] By the end of 1992 the Leninabad–Kulyab alliance of old communists and quasi-criminal warlords had, with some support from Uzbekistan and local Russian forces, retaken Dushanbe and were busy seeking to 'restore order', albeit by means of retribution rather than attempts at national reconciliation.[99] Their task was made easier by the fact that the new regime and its external backers could defend their harsh

[97] See the discussion in *Nezavisimaya gazeta* 3 Mar. 1993.
[98] It is interesting to note that despite including the Tajik part of the Fergana valley, a traditional centre of Islamic activism, the Leninabad region had been largely untouched by the efforts of the IRP.
[99] *Le Monde* 2 Feb. 1993 includes an account of the brutalities associated with this restoration of order based upon revenge and the settling of old scores.

measures in terms of preventing the spread of 'fundamentalism'. Ironically propaganda of this sort alongside harsh repressive measures directed against anyone linked to the opposition or even from the wrong region of the republic created tens of thousands of refugees, the majority of them fleeing to Afghanistan where they linked up with the mujihaddin and where their commitment to radical forms of Islam was only strengthened. And by mid-1993 the resurgence of the opposition which launched attacks into Tajikistan was drawing Russia back into a regional conflict of a type it had hoped not to see again.

Even this cursory treatment of the Tajik issue illustrates some of the problems raised by attempts to separate out the role of religion in contemporary Central Asian politics, and points to the cross-cutting cleavages that affect many of the newly independent states – ethnic, regional, tribal, religious and political – as well as pointing to some of the international aspects of these tensions. And even when speaking of the role of Islam in Central Asia there is no one Islam to which one can point. In Tajikistan, for example, the predominantly Sunni Muslims of the IRP were joined, to some degree, by the Ismaili's (a Shiite sect) of the Gorno-Badakhshan region in a struggle against the warlords in the southern Kulyab region who could produce their own mullahs to support their campaign against 'fundamentalism'.[100] After the defeat of the Islamic-democratic opposition the latter were quick to ensure the 'election' of a new, more compliant mufti for Tajikistan who promised to keep religion out of politics and to support the new government.[101]

Orthodoxy and politics in Russia

In various interviews given from late 1990 onwards Russian Orthodox Patriarch Aleksii II developed a cautious approach to political life, one consistent with both his training as a Soviet priest and the tenor of Orthodox social teaching. Repeatedly he stressed the need for responsible politics, in which democracy was not understood as the right to make any demand, and in which pluralism operated within certain limits.[102] In an interview published towards the end of 1990 he seemed to support Mikhail Gorbachev's shift 'to the right', yet simultaneously appeared to accept that the Soviet Union might not be there for ever – 'there is no social structure, no state and no nation which could have been created by

---

[100] The imam of Khasib mosque in Kulyab, Gaidar Sarifzoda, suggested that the *kazi's* prime aim was power and that he was not even a proper Muslim, being of the Wahhabite sect. For Sarifzoda it was clear that Abkhar Toradzhon aimed at creating an Islamic republic on Iranian lines, something he felt inappropriate in Tajik conditions. *Nezavisimaya gazeta* 5 June 1992.   [101] *Moskovskie novosti* 21 Feb. 1993.

[102] *Pravda* 17 July 1990.

God for eternity'.[103] He amplified this position further after the March 1991 referendum by suggesting that whilst he remained committed to support the forces working for union, this did not necessarily entail simply a revised USSR.[104]

This tendency to caution was clear at the time of the August 1991 coup attempt. According to some reports certain members of the Orthodox synod welcomed the coup and resisted Patriarch Aleksii's attempt to denounce it. The Patriarch later denied this account but it was only on 21 August, when the plotters were fleeing, that he publicly attacked those involved in organising the events of that month.[105] Non-conformist Orthodox clerics were far more forthright during this period, with deputies such as Frs Gleb Yakunin and Vyacheslav Polosin, chairman of the Russian parliament's committee on freedom of conscience, making clear their solidarity with the defenders of the Russian parliament.

In the months following the coup the Orthodox Church maintained its public commitment to a renegotiated union,[106] though hierarchs also cultivated their links with representatives of the new order. Over the following year the Patriarch sought to establish close personal ties with Boris Yel'tsin, to this end following the time-honoured tradition of steering clear of political parties, movements or programmes, whilst issuing generalised appeals to the population to work conscientiously for the good of the nation. Often such statements suited the state in stressing 'responsible action' by politicians in easing tensions between the newly independent states.[107] In July 1992, for example, the Patriarch issued an appeal to Orthodox Christians in Moldova describing all sides as in some sense guilty for the conflicts in the region, and calling upon military units to avoid shedding blood if at all possible.[108] But in general the church sought to avoid adopting explicit positions on the issues of the time and during the Russian constitutional crisis of early 1993 studiously avoided taking sides, though on the eve of the bloody siege of the White House building in early October 1993 it did seek to find a way out of the crisis, by offering its services as mediator between parliament and president.[109]

---

[103] *Izvestiya* 30 Dec. 1990; in a comment on the killing of Lithuanian demonstrators in early 1991 the Patriarch coupled a call for moderation from all involved with a condemnation of the use of military force 'as a major political mistake. In church language, a sin.' *Izvestiya* 15 Jan. 1991.

[104] *Komsomol'skaya pravda* 6 Apr. 1991.

[105] See O. Antic, 'Church Reaction to the Coup', *RFE/RL Report on the USSR* 20 Sept. 1991, pp. 15–17.

[106] See Aleksii's speech to the Extraordinary Congress of People's Deputies of the USSR on 2 Sept., reported in *Khristianskie novosti* 41, 8 Sept. 1991, pp. 11–14.

[107] An appeal issued by the bishops' council meeting in Apr. 1992, published in *Russkaya mysl'* 17 Apr. 1992.   [108] *Nezavisimaya gazeta* 9 July 1992.

[109] *Izvestiya* 16 Apr. 1993.

In entering the political arena, however cautiously, the Russian Orthodox Church was acting within the context of pluralistic society in which it was but a single voice amongst many. It may have possessed a large constituency, and one hotly pursued by politicians in need of votes, but it was by no means clear that the church could shape the political views and behaviour of believers. Though the political views of Russian believers were far from monolithic, various surveys carried out in 1991 suggested that on the whole they inclined to conservative positions on many issues. A survey of some 2,000 Russians living in the Russian Federation, carried out during September 1991, reported that of those interviewed some 41 per cent considered themselves believers (95 per cent Orthodox) , and on almost all political issues they expressed more conservative opinions than non-believers. The majority of the believers were rural dwellers with low levels of education, although the survey included a 'metropolitan minority' of Muscovites. Believers were more likely to stress law and order than non-believers, for example favouring as authority figures Nicholas II and Stalin; they were generally less tolerant than non-believers, being more prepared to ban certain books or isolate AIDS patients; they were less likely to accept the need for multi-party politics and more sceptical of economic reform proposals; and they were more likely to support forces at either end of the political spectrum (communist or nationalist). On only two issues were believers more 'liberal' than non-believers, in relation to the question of whether they agreed with the statements that the environment was a matter of pressing concern and that women were still oppressed. And on all issues the metropolitan minority of largely well-educated women were more liberal than the main body of religious adherents.[110] Such results pointed to the innate conservatism of the average Orthodox believer and suggested that even if religious leaders were to evolve a greater commitment to liberal political options they might not be able to take their flock with them.

Whilst religious leaderships sought to steer clear of overt political commitment, there were those within their communities who felt that religion did point in a particular political direction and hoped that religious bodies would back their attempts to give such aspirations

---

[110] This summary is based entirely upon M. Rhodes, 'Religious Believers in Russia', *RFE/RL Research Report* 3 Apr. 1992, pp. 60–4. Studies carried out over the last three years by Sergei Filatov at the Institute of USA and Canada reveal similar results, whilst also revealing that amongst many self-designated believers there was a remarkably vague knowledge of religious doctrines and teachings. I am grateful to him for showing me some of the results of his work. Some of this can be found in S. B. Filatov & D. F. Furman, 'Religiya i politika v massovom soznanii', in *Sotsiologicheskie issledovanie* 7, 1992, pp. 3–12.

institutional form. Amongst such groups might be included the various Christian Democratic groupings and some Russian nationalists.

Within the Russian republic the formation of Christian Democratic groupings from 1989 represented the first attempt at developing a specifically religious approach to political life.[111] The first to appear was the Christian Democratic Union of Russia (CDUR) created in August 1989 by a group of Orthodox activists associated with the former political prisoner Aleksander Ogorodnikov. At a conference that month a general statement was issued committing the organisation to work on the basis of the moral and philosophical principles laid down in the gospel.[112] Subject to various splits during the winter of 1989–90, the CDUR saw only a handful of its members elected onto local councils in the spring 1990 elections, and by mid-1990 it had perhaps 300 members. From that point onwards the Christian Democrats were more prominently engaged in educational and charitable work than in the mainstream of Russian politics.

In April 1990, just as the CDUR was undergoing its first splits, three newly elected deputies to the Russian parliament – Viktor Aksyuchits, Fr Vyacheslav Polosin and Fr Gleb Yakunin – initiated the Russian Christian Democratic Movement (RCDM). At the opening conference co-chairman Gleb Anishchenko spoke of politics as another form of charity and of the chief aim of the RCDM as 'an attempt to create a political bastion against the forces of evil'.[113] Over the following months the RCDM sought to build up organisations throughout the Russian republic, and by late 1990 was claiming branches in 96 towns, and over 16,000 members. With six deputies in the Russian parliament, the chairmanship of that body's Committee on Freedom of Conscience and Charitable Activity, and representation on a number of town soviets, the RCDM appeared to be putting down roots within the new political structures. More importantly, it participated in the 'Democratic Russia' movement which sought to unite all democratic forces in the electoral campaigns of 1990 and coordinated the struggle against CPSU dominance of political life.

The programme of the RCDM quite explicitly aimed at a Christian

---

[111] I have provided a much fuller discussion of the emergence of the Christian Democrats in an unpublished conference paper (revised in March 1992) entitled 'Christian Democracy on the Orthodox Fringe – the Case of Russia'. See also R. Sakwa, 'Christian Democracy in Russia', *Religion, State and Society*, vol. 20, no. 2, 1992, pp. 135–200.

[112] On the founding of the CDUR see *KNS 333* (7 Sept. 1989), p. 11; the programmatic statement can be found in *Vestnik khristianskoi demokratii* 10 May 1990, p. 1.

[113] *Vestnik khristianskogo informatsionnogo tsentra, 29 (87),* 10 Apr. 1990, contains a lengthy report on the first congress and summarises the main speeches.

revitalisation of Russian politics. Rejecting communism as an alien flower upon Russian soil it attacked the Bolshevik attempt to build heaven upon earth and the destruction of the spiritual dimension of human existence. The only way out of the crisis was a Christian one, involving a religious and moral rebirth based upon repentance for past sins. In this situation Christian politics was less about the promotion of particular structures than 'the confirming and strengthening in society of the ideal of freedom and creative responsibility which was Christ's gift to man'.[114] In practical terms this meant re-establishing the public (but not supremacist) role of religion, for example through the celebration of religious holidays or the freedom to develop religious education in schools.

The programme of the RCDM[115] included a commitment to a 'social market economy' based upon 'private property and Christian justice', though in practice they were to split over the question of marketisation in late 1991. On the question of political structures the Christian Democrats were more ambiguous, stressing their commitment to democratic forms on the one hand, but suggesting that this was a transitional phase. They believed that a National Council was necessary to find the form of government most appropriate to Russian traditions and 'to restore the continuity of legislative ruling power which was interrupted by the revolution'. This ambiguity was also apparent in their treatment of the national question, where a professed commitment to the right to self-determination, was counterbalanced by the suggestion that in a democratic state there might be less need to secede given that communism was at the heart of national discord.[116]

Many of these ambiguities and the presence of conflicting trends were reflected in the speeches at the opening conference of the RCDM in April 1990. Fr Gleb Yakunin, for example, argued that whilst a 'slavophile' in spiritual terms, he was suspicious of the 'social-patriotic' movements with their chauvinistic and anti-semitic tendencies. Moreover, he went on to say that in political and economic terms he was a 'westerner', supporting the necessary introduction of a market economy and arguing that democracy was perhaps the secular form of government most compatible with Christian values in that it recognised human frailty and sought to create a plurality of power centres. At the other end of the scale

---

[114] *Rossiiskoe khristianskoe demokraticheskoe dvizhenie – sbornik materialov* (Moscow, 1990).

[115] See Anderson, 'Christian Democracy on the Orthodox Fringe'; Sakwa, 'Christian Democracy in Russia'.

[116] *Khristianskaya demokratiya 13*, 1991, p. 26. This is an English language translation of CD documents produced by the Christian Democratic International in Belgium.

Vladimir Karpets told the conference that at this stage the RCDM should not commit itself irrevocably to a democratic orientation, for monarchy still enjoyed some support in society.[117]

These tensions came to a head at the time of the coup and in the following months as the democratic camp split into 'liberal' and 'conservative' factions. In April the movement had gone into alliance with the Russian Democratic Party and the Constitutional Democrats to form a conservative 'People's Concord Bloc'. Not all CDs supported this move to the 'right' and only days before the coup Fr Gleb Yakunin and others resigned from the RCDM, later joining forces with various regional groups to form a Russian Christian Democratic Union (RCDU). This latter group maintained its links with 'Democratic Russia' when the RCDM walked out of that bloc in November 1991. Since then the main body of the Christian Democrats associated with Aksyuchits has participated in various groupings on the 'patriotic' side of Russian politics, being instrumental, for example, in the calling of a conference of Civic and Patriotic Forces in February 1992. By mid-1992 the RCDM was in clear opposition to the Russian government and within the Russian parliament was in alliance with a variety of 'patriotic' forces, from Russian nationalists to hardline communists, all united by their commitment to what Aksyuchits considered the chief political task of the present moment – the 'restoration and strengthening of Russian state-hood'.[118]

Though explicitly committed to Christian politics, the relationship between the RCDM and religious organisations in Russia was far from clear. Certainly, if we were looking for a 'natural' constituency of support for the CDs we would probably start by looking in the direction of the millions of citizens who identify themselves to some degree with the Russian Orthodox Church. If this group could be harnessed to the cause the CDs would undoubtedly become a major actor in Russian politics. But acquiring the support of this group is problematic, even though the polls quoted earlier suggested that believers were more likely to incline to the 'patriotic' camp than any other. This 'natural' link might be strengthened were the Russian Orthodox hierarchy explicitly to endorse the CDs. On many issues the natural inclinations of a patriotic and cautious hierarchy and the conservatism of many believers are consonant with many of the programmatic statements of the RCDM. And in the past the church hierarchy and the Christian Democrats have collaborated, for example in the passage through parliament of various

---

[117] *Vestnik khristianskogo informatsionnogo tsentra* 29.
[118] Cf. *Nezavisimaya gazeta* 23 June 1992 & 30 July 1993; *Moskovskie novosti* 16 Aug. 1992.

pieces of legislation affecting religious groups. Yet in practice – and despite conversations between the church and the various Christian Democratic groupings[119] – the Orthodox Church, and the Patriarch in particular, has sought to avoid endorsing any party, arguing that the church as an institution cannot identify with any group and that Christians should accept as normal political disagreements within their own ranks.[120]

The gradual shift of one of the Christian Democrat organisations towards a 'patriotic' stance draws attention to another aspect of political life with which the Russian Orthodox Church has had to deal. For centuries the church identified itself with Russian nationalism and the state, and in the post-war years it sought to make use of the connection in ensuring some degree of institutional survival. Under Brezhnev this approach coincided with a wider revival of Russian nationalism amongst the intelligentsia, whether in quasi-establishment literary form or dissent of a wide variety of forms. With the lifting of censorship and repression under Gorbachev the political expression of national identity became possible, and the late 1980s spawned a plethora of nationalist groups, including some of an extremely chauvinistic nature. Though some of the latter preferred Russia's pagan heritage, many looked to the Orthodox Church as a source of inspiration and support. Groups such as Pamyat' paraded the streets of major cities with crosses, icons and, more recently, with priests in attendance. These groups often saw themselves as the true representatives of the Russian tradition, yet their commitment was to an Orthodoxy of a certain kind, subordinate to the state and promoting a Russian nationalism which relied heavily upon negative feelings towards other national groups, in particular the Jews.

Simultaneously the church had to cope with those who viewed true Orthodoxy as innately linked to monarchy, and who suggested that democracy within the state and political disagreements amongst church members were abnormal phenomena, if not demonic.[121] Others were less convinced, with one historian addressing a letter to the leaders of the Russian Orthodox Church suggesting that perhaps canonisation of the tsar and his family as martyrs was inappropriate given that it was Nicholas II's own policies which played a major part in causing the tragedy of 1917.[122]

Many of these issues came together in 1992 as the church had to respond to the growth of nationalist sympathies, some of an extremely

---

[119] *Moskovskie novosti* 13 Dec. 1992.
[120] See the article by Fr Vsevolod Chaplin in *Moskovskie novosti* 31 May 1992.
[121] See the comments of Fr Aleksii Ostaev from Tver region, and the reply from Fr Chaplin in *Moskovskie novosti* 15 Nov. 1992.   [122] *Ogonyok* 42–3, 1992, p. 5.

chauvinistic nature. Typical of the controversies was that surrounding an address which Patriarch Aleksii II had given to a gathering of New York rabbis in November of the previous year. Here he had outspokenly condemned anti-semitism, not for the first time, and suggested that those Orthodox who expressed such feelings were doing so on a basis other than religious.[123] Sharp responses came from representatives of the Union of Orthodox Brotherhoods, charitable and educational bodies created with the Patriarch's blessing in 1990. By 1992 it was clear that many of these brotherhoods, dominated by that based at the Trinity St Sergius monastery at Sergiev Posad (Zagorsk), represented an extremely conservative trend within Orthodoxy. Interviewed in May 1992 the chairman of the brotherhoods Hieromonk Kirill denied that they were anti-semitic, but was critical of Aleksii's comments and asked how it was possible for believers to be happy when they saw the Jewish festival of hannukah being celebrated in the grounds of the Kremlin, a place sacred to the Orthodox.[124] A journalist reporting a conference of the brotherhoods in the summer of 1992 noted a banner over the meeting hall proclaiming 'cease the ritual murder of the Orthodox Serbs'. This same gathering discussed the canonisation of the tsar and his family as 'martyrs to the Jews' and of Andrei Olshinsky, whose alleged ritual murder by Jews had sparked the Beilis case in 1911.[125] Similar sentiments were expressed by leaders of the Orthodox brotherhoods in an open letter to the patriarch published in the conservative paper *Sovetskaya rossiya* in February 1993 which attacked his flirtation with 'the judaising heresy' and his willingness to allow the 'heretic baptists' to use a former Orthodox church for their services.[126]

Such tendencies were sharply rejected by the patriarch, some hierarchs and members of the laity,[127] but nationalist expressions of this type were not untypical amongst sections of the church. In 1993 the question of the Orthodox Church's relationship to extreme nationalism came to a head as a result of a series of articles published in the 'conservative' press by Metropolitan Ioann of Leningrad and Ladoga. Here this senior hierarch developed a critique of much that was happening in Russia and clearly expressed his sympathy with the anti-Western and anti-semitic inclinations of the 'patriotic' camp in Russian politics. In particular, basing himself on the forged 'Protocols of the Elders of Zion' he pointed to a conspiracy directed against Russia which brought together freemasons,

---

[123] *Moskovskie novosti* 26 Jan. 1992.   [124] *Nezavisimaya gazeta* 21 May 1992.
[125] *Nezavisimaya gazeta* 11 July 1992.   [126] *Sovetskaya Rossiya* 18 Feb. 1993.
[127] See the declaration condemning anti-semitism issued by a group of clergy and laity in *Nezavisimaya gazeta* 12 Aug. 1992, and Patriarch Aleksii's comments on the incompatibility of nationalism based upon hatred for others with true Christian patriotism. *Megapolis ekspress* 21 Oct. 1992.

Roman Catholics, the leading Western powers, Marxism and Zionism.[128] To combat the possible destruction of Russia he spelt out his own prescriptions for Russian state-building in the pages of *Sovetskaya rossiya* in May 1993. These included the rebuilding of the nation upon collective forms of life rooted in the Orthodox world-view, the re-establishment by the state of control over the economy, the evolution of strong and united leadership rather than the absurd notion of a 'separation of powers', a 'moral censorship' of the press which prevented the publication of materials damaging to the morals and the national interest of the country, and the restoration of Russia to its natural boundaries by persuading Ukraine and Belarus to join together again.[129]

Though such views were rejected by many within the church, including the patriarch who reportedly banned articles by the Metropolitan from the church press,[130] they had their supporters amongst the hierarchy and influential clerical politicians such as Fr Polosin, chairman of the Russian parliament's commission on freedom of conscience. Sections of the *emigré* church also expressed sympathy for extreme right-wing groups, a trend perhaps strengthened by their church's hostility towards ecumenism and towards the leader of the patriarchal church.[131] By mid-1993 it seemed that the church was as divided as the rest of society on the issue of where Russia was headed and how the current crisis could be resolved.

Conclusion

In the immediate post-Soviet period certain trends began to emerge. Firstly, none of the new states retained policies aimed at the emasculation of religious influences and institutions, though in some minority groups do not always enjoy the same freedoms as the 'national religions'. In most of the successor states religion enjoyed new rights in the public sphere, and it was not uncommon to find black robed priests and other clerics at public functions or even sitting in legislative bodies. Yet despite the fears of some it remained impossible to speak of a clericalisation of public life, or to provide evidence of an influence on political life comparable to that apparently demonstrated by the Catholic Church in Poland during the late 1980s and early 1990s. Moreover, those few

[128] Quoted in *Moskovskie novosti* 25 July 1993.
[129] *Sovetskaya Rossiya* 13 May 1993.   [130] *Sovetskaya Rossiya* 18 Feb. 1993.
[131] The Church-in-Exile's ambiguous position on these issues was evident in its handling of those of its clerics in Russia who associated with Pamyat', initially condemning them but later appearing to condone their activities. *Nezavisimaya gazeta* 8 Apr. 1992, 29 Oct. 1992, 5 Nov. 1992, & 20 May 1993; *Russkaya mysl'* 20 Nov. 1992; *Moskovskie novosti* 18 Apr. 1993.

political parties formed upon the basis of religious ideas have – with the possible and brief exception of the IRP in Tajikistan – exhibited few signs of becoming major political actors.

Secondly, the new states to varying degrees began to evolve a more open policy making process and one in which governments cannot simply determine centrally how to treat religion, but have to consult more widely and, at least in some of them, face potential criticism from elected politicians, the press and religious communities themselves. This has not prevented political elites from granting certain religious communities a *de facto* privileged position, but ensured that this remained open to question – Uzbekistan and other parts of Central Asia providing partial exceptions to this latter qualification.

Thirdly, religious communities themselves had to adapt to the radical changes brought about by political, cultural and religious pluralism. Not all were happy with the products of the new order, and some longed for the old certainties and the degree of social control over sects and the press characteristic of the old regime. Simultaneously, many religious communities have found it hard to adapt and reform so as to meet the new challenges posed by religious freedom, finding it easier to concentrate their attention on inter-religious conflicts than on developing their own spiritual life.

Whilst much has changed in the relationship between religion and the political order, there remain continuities. The disposition to control remains strong amongst many of the new political regimes, and not just amongst those of more autocratic bent such as Uzbekistan. Many of those previously involved in the regulation of religious life retain similar, if formally different, roles in the new democratic orders. Nationalist and democratic politicans still find it useful to be seen as close to religious leaders or institutions, whilst political parties and movements seek to secure religious support for their programmes. In the vast majority of cases this linkage is utilitarian, with religion's use defined and controlled by political institutions rather than on its own terms. In this sense it might be suggested that Marx's critique of religion as a tool of the ruling classes is not without validity in post-communist society. But equally it might be argued that when society is undergoing radical surgery, even opium has its uses.

8   Conclusion

The aim of this book has been threefold: to provide an overview of religious policy from the death of Stalin to the years immediately following the collapse of communism, to explore the nature of the policy process as it affected religion, and to isolate some of the long-term trends which contributed to the gradual change in the attitude of the state towards religion as well as certain continuities which might serve to influence the future development of relations between them.

To this end I have first of all sought to provide a work of synthesis, bringing together the best of the existing literature on the subject whilst supplementing it with my own understanding based upon reinterpretation and new research. In particular I have focused to a greater extent than many works on official sources, and have been able to make use of some archive materials not available to previous writers. On occasion I have updated and revised our understanding of religious policy, although not all will agree with my conclusions. In such a short space it has been impossible to be comprehensive, and some parts of the country and some religious groups have received more coverage than others. But at the same time I have sought to present a more systemic account of policy which focuses equally on state and religious organisations, on central decision making bodies and on local implementers.

During the course of the study I have traced the evolution of religious policy since the time of Khrushchev's renewed assault on religion, foreshadowed in the brief 1954 campaign but launched with fresh intensity in the autumn of 1958. Having noted the crucial role of Khrushchev's personal commitment to the building of communism, chapters 2 and 3 explored the way in which policy was worked out and in which it was announced to those official bodies responsible for putting theory into practice. They went on to outline the systematic campaign of propaganda, education, control and repression aimed at the reduction of the influence of both religious ideology and institutions. In particular we noticed the way in which the Orthodox Church in the Slavic heartlands bore the brunt of the institutional attack, and produced figures from the

CRA archives revealing the quantitative impact (less than earlier believed, though still substantial) on the number of legally functioning places of worship in the USSR.

Chapters 4 and 5 explored the development of religious policy under Brezhnev, Andropov and Chernenko. Though the new leadership initially permitted some discussion of the religious question, by 1966 it appeared to have settled into a policy of Khrushchevism minus excess. The mass closure of churches came to an end, as did the cruder form of anti-religious propaganda, but the educational and propaganda programmes set in motion during the early 1960s remained in place and were, at least on paper, further developed under Brezhnev. In general the ageing leadership of the 1960s and 1970s proved more flexible in its dealings with religion, willing to delegate day to day administration in this area to other bodies. Yet increasingly they faced new problems, with challenges posed by religious vitality, dissent, nationalism and foreign pressures. In meeting these new challenges they relied on a combination of traditional measures such as denunciation, tightened control and repression, and a willingness to make concessions in areas such as registration of religious communities with the result that there were more registered communities when Brezhnev died than when he came to power.

Many of these problems and changes reflected a wider process taking place in a Soviet society where economic decline coincided with the emergence of a population ever more alienated from official structures and ideologies. During the early 1980s the ageing leadership tried to deal with this by tightening the screws, by keeping the lid on whilst attempting cautious and partial reform. Only with the accession of Mikhail Gorbachev was the real depth of the problems facing the Soviet Union understood and an attempt, initially cautious, made to deal with them. In the religious sphere this entailed a recognition not only of the continued vitality of the believing sector of the population, but of the need to extend the humanisation of Soviet society to all citizens, and the potential utility of religious believers to the reform programme. Consequently the late 1980s witnessed the liberalisation of both official attitudes towards religion and a change in the practical and legal status of religious bodies. Such changes met with some resistance from party and state workers, but the focus of conservative opposition to reform was never seriously on religion, because of both the natural linkage between conservatism and Russian nationalism, with its more benevolent attitude to Orthodoxy, and in part perhaps because much of the religious sector was inclined to conservative political attitudes.

By 1990 a *de facto* and *de jure* freedom of conscience had emerged within the USSR, at the same time as that particular state formation was fragmenting. The August 1991 coup merely sealed the process, permitting in the religious sphere the replacement of a single approach to the question with fifteen or more new ways of dealing with religion. Most of the newly independent states were content to leave religion to its own devices, though some political leaders – in government and opposition – sought religious legitimation. In practice, however, it is too soon to speak of the emergence of state religions, let alone religious states, and most religious groups have distanced themselves from identification with particular political programmes, even those promoted by ostensibly religious parties. For many the main problem in this transitional phase is not dealing with the state, but coming to terms with the past and reforming themselves. What they want from the state is benevolent neutrality, some support for rebuilding their structures and perhaps protection against what they see as certain undesirable consequences of pluralism. What they do not want, with some notable exceptions, is a revival of a state system that seeks to control and direct their everyday activities.

In terms of the religious policy making process it is possible to draw a number of conclusions. Firstly, it appears that policy in the post-Stalin era was increasingly dependent upon contingent factors rather than the product of a party-state driven by its hostility towards religion. As in previous periods, and as Lenin always stressed, the treatment of religion had to be subordinated to the wider concerns of creating a socialist society. Under Khrushchev the teleological imperative made a brief reappearance, but this was very much an abberation during the post-Stalin years, and one whose practical realisation was unlikely in an organisational and political setting where the centre did not always have the means to effect its desires. After 1964 the generalised aim of weakening religious influence remained, but day-to-day policies were largely dependent upon the needs of the day – the control of dissent and nationalism, the neutralisation of foreign criticisms etc. By the mid-1980s the state had fundamentally changed its approach to religion and by opening up the policy process as a whole permitted the emergence of a pluralism of views on the correct place of religion in Soviet and post-Soviet society.

Our study of the policy process has revealed the existence of some debate on the religious question within the broad 'policy community', although until the late 1980s its capacity for public expression was extremely limited. Such arguments as there were under Khrushchev have on many questions to be deduced from comments and criticisms levelled by the writers of that time, although on certain issues – for example, the introduction of new rites – such debates came out into the open. But whilst pointing tentatively to the presence of discussion and argumentation, a number of qualifying points need to be made. It is not always easy to identify with any degree of precision either the precise policy difference or the individuals advancing them. Familiar refrains – the need to balance education and social change, the warnings against administrative abuses – resonate through most of the writings of the 1950s through 1970s, yet these are emphasised in a variety of ways. It is also the case that not all individuals take the same stance on every issue, although writers such as Klochkov and Lisavtsev do have a tendency to take hard line views whilst literary figures were often to be found in the moderate camp. But other figures are more complex. Yuri Rozenbaum, a 'liberal' in 1965 and then in the late 1980s, comes across as extremely 'conservative' in material contained in the CRA archive. In his case this perhaps reflected a commitment to a rigorous approach but one that was imposed via legal channels. It is equally the case that policy prescriptions cannot always be identified with specific institutions, although as Bociurkiw pointed out in his description of 'fundamentalists' and 'pragmatists', one was more likely to find the hardliners in the party and komsomol apparatus. Yet even this generalisation needs to be treated with some caution, for as we saw in chapter 6, when the Dneprodzerzhinsk believers campaigned for the opening of a cathedral closed under Khrushchev, it was sometimes the communist leaders who took the permissive line against a state official (in this case the mayor) who tried to prevent change (pp. 173–74).

With regard to the question of bureaucratic and interest group politics, this study supports a cautious approach which accepts that such politics did take place but stresses the limitations which curbed its full development. Certainly during the period there is some evidence to suggest a growing sensitivity to specialist advice, for example in the 1965 debates over how to manage the Baptist problem, in the awareness shown by political elites during the 1980s of the changing dynamics of the religious section of the population, and above all in the radical rethinking of religious policy of the late 1980s. There is also some evidence to support the common sense view that within the anti-religious establishments there were conflicts – for example between the two councils controlling religious affairs in 1964–5, or as evidenced by the coming to the fore of such tensions in the very different circumstances of the late 1980s.

But this was a limited and licensed debate for a number of reasons. Two of these were pointed to by Schwartz and Keech in their 1968 article on the role of groups in the Soviet policy process. They hypothesised that the greater the degree of dispute over policy issues within the political elite, the greater the possibilities for groups to become involved and to be listened to by individual politicans seeking evidence to back up their case. In the case of religion we have little evidence to suggest major differences within the elite until the Gorbachev years, by which time the policy process was becoming more open anyway. In such circumstances different tendencies within the anti-religious establishment were unlikely to emerge clearly. This was particularly so during the Khrushchev years when a firm lead on the religious question was being given by the political leadership. Secondly, Schwarz and Keech noted that political elites were more dependent upon specialist groups in situations where technical advice was essential and where political nous would not suffice.[1] From the leaders' perspective, many of the decisions affecting religion would certainly have appeared to require the exercise of common sense tempered by ideological and control needs, rather than the appeal to experts. To these factors one might add two others. In the case of religion there were not huge resources to be competed for, although like any other set of organisations, those involved in anti-religious work did hope for an expansion of their activities and agitated accordingly – witness the Furov report's combination of reporting success and stressing the work still to be done. And related to this was the fact that a major actor in this policy sphere, the religious communities themselves, had no political defender or bureaucratic champion.

A further point about the policy process we have perhaps stressed more than hitherto has been the degree of autonomy of implementing agencies during much of our period. Even under Khrushchev we noted that local authorities put theory into practice in different ways, evident for example in the differing rates of church closures. Under Brezhnev this trend became more pronounced as certain central agencies such as the CRA and KGB enjoyed relatively greater autonomy in interpreting party directives, and as republican, regional and local authorities became ever more bosses in their own lands. This latter tendency coincided with certain systemic political features to produce differing treatments of religious communities across much of the country, although it is impossible to deny that on the whole religious groups were not treated with any degree of justice or equity. But the dual institutional loyalties of the regional CRA commissioners, to their Moscow bosses and regional nomenklatura superiors, combined to produce differing results. In many areas the political cheapness of attacking religion combined with long traditions of harsh attacks in non-conformity to produce significantly

---

[1] J. Schwartz & W. Keech, 'Group Influence and the Policy Process in the Soviet Union', *American Political Science Review*, vol. 62, no. 3, 1968, pp. 840–51.

harsher policies than those perhaps intended by the centre – and in this sense official attempts to blame problems on local officials were not without some truth, though by no means the whole truth.[2] But such structures could also produce regions where policy was interpreted liberally, where churches were not closed (including Gorbachev's Stavropol according to one source),[3] and where believers were not subject to overt discrimination.

Finally, under Gorbachev the whole policy process became more open, as a more radical and investigative journalism developed, as the number of bodies and groups consulted grew, and as quasi-parliamentary institutions evolved. Though the bureaucracy was for a while able to obstruct the liberalisation of policy and law regarding religion, it could no longer do so unopposed and unquestioned, whilst the increasing transparency of the process enabled observers and scholars to comprehend more fully the ways in which Soviet and post-Soviet religious policy was being shaped.

A third theme of this book has been the tracing of patterns of continuity and change in the evolution of religious policy. In our study of some of the arguments and debates underlying policy over the last four decades certain themes have constantly resurfaced, albeit not always in the same form nor approached from the same perspective. From Khrushchev to Gorbachev, and indeed after, scholars and citizens have debated the proper role of religion in society. They have argued over the nature of religion – was it by definition reactionary, did it have any social roots in socialist society, was it something that would always be with us. At various times they came up with different answers – for example, in the mid-1960s most would have argued that religion was doomed to extinction, though some suggested that certain features of religion such as rites were an essential part of the human experience. There were ongoing debates over the relationship between religion and culture, dismissed under Khrushchev and during Andropov's ascendancy, but explored (tentatively) in the early 1970s and (overtly) in the late 1980s. Questions also arose over the links of religion and morality, a link condemned when put forward during the Khrushchev years, but increasingly stressed from 1987 onwards. Such questions raised their head with increasing frequency throughout our period and were met with changing answers as the years passed.

---

[2] As I was finishing this manuscript I came across an article by James Warhola which explores similar territory and makes some useful points about centre–local relations in this sphere. 'Central versus Local Authority in Soviet Religious Affairs, 1964–89', *The Journal of Church and State*, vol. 34, no. 1, Winter 1992, pp. 15–37.

[3] G. Sheehy: *Gorbachev – A One Man Revolution* (London, 1990), p. 117.

There were also social processes underway during these years that contributed to the fundamental change in the nature of religious policy that took place under Gorbachev. Whilst the anti-religious establishment remained geared up, at least in its popular atheism, to the mass, semi-educated audiences of the past, social change was producing a different type of religious community. On the one hand the quantity of self-confessed believers was much smaller, thus rendering mass measures less appropriate; on the other, Soviet social policies had produced a better educated populace, with many congregations changing their demographic make-up so as to reduce the dominance of elderly, poorly educated, female homeworkers and to create 'a new type of believer'. By the early 1980s it was clear that the atheist establishment was poorly equipped to deal with a religious sector that whilst weakened retained a certain vitality in many parts of the country. It was also increasingly unclear to many intelligent people why the overwhelmingly loyal, believing population should be subject to persistent harassment.

When change did come it was radical in that it freed religious organisations of many of the shackles that previously bound them and witnessed the state's conversion to a position of benevolent neutrality in religious matters. Conflict was replaced with cooperation as both sides sought to meet the challenges facing them. Yet traces of the past remained: in officials and institutions responsible for administering the new laws on religion, in the tendency of individual states to favour particular religious groups – in Ukraine, in Russia, in Georgia and in parts of Central Asia – or come close to resurrecting state religions. Above all one saw the maintenance of old assumptions amongst many of those involved in religious matters. State officials continued to take for granted that to some degree it was their responsibility to 'control' religious life.

The future place of religion in the Soviet successor states remains far from certain. The old hostility to religion has gone, although in some states minority religions may face restrictions, but the tendency of many officials to interfere in the daily life of religious communities is one that may take some time to unlearn. Good relations between religion and the state have not always been helped in this regard by the maintenance in position of some of the very people who previously persecuted believers. Tensions also remain where the state inclines to religious favouritism, a temptation which the larger national churches or religions may find hard to resist. Nonetheless, religious groups have been freed from the oppressiveness of the old regime and have an opportunity to recoup, rebuild and develop their spiritual lives in a new situation. This cannot be an easy task, but it is now up to them whether they choose to seek a continuation of dependency, to focus on side issues, or petty conflicts with other religious groups, or whether they go for spiritual revitalisation and a stance independent and, if necessary, critical of the new political orders emerging in the fifteen successor states. And how the new states treat religious groups will provide one of the criteria for judging whether they have moved from a political culture that views citizens and social organisations as subjects to one that sees them as fellow participants in the creation of a truly pluralistic society.

Bibliography

DOCUMENTARY SOURCES

Arkhiv samizdata (AS): a numbered collection of samizdat documents produced by Radio Liberty

Material from the archives of the Communist Party's Central Committee now contained in the Centre for the Preservation of Contemporary Documentation (TsKhSD) in Moscow. Documents are available for the whole of the period 1953–91, but accessibility is limited and certain types of documents, including Politburo minutes and KGB reports are unavailable.

Chronicle of Current Events (English translation of the samizdat bulletin published in London by Amnesty International)

Chronicle of the Lithuanian Catholic Church (English translation of the Lithuanian samizdat publication produced in New York)

Materials from the archive of the Council for Religious Affairs situated in Moscow's Central State Archive of the October Revolution (TsGAOR), f. 6991s. I had access to the open section of this archive including material dating from the period 1943–65

Current Digest of the Soviet Press (Extensive use of this source was made for the Khrushchev chapters, although where quotes are used I have checked Russian texts)

Documents of the Christian Committee to Defend Believers' Rights (photocopies of documents produced by the Christian Committee with English translation of a small minority)

Materials from the Keston College library and archive, including official documents, books, laws and instructions, samizdat, and press cuttings; in late 1993 the renamed Keston Research, now in Oxford, acquired copies of some materials from the archives of CRA commissioners in various Russian regions

Konstitutsiya (osnovnoi zakon) SSSR (Moscow, 1983)

Kuroedov, V. A. & A. Pankratov, eds., *Zakonodatel'stvo o religioznykh kul'takh* (Moscow, 1971); a collection of documents on religious policy, some unpublished, produced in numbered copies issued 'for official use only'. A copy of the original text is in the Keston College archive, and the edition used here is that produced by Chalidze press in New York, published in 1981

KPSS v resolyutsiyakh i resheniyakh s'ezdov, konferentsii i plenumov TsK, vol. 7, 1955–59 (Moscow, 1971)
O religii i tserkvi (Moscow, 1977); a collection of party, state and legal documents on religion from the time of the revolution to the mid-1970s
Ugolovnoe kodeks RSFSR (Moscow, 1975)
Vneocherednye XXI s'ezd KPSS (Moscow, 1959)

BOOKS AND ARTICLES

Aitmatov, Ch., *The Day Lasts more than a Thousand Years* (London, 1982)
Aktual'nye voprosy ateisticheskogo vospitaniya na sovremennom etape (Moscow, 1986)
Alekseev, V., '*Shturm nebes' otmenyaetsya* (Moscow, 1992)
Anashkin, G., 'O svobode sovesti i soblyudenii zakonodatel'stva o religioznykh kul'takh', *Sovetskoe gosudarstvo i pravo*, 1965/1, pp. 39–45
Anderson, J., 'The Campaign that Never Was,' *Religion in Communist Lands*, vol. 15, no. 2, 1987, pp. 182–9
  'The Council for Religious Affairs and the Shaping of Soviet Religious Policy', *Soviet Studies*, vol. 43, no. 4, 1991, pp. 689–710
Aptekman, D. M., 'Problemy effektivnosti v rabote soveta po ateisticheskomu vospitaniyu pri raikome partii', in *Voprosy nauchnogo ateizma*, vyp. 19 (Moscow, 1976), pp. 53–63
Ashirov, N., *Evolyutsiya islama v SSSR* (Moscow, 1972)
  Islam i natsiya (Moscow, 1975)
Bachrach, P. & M. Baratz, 'Decisions and Non-Decisions – An Analytical Framework', *American Political Science Review*, vol. 57, no. 3, 1963, pp. 632–42
Bairamov, E., 'Islam i natsional'nye traditsii', *Agitator* 1966/24, pp. 42–45
Bairamsakhatov, N., *Novye byt i islam* (Moscow, 1979)
Barmenkov, A. I., *Svoboda sovesti v SSSR* (Moscow, 1979)
Baturin, N., 'Novye sovetskie traditsii – vazhnoe sredstvo kommunisticheskogo vospitaniya molodezhi', in *Voprosy nauchnogo ateizma*, vyp. 3 (Moscow, 1967), pp. 245–54
Belov, A. & D. Shilkin, *Diversiya bez dynamita* (Moscow, 1972 & 1976)
Belyaev, V., *Ya obvinyayu* (Moscow, 1984)
Bennigsen, A., 'Soviet Islam since the Invasion of Afghanistan', *Central Asian Survey*, vol. 1, no. 1, 1982, p. 66
Bennigsen, A. & M. Broxup, *The Islamic Threat to the Soviet State* (London, 1983)
Heprimirimost k burzhuaznoi ideologii perezhitkam natsionalizma (Moscow, 1982)
Binns, C., 'Soviet Secular Ritual – Atheist Propaganda or Spiritual Consumerism', *Religion in Communist Lands*, vol. 10, no. 3, 1982, pp. 298–309
Blane, A., 'A Year of Drift', *Religion in Communist Lands*, vol. 2, no. 3, 1974, pp. 9–15
Bociurkiw, B., 'The Shaping of Soviet Religious Policy', *Problems of Communism*, May–June 1973, pp. 37–51
Bourdeaux, M. A., *Religious Ferment in Russia* (London, 1968)

Patriarchs and Prophets – Persecution of the Russian Orthodox Church (London, 1970)

Gorbachev, Glasnost' and the Gospel (London, 1990)

Brazhnik, I., 'Ateisticheskoe vospitanie – obshchepartiinoe delo', *Partiinaya zhizn'* 24, 1963, pp. 21–6

Breslauer, G., *Khrushchev and Brezhnev as Leaders – Building Authority in Soviet Politics* (London, 1982)

Brezhnev, L. I., *Leninskim kursom*, vol. 4 (Moscow, 1974)

Brown, A., 'Policy Making in the Soviet Union', review article, *Soviet Studies*, vol. 23, no.3, 1971, pp. 120–148

Bruce, J., *The Politics of Policy Formation – Khrushchev's Innovative Policies in Education and Agriculture* (Denver, 1976)

Bukin, V., 'Preodolenie religioznykh chuvstv', *Kommunist* 2, 1963, pp. 71–4

Carrere d'Encausse, H., *Decline of Empire – The Soviet Republics in Revolt* (New York, 1979)

Cherkashin, P., 'O sotsial'nykh kornyakh religii', *Voprosy filosofii* 6, 1958, pp. 29–41

Corley, F., *Armenia and Karabakh – Ancient Faith, Modern War* (London, 1992)

Dmytruk, K., *Swastikas on Soutanes* (Kiev, 1981)

Dunlop, J., *The Faces of Contemporary Russian Nationalism* (Princeton, 1983)
The New Russian Nationalism (New York, 1985)

Ellis, J., *The Russian Orthodox Church – A Contemporary History* (London, 1986)

Fedoseev, P. N. & M. N. Sheinman, eds., *Nauka i religiya* (Moscow, 1957)

Fireside, H., *Icon and Swastika – the Russian Orthodox Church under Nazi and Soviet Control* (Cambridge, Mass., 1971)

Fletcher, W., *Nikolai – Portrait of a Dilemma* (London, 1968)
Religion and Soviet Foreign Policy, 1945–70 (London, 1973)

Freedman, R. O. ed., *Soviet Jewry in the 1980s – The Politics of Antisemitism and Emigration, and the Dynamics of Resettlement* (London, 1989)

Gerstenmaier, C., *The Voices of the Silent* (New York, 1972)

Gol'st, G. P., *Religiya i zakon* (Moscow, 1975)

Gordienko, N., *Kreshchenie Rusi – fakty protiv legend i mifov* (Leningrad, 1983)

Grishin, V., *Voprosy partiinogo-organizatsionnoi i ideologicheskoi raboty* (Moscow, 1984)

Grossman, J. Delaney, 'Khrushchev's Anti-Religious Policy and the Campaign of 1954', *Soviet Studies*, vol. 24, no. 3, 1973, pp. 374–86

Gustafson, T., *Reform in Soviet Politics – Lessons of Recent Policies on Land and Water* (Cambridge, 1981)

Hahn, W., *Post-War Politics – The Fall of Zhdanov and the Defeat of Moderation* (Cornell, 1982)

Hajda, L. & M. Beissinger, eds., *The Nationalities Factor in Soviet Politics* (Harvard, 1990)

Hamm, C. & M. Hill, *The Policy Process in the Modern Capitalist State* (Brighton, 1984)

Hogwood, B. & L. Gunn, *Policy Analysis for the Real World* (Oxford, 1984)

Il'ichev, L. F. 'XXI s'ezd KPSS i nekotorye voprosy ideologicheskoi raboty', *Kommunist*, 2, 1959, pp. 18–32

'Ocherednye zadachi ideologicheskoi raboty partii', in *Plenum tsentral'nogo komiteta kommunisticheskoi partii sovetskogo soyuza, 18–21 iyunya 1963g. Stenograficheskii otchet* (Moscow, 1964), p. 40

Individual'naya rabota s veruyushchimi (Moscow, 1967 & 1974)

International Who's Who 1982–3 (London, 1982)

Istoriya evangel'skikh khristian-baptistov v SSSR (Moscow, 1989)

Juviler, P. & H. Morton, eds., *Soviet Policy Making – Studies of Communism in Transition* (London, 1967)

Kampars, P. P. & M. N. Zakovich, *Sovetskaya grazhdanskaya obryadnost'* (Moscow, 1967)

Karklins, R., *Ethnic Relations in the USSR – The View from Below* (London, 1985)

Keeble, C. ed., *The Soviet State – The Domestic Roots of Soviet Foreign Policy* (London, 1985)

Keleher, S., 'Catholic Ostpolitik and the legalisation of the Ukrainian Greek Catholic Church' (unpublished conference paper).

Keston College, *Religious Prisoners in the USSR* (Keston, 1985)

Khrushchev, N. S., *Khrushchev Remembers*, vol. 1 (London, 1971)

Khrushchev on Khrushchev (London, 1990)

Klochkov, V. V., 'Kontseptsiya svobody sovesti v burzhuaznom i sotsialist-icheskom mirovozzreniyakh i zakonodatel'stve', *Sovetskoe gosudarstvo i pravo*, 9, 1974, pp. 29–38

Religiya, gosudarstvo, pravo (Moscow, 1978)

Knight, A., *The KGB – Police and Politics in the Soviet Union* (London, 1988)

Konavelev, V., 'Ateizm v sotsialisticheskom obshchestve', in *Voprosy nauchnogo ateizma*, 25 (Moscow, 1980), pp. 244–66

Koval'skii, N. A., *Imperializm, religiya, tserkov'* (Moscow, 1986)

Kurochkin, P. K., 'K otsenke protsessa modernizatsii religii v sovremennykh usloviyakh', in *Voprosy nauchnogo ateizma*, 2 (Moscow, 1966), pp. 5–38

Evolyutsiya sovremennogo russkogo pravoslaviya (Moscow, 1971)

Kuroedov, V. A., 'Neot'emlimaya konstitutsionnaya norma sotsialisticheskogo gosudarstva', *Kommunist*, 5, 1980, pp. 45–55

Lane, C., *The Rites of Rulers – Ritual in Industrial Society* (Oxford, 1981)

Lazareff, H. & P. Lazareff, *The Soviet Union between the 19th and 20th Party Congresses, 1952–56* (The Hague, 1959)

Levin, M., *The Gorbachev Phenomenon – A Historical Interpretation* (London, 1988)

Lisavtsev, E. I., *Novye sovetskie traditsii* (Moscow, 1966)

Lobacheva, N. P., 'O protsesse formirovaniya novoi semenoi obryadnosti', *Sovetskaya etnografiya*, 1, 1972, pp. 3–13

Lyalina, G. S., *Baptizm – illyuzii i real' nost'* (Moscow, 1977)

McAuley, A., 'Nations and Nationalism in Central Asia', C. Keeble, ed., *The Soviet State – The Domestic Roots of Soviet Foreign Policy* (London, 1985)

McLellan, D., *Marxism and Religion* (London, 1988)

Marshall, R. ed., *Aspects of Religion in the Soviet Union, 1917–1967* (Chicago, 1971)

Matthews, M. ed., *Soviet Government – A Selection of Official Documents on Internal Policy* (London, 1974)

'Perestroika and the Rebirth of Charity', in A. Jones, W. Connor & D. Powell, eds., *Soviet Social Problems* (Harvard, 1991), pp. 154–71

Medvedev, R., *Khrushchev* (London, 1982)

Minkyavicius, Ya. V., *Katolitsizm i natsiya* (Moscow, 1971)

Mishutis, P. N., 'Opyt sozdaniya sistemy ateisticheskogo vospitaniya v Litovksoi SSR', in *Voprosy nauchnogo ateizma*, 1 (Moscow, 1966), pp. 200–20

Morrison, J., *Boris Yel'tsin* (London, 1991)

Nikishov, S. I., *XXIV s'ezd KPSS i zadachi ateisticheskogo vospitaniya* (Moscow, 1972)

Aktual'nye problemy propagandy ateizma v razvitom sotsialisticheskom obshchestve (Moscow, 1982)

Nyunka, V., 'Vostochnaya politika Vatikana', *Kommunist* (Lithuania), 2, 1982, pp. 62–6

Ob ideologicheskoi rabote KPSS – sbornik dokumentov (2nd edition, Moscow, 1983)

Okulov, A., 'Za glubokuyu nauchnuyu razrabotku sovremmenykh problem ateizma', in *Voprosy nauchnogo ateizma*, 1 (Moscow, 1966), p. 13

Oleshchuk, F. N., 'Religioznye perezhitki i puti ikh preodoleniya', in *Voprosy filosofii*, 6, 1954, pp. 76–88

O nauchnom ateizme i ateisticheskom vospitanii (Moscow, 1974)

Partiinaya organizatsiya i ateisticheskoe vospitanie (Moscow, 1975)

Petlyakov, P. A., *Uniat'skaya tserkov' – orudiye anti-kommunizma i anti-sovetizma* (Lvov, 1982)

Peris, D., 'The 1929 Congress of the Godless', *Soviet Studies*, vol. 43, no. 4, 1991, pp. 711–32

Pishchuk, Yu. B. & V. G. Furov, 'Ob otnoshenii k kul'turnomu naslediyu proshlogo', in *Voprosy nauchnogo ateizma*, 22 (Moscow, 1978), pp. 217–32

Platonov, R. P., *Vospitanie ateisticheskoi ubezhdennosti* (Minsk, 1973)

Polok, I. V., 'O praktike raboty po protivodeistviyu katolicheskoi i uniatskoi propagande', in *Voprosy nauchnogo ateizma*, 28 (Moscow, 1982), pp. 84–104

Pospielovsky, D., *The Russian Orthodox Church under the Soviet Regime, 1917–82* (2 volumes, New York, 1984)

A History of Soviet Atheism in Theory and Practice, and the Believer (3 volumes, London, 1987–8)

Powell, D., *Anti-Religious Propaganda in the Soviet Union* (London, 1975)

Pravdin, A., 'Inside the CPSU Central Committee', *Survey*, vol. 20, no. 4 (1974), pp. 94–104

Ramet, P. ed., *Religion and Nationalism in Soviet and East European Politics* (London, 1989)

Ramet, S. P. ed., *Religious Policy in the Soviet Union* (Cambridge, 1993)

Remnek, R. ed., *Social Scientists and Policy Making in the USSR* (London, 1977)

Rossiskoe khristianskoe demokraticheskoe dvizhenie – sbornik materialov (Moscow, 1990)

Rudakov, N., 'Osobennosti ateisticheskoi raboty sredi posledovatelei nekotorykh techenii baptizma', in *Voprosy nauchnogo ateizma*, 19 (Moscow, 1976), pp. 244–56

Rudnev, V. A., *Sovetskie prazdniki, obryady, ritualy* (Leningrad, 1979)

Rywkin, M., *Moscow's Muslim Challenge* (London, 1982)

Salo, V., 'Anti-Religious Rites in Estonia', *Religion in Communist Lands*, vol. 1, nos. 4–5, 1973, pp. 28–34

Sapiets, M., *True Witness – The Story of the Seventh Day Adventists in the Soviet Union* (Keston, 1990)

Saprykin, V., *Sotsialisticheskii kollektiv i ateisticheskoe vospitanie* (Alma Ata, 1983)

Sawatsky, W., 'Secret Soviet Lawbook on Religion', *Religion in Communist Lands*, vol. 4, no. 4, 1976, pp. 24–34

Soviet Evangelicals since World War II (Ontario, 1981)

Schwartz, J. & W. Keech, 'Group Influence and the Policy Process in the Soviet Union', *American Political Science Review*, vol. 62, no. 3, 1968, pp. 840–51

Shamaro, A., 'Pamyatniki tserkovnogo zodchestva v ateisticheskom vospitanii', *Voprosy nauchnogo ateizma*, 30 (Moscow, 1982)

Shepetis, L. K., 'Ateisticheskomu vospitaniyu – deistvennost' i nastupatel' nost'', *Voprosy nauchnogo ateizma*, 32 (Moscow, 1985)

Shirley, E. & M. Rowe, eds., *Candle in the Wind – Religion in the Soviet Union* (Washington, 1989)

Skilling, H. & F. Griffith, eds., *Interest Groups in Soviet Politics* (Princeton, 1971)

Stewart, P. 'Soviet Interest groups and the Policy Process – The Repeal of Production Education', *World Politics*, October 1969, pp. 29–50

Stricker, G. 'Mennonites in Russia and the Soviet Union', *Religion in Communist Lands*, vol. 12, no. 3, 1984, pp. 293–314

'German Protestants in Tsarist Russia and the Soviet Union', *Religion in Communist Lands*, vol. 15, no. 1, 1987, pp. 32–53

Struve, N., *Christians in Contemporary Russia* (London, 1967)

Taheri, A., *Crescent in a Red Sky – The Future of Islam in the Soviet Union* (London, 1989)

The 24th Congress of the CPSU – Documents (Moscow, 1971)

Tsameryan, I. ed., *Stroitel'stvo kommunizma i preodoleniya religioznykh perezhitkov* (Moscow, 1966)

Thrower, J., *Marxist–Leninist Scientific Atheism and the Study of Religion and Atheism in the USSR* (Berlin, 1983)

Ugrinovich, D., 'Neobkhodima produmannaya sistema nauchno-ateisticheskogo vospitaniya', *Kommunist*, 9, 1962, pp. 93–100

Obryady – za i protiv (Moscow, 1975)

Voslensky, M., *Nomenklatura* (New York, 1984)

Warhola, J., 'Central versus Local Authority in Soviet Religious Affairs, 1964–89', *Journal of Church and State*, vol. 34, no. 1, Winter 1992, pp. 15–37

White, S. & A. Pravda, eds., *Ideology and Soviet Politics* (London, 1988)

Wood, J. ed., *Readings on Church and State* (Waco, 1989), pp. 303–18

Yablokov, I. N., *Metodologicheskie problemy sotsiologii religii* (Moscow, 1972)

Zakovich, M. N., *Sovetskaya obryadnost' i dukhovnaya kul'tura* (Kiev, 1980)

Zalesski, A. ed., *Prichiny sushchestvovaniya i puti preodoleniya religioznykh perezhitkov* (Moscow, 1965)

Zaslavsky, V. & R. Brym, *Soviet Jewish Emigration and Soviet Nationality Policy* (London, 1983)

Za vysokoe kachestvo i deistvennost' ideologicheskoi raboty (Moscow, 1981)

Zemlyanskii, D. & S. Mezentsev, 'Ideologicheskie komissii partiinykh komitetov', *Kommunist*, 5, 1962, pp. 78–84

SOVIET (RUSSIAN) JOURNALS AND NEWSPAPERS

Agitator
Argumenty i fakty
Den'
Glasnost'
Gudok
Izvestiya
Izvestiya TsK KPSS
Kazakhstanskaya pravda
Khristianskie novosti
Kommunist
Kommunist (litva)
Kommunist Tadzhikistana
Komsomol'skaya pravda
Leningradskaya pravda
Literatura i zhizn'
Literaturnaya gazeta
Lyudyna i svit
Meditsinskaya pravda
Megapolis express
Molodoi kommunist
Molodezh Moldavii
Moscow News
Moskovskie novosti (Russian edition of above, sometimes with differing texts)
Moskovskaya pravda
Muslims of the Soviet East
Nauka i religiya
Nedelya
Nevskoe vremya
Nevsky dukhovnyi vestnik
Nezavisimaya gazeta
Nezavisimaya Moldova
Ogonyok
Partiinaya zhizn'
Pravda
Pravda Ukrainy
Pravda vostoka
Pravitel'stvenny vestnik
Rossiiskie vesti
Sotsialisticheskaya zakonnost'
Sovetskaya Belorossiya
Sovetskaya etnografiya
Sovetskoe gosudarstvo i pravo
Sovetskaya Yustitsiya

Sovetskaya Kirgiziya
Sovetskaya Latviya
Sovetskaya Litva
Sovetskaya Rossiya
Trud
Turkmenskaya iskra
Uchitel'skaya gazeta
Vestnik khristianskogo informatsionnogo tsentra
Voprosy filosofii
Zarya vostoka
Zhurnal moskovskoi patriarchii

WESTERN JOURNALS AND PAPERS

American Political Science Review
Central Asian Survey
The Guardian
The Independent
The Journal of Church and State
Keston News Service
Nationalities Papers
Problems of Communism
Radio Liberty Research Report on the USSR
Religion in Communist Dominated Areas
Religion in Communist Lands
Russkaya mysl'
Slavic Review
Soviet Jewish Affairs
Soviet Studies
Survey
Vestnik RKhD
World Politics

Index

Lightning Source UK Ltd.
Milton Keynes UK
17 November 2010

162993UK00001B/154/A